CONTENTS

PROFESSIONAL WRITING IN SPEECH-LANGUAGE PATHOLOGY AND AUDIOLOGY

Third Edition

Robert Goldfarb, PhD
Yula C. Serpanos, PhD

5521 Ruffin Road
San Diego, CA 92123

email: information@pluralpublishing.com
website: http://www.pluralpublishing.com

Typeset in 11/13 Garamond by Flanagan's Publishing Services, Inc.
Printed in the United States of America by McNaughton & Gunn, Inc.

Library of Congress Cataloging-in-Publication Data

Names: Goldfarb, Robert (Robert M.), author. | Serpanos, Yula Cherpelis, author.
Title: Professional writing in speech-language pathology and audiology / Robert Goldfarb, Yula C. Serpanos.
Description: Third edition. | San Diego, CA : Plural, [2020] | Includes bibliographical references and index.
Identifiers: LCCN 2018028839| ISBN 9781635500134 (alk. paper) | ISBN 1635500133 (alk. paper)
Subjects: | MESH: Medical Writing | Speech-Language Pathology | Audiology
Classification: LCC RC423 | NLM WZ 345 | DDC 808/.066616--dc23
LC record available at https://lccn.loc.gov/2018028839

INTRODUCTION

"If you didn't document it, you didn't do it." Competent professional writing is a necessity, not a luxury. Third-party payers, such as insurance companies, may deny payment if the documentation for professional services is incorrect or incomplete. Medical chart notes, diagnostic evaluations, progress reports, and discharge summaries are all legal documents that may be used in court. The Code of Ethics of the American Speech-Language-Hearing Association (ASHA, 2016) states that individuals shall provide all services competently, and that includes documentation of services rendered.

The authors were motivated to write the present book to address writing problems exhibited by undergraduate and graduate students in communication sciences and disorders (CSD), lax documentation by clinicians, and general slovenliness in professional discourse. Since the second edition was published in 2014, we have figuratively blown our tops at students' overuse of *literally* in conversation, although this trend has not (yet) infected their professional writing. We continue to remind students that they are off base if they write *based off of* instead of based on. Lastly, we understand the reasons for accepting a singular form of *they* in spoken discourse, but reject its use in professional writing. The *Third Edition* includes expanded exercises in all sections, in response to reviewers who used the second edition and requested more practice opportunities. We include a more accessible website instead of a bundled CD for additional materials. We also responded to feedback from students who enrolled in a Professional Writing Boot Camp at Adelphi University that led to some changes and adjustments in the present volume. Guidelines for instituting writing boot camps at other colleges and universities appear in the website. In addition, RG field-tested portions of the second edition as a Fulbright Senior Specialist in Linguistics in Bogota, Colombia. The graduate TEFL students attended research methods and academic writing lectures in English, and provided valuable feedback regarding both English and Spanish materials provided in the courses.

In the past few years, we have had our concerns about professional writing shared by site visitors from the National Council for Accreditation of Teacher Education programs (NCATE). Within our own disciplines, the Council of Academic Accreditation (CAA) evaluators of our graduate program in speech-language pathology, the CAA site visitors of our consortial doctor of audiology program, and the CAA teams that joined RG on site visits to other colleges and universities echoed the need for improvement in professional writing. In all cases, we were assured that the decline in professional writing was a national concern.

At a recent meeting of the Council of Academic Programs in Communication Sciences and Disorders, we were eager to learn how other CSD programs assessed professional writing. We learned that while some programs denied admission to students applying for matriculation in graduate degree programs based on poor professional writing, other programs ignored professional writing, and one program director was honest enough to admit, unofficially, that writing requirements were "dumbed down" to give the program a perceived competitive advantage in recruitment. All programs welcomed a resource for professional writing that was comprehensive and scholarly.

In our research for the present book, we have discovered some fine style manuals for research reports and professional writing, as well as workbooks focusing on drill work. In this volume, we hope to provide reasons and explanations for the suggestions we make, and to support our claims with relevant professional citations. We do not think our students need to attend "remedial graduate school," nor do we doubt that every CSD student and professional practitioner can learn to write competently. We also think that learning to be a better professional writer does not have to be drudgery and have attempted to leaven our instruction with humor and stories.

Chapter 1 has some material that is new to the third edition, and includes an overview of English mechanics underlying syntax. In addition to a review of parts of speech, the chapter includes information about sentence structure, syntactic development, and disorders of syntax.

In Chapter 2, we describe language as our favorite toy, where even punctuation can be funny. Other topics include the alphabet soup of abbreviations that we use professionally; the mutability of language, especially among young adult users; and such thorny issues as gender neutrality and cultural differences. There are examples of correct and incorrect forms of usage throughout the chapter, as well as exercises at the end that review some of the themes. We have included many exercises and worksheets to address common errors in written expression; a list of common abbreviations that we use in professional writing; and have added to the website sections on strong language, "Mondegreens," and a game to use Shakespeare's insults to improve vocabulary. When students ask why there is so much professional jargon in our disciplines, we sometimes give the flip answer, "So you can charge more." The reality is that every trade and professional group uses jargon, whether it's "Adam and Eve on a raft" (two sunny-side up eggs on toast) in a local diner, or the contents of a legal document.

The focus of Chapter 3, evidence-based writing, is to provide the reader with strategies to answer the "why" questions about professional writing. We include annotated samples of students' evidence-based writing. We take you through the stages of writing a journal article. Our goal for most readers is to help them become educated consumers of research, not necessarily producers of research. We would also like to foster a cognitive shift away from the educational model in preparing therapy plans and reporting treatment to one where the clinician is testing hypotheses. After all, if you are following a curriculum, you may continue with it even if it doesn't seem to be working, whereas, if your hypothesis is falsified, you can begin testing another one.

As noted above, the ASHA Code of Ethics (revised in 2016) requires that we discharge our duties honorably and document our services appropriately. In Chapter 4, we review the Principles of Ethics that relate to professional writing, the constraints imposed by the Health Insurance Portability and Accountability Act of 1996 (HIPAA), and the guidelines for writing a successful research proposal to an Institutional Review Board. Since 2000, anyone seeking federal grant support is required to have a current certificate indicating a passing grade (currently 80%) on the web-based training program on the protection of human research participants administered through the National Institutes of Health. Students and professionals in communication sciences and disorders (CSD) are obliged to learn ASHA's code of ethics. There are many other websites related to ethics, and we provide the links for instruction about ethics in areas related to CSD.

Using library resources, discussed in Chapter 5, begins with a history of the library, followed by a discussion of collections and services. Those of us who enjoy the musty smell of the stacks can still indulge in this activity, but we also need to know how to conduct electronic searches. As instructors often use a course pack to supplement or substitute for a traditional textbook, we considered it worth noting. We also include sections on copyright and plagiarism. We would like a field trip to a college or university library to be part of the requirements for Chapter 5. Although we can access most of what the library has to offer through a desktop computer at home, we find the "bricks-and-mortar" experience of being in the building to be stimulating and informative. There is an extended set of exercises in correct use of APA 2010 style for referencing.

As we say in Chapter 6, on using Internet resources, welcome to the new way of doing business, meeting your life partner, succeeding in academia, and conducting your clinical practice. The syntax, semantics, and jargon associated with the

Internet today may appear out of date and even quaint by the time this chapter gets to the reader, but the section on uses and abuses of the Internet should remain relevant. We continue the discussion about research-based writing in this chapter. We recommend Internet resources to use, as well as those to avoid; explain the peer-review process for both print and electronic media; and recommend sites and strategies for database searches.

We have not seen a section on writing for oral presentation, which is covered in Chapter 7 in the current volume, in other professional writing books. Preparing an oral presentation is a topic of importance in basic books on rhetoric and public address, but we include it here to show how to develop a speech and to outline the presentation. In delivering the oral presentation, particularly one that includes computer-generated visual aids, we differentiate what should appear on the slides compared to what should be included in effective speech delivery. An oral report in class, a demonstration of a diagnostic test in clinical practicum, and a short course at ASHA are all based on written preparation. As the poster presentation is popular as an assignment for demonstrating evidenced-based practice in university clinics, as well as for disseminating research findings at professional conventions, we devote considerable attention to preparing a poster, and include examples on the accompanying website.

The diagnostic report, Chapter 8, is one of the lengthier sections of the book, divided into two parts. The first part specifies and describes five rules for diagnosis. For example, we address the second rule, *Be an Educated Consumer of Tests and Measures*, to all audiologists and speech-language pathologists who must understand research methodology even if they do not actively produce research. The guidelines for writing diagnostic reports in speech-language pathology and audiology, in the second part of the chapter, include specific instructions and examples for diagnostic protocols and report formats. Exercises start with the building block of phonetic transcription, which includes solving and writing a crossword puzzle in phonetics. Following that are original and edited diagnostic reports in speech-language pathology and audiology, and exercises for editing reports.

Chapter 9, clinical goals, reports and referrals, includes templates and samples of a treatment plan, progress report, and chart note, as well as forms of professional correspondence. We review issues in clinical writing related to terminology, ethics, and software. Exercises include writing cover letters for professional reports, writing letters as reports, completing an audiometric profile, and entering log notes in medical charts. We take you through the step-by-step process of evaluating background information, including test results, and making recommendations.

We end the book with an updated Chapter 10 on writing for professional advancement, because the format and number of questions have changed on our national examinations. The graduating student seeking a clinical fellowship, and the seasoned professional moving forward in a rewarding career, need strategies for developing professional documents. The chapter concludes with an analysis of multiple-choice tests, those used in the Praxis II exam as well as those prepared by course instructors. Exercises include developing a personal resume, preparing a professional cover letter, and developing a professional portfolio.

In recognizing the many people who helped us with this project, we want to pay a special tribute to the late Dr. Sadanand Singh, the founder of Plural Publishing, Inc. Singh (there is no disrespect intended; that is how he asked many of us to address him) also indicated that, although he could not read all manuscripts submitted or published, he did read our earlier one and enjoyed it very much. Angie Singh currently carries the torch at Plural, and she has been a wonderful source of support for us.

We are grateful for the assistance of Professor Suzy Lederer and Ms. Dawn Cotter-Jenkins at Adelphi University in providing some of the clinic forms used in this book. Professor Susan Behrens, a linguistics professor in the CSD Department at Marymount Manhattan College, spent a great deal of time with us to make sure that all appropriate grammatical rules were included in the third edition, and that our examples in the exercises were clear and appropriate. Our editors at Plural Publishing, Inc.—Kalie Koscielak and

Valerie Johns—have provided encouragement, cheerleading, and welcome deadlines throughout the writing project. Terry Gozdziewski field-tested the earlier editions in her writing classes and offered valuable suggestions. Our graduate research assistant, Yulia Kovalenko, painstakingly checked all chapters for clarity, ease of flow, and accuracy. Another graduate student, Monica Fernandes, corrected the Spanish version of the book that *Google Translate* yielded to produce a coherent Spanish version of the chapters used in Bogota. Our students' excellent work has inspired us, and their not-quite-so-excellent writing has motivated us, in preparing composite examples of diagnostic and treatment reports.

To Shelley and Elizabeth Goldfarb, Matt Simon and Tessera Rose; and to Andreas, Marie, and Ariana Serpanos, Luke Hardcastle, and Mark McClean—we love you madly. To Shelley and to Elizabeth V. Goldfarb, Matthew D. Simon, and to . . . (as written).

We invite readers to send comments and suggestions to us by email at:

Goldfarb2@adelphi.edu

Serpanos@adelphi.edu

To our daughters and their husbands.

Getting Started

Language is our favorite toy. We encourage you to play with it, develop your own skill set, and have fun inventing and reinventing your unique use of it. At the same time, we want you to develop a consistently excellent professional writing (and speaking) style, using conventions universally understood by speech-language pathologists and audiologists. The professional and personal language you use will be quite different from what we wrote and said as undergraduate and graduate students. Emerging technology, especially in audiology, but also in areas of speech-language pathology such as alternative and augmentative communication, has resulted in a new and richer vocabulary, with terms borrowed from computer science, engineering, and medicine.

Nowhere is the flux of language more evident than in the words used by young adults to represent something or someone in exceedingly positive terms. These have evolved from "the cat's pajamas" to "groovy," "far out," and "def." The last term gives us an opportunity to examine what is claimed here to be a misunderstanding based on vernacular English. The term *def* does not refer to hearing loss; rather, as it originated in inner cities, it refers to *death* in an ironic way. There is a phonological rule in African American Vernacular English (AAVE) where the sound made by the voiceless *th* (theta), when appearing after a vowel, is pronounced as the sound made by the letter *f*. We write the rule as follows: postvocalic /θ/→/f/. This rule, as legitimate as any other in phonology, represents the accepted practice of a large linguistic community. It is important to note the difference between vernacular English and language disorder, as Jones, Obler, Gitterman, and Goldfarb (2002) indicate in a comparison of AAVE to agrammatism in aphasia. We can see now that the use of *def* actually corresponds to a phrase—*the livin' end*—used as a superlative several generations ago, for what is the end of life (*the livin' end*), but *def*?

Finally, as you play with your new language toy, resist the urge to turn nouns into verbs or verbs into nouns. Former President George W. Bush caused himself political harm by creating a noun from the verb *to decide*. Calling himself "the decider" resulted in a cascade of political cartoons, usually with a superhero in cape and tights (and the President's face) and a capital *D* emblazoned on his chest. The President would have been much better served by using the term *commander-in-chief* or even *the boss*. Similarly, creating a verb form of *clinician* is not the most apt way of expressing the notion that a speech-language pathologist or audiologist should be well rounded, as in, "To be a good clinician, you should *cliniche* with all types of cases."

Beginnings of Speech-Language Pathology

This section is devoted to the beginnings of the field of speech-language pathology as well as the professional titles we use when referring to our colleagues and ourselves. The origins of speech-language pathology are usually traced to physicians in German-speaking countries in Europe during the early 1900s and shortly thereafter to the University of Iowa in the United States

(Goldfarb, 1985). In 1918 the University of Vienna appointed Emil Froeschels to serve as chief physician and *speech pathologist* (emphasis added) in the department of speech and voice disorders at the Central Hospital in Vienna. Together with Hugo Stern, his counterpart in the phoniatrics department, Froeschels convoked a meeting of what he dubbed the First International Congress of Logopedics and Phoniatrics. That meeting, held on July 3 to 5, 1924, at the Vienna Institute of Physiology, attracted some 65 specialists from the fields of laryngology, psychology, and pedagogical subjects. All but two of the participants were German-speaking Central Europeans.

At roughly the same time, across the seas in the United States, efforts were begun to develop the study and treatment of speech and hearing problems as a nonmedical field of professional specialization. Carl Emil Seashore, a psychologist and Dean of the Graduate College at the University of Iowa, selected a promising graduate student to develop a new program. This student, Lee Edward Travis, was probably the first individual in the world to be trained at the PhD level to work experimentally and clinically with speech and hearing disorders. His preparation involved study in the departments of psychology, speech, physics, psychiatry, neurology, and otolaryngology. In 1927, Travis became the first director of the University of Iowa Speech Clinic.

At the present time the International Association of Logopedics and Phoniatrics (IALP) convenes a congress every three years. The American Speech-Language-Hearing Association (ASHA), which is affiliated with IALP, presently lists more than 190,000 members (ASHA, 2018a). The professional titles of *logopedist* and *phoniatrist* have not been adopted in the United States. These titles and others are used primarily in Europe. For instance, the professional title of *orthophoniste* is used in France, as noted in Jean-Dominique Bauby's 1997 account of his brainstem stroke, *The Diving Bell and the Butterfly*. If they were used in the United States, the first author of this book would have to be called a *logogerist*, because he works with the elderly. Instead, in the United States, there has been a shift from identifying our practice as *speech correctionists* to *speech-language pathologists*, a shift that is traceable to the end of World War II. When injured soldiers, sailors, and marines returned to Veterans Administration Hospitals (now VA *Medical Centers*) with speech and language disorders secondary to head trauma, the attending psychiatrists and psychologists found they were not equipped to deal with these communication impairments. Some psychologists, notably Jon Eisenson, acquired expertise in both psychology and speech-language pathology, but the American Speech and Hearing Association (as it was called then) began emphasizing language in the scope of practice of its members. The addition of *Language* to the title came in the 1970s, when Norma Rees was president of ASHA (which preferred to keep its acronym rather than changing it to the unwieldy ASLHA).

Beginnings of Audiology

Audiology emerged as a distinct profession in the United States during World War II, where noise exposure to the modern weapons of the times created the necessity of diagnostic and rehabilitative services for many returning military personnel. At the time, audiologic services were administered by professionals in related areas, mostly otologists and speech-language pathologists, and included psychologists and teachers of the deaf, who ultimately became the first audiologists. The term *audiology* given to the new profession meaning "the study of (*logos*: Gr.; *audire*: L.) hearing" (Martin & Clark, 2012, p. 4) is attributed to otolaryngologist Norton Canfield and speech-language pathologist Raymond Carhart.

Robert West, a speech-language pathologist, is credited with expanding the discipline of speech correction to include hearing services (Bess & Humes, 2003). Audiologic services were officially recognized within the profession's purview by ASHA (then known as the American Academy of Speech Correction) in 1947, where the organization voted to include the term *hearing* in the association's title (Paden, 1975). At present, ASHA is the largest organization representing audiologists, with over 12,000 certified members, a number that is substantially lower than the membership of over 165,000 certified speech-language pathologists also represented by ASHA (ASHA, 2018b).

A movement to create an independent organization for audiologists resulted in the formation of the American Academy of Audiology (AAA) in 1988 with a mission to "promote quality hearing and balance care by advancing the profession of audiology through leadership, advocacy, education, public awareness and support of research" (AAA, 2018). With over 12,000 members, the AAA is currently the largest independent professional organization operated specifically by and for audiologists. Like ASHA, the AAA offers clinical certification to its qualified members, publishes a scientific journal, professional position statements, and practice guidelines in addition to consumer information, and conducts an annual national conference. There are numerous other organizations for the varying areas of audiology specializations, including hearing aid dispensing and pediatric and rehabilitative audiology.

About the Deaf Community and *Hearing Impairment*

There are many terms used to describe individuals with hearing loss, including *hard of hearing* or *hearing impaired*. The use of such terms may vary depending on the severity of the loss or the communicative method used by the individual, such as manual, spoken, written forms, or their combinations. The term *deaf* is specifically used to describe an individual with a severe to profound degree of hearing loss, such that hearing cannot be used as a principal means of receiving communication. Individuals who are deaf and communicate primarily using manual language (e.g., American Sign Language, or ASL), sharing a culture of similar traditions and values, are part of what is referred to as the *Deaf community* (differentiated by the term *deaf* with a capital D). At issue with its members is the connotation of disability or handicap often associated with terms relating to hearing loss. The Deaf community does not consider deafness a deficit but rather a characteristic of an individual's hearing acuity (Debonis & Donohue, 2008; Martin & Clark, 2012).

Current Issues

There are physical, occupational, and respiratory therapists; why are we not speech or hearing therapists? Currently, the master's degree is the minimum level of education for best practice in speech-language pathology, whereas the doctoral degree is required for practice in audiology. Accordingly, speech-language pathologists and audiologists do their own diagnosis, treatment, and discharge planning. There is no medical specialty with greater expertise in communication sciences and disorders than that of ASHA-certified practitioners. Although we may provide speech, language, and aural rehabilitation, we are not therapists. A therapist's professional duties are prescribed by a physician; take, for example, the activities of daily living skills for the occupational therapist (OT) and range-of-motion exercises for the physical therapist (PT). Referral from a physician to a speech-language pathologist, required for some insurance reimbursement, should properly indicate no more than "evaluate and treat."

The confusion continues when we try to describe the people we treat. Those of us who work in hospitals and medical centers may refer to our *patients*. In university speech and hearing centers, our graduate students tend to see *clients*. When they go off on externships in schools, they may work with *students*. If the placement is in a day treatment center for individuals with developmental disabilities (formerly referred to as *mentally retarded*), they become *providers* working with *consumers*.

English Mechanics

One interpretation of the title of the present section is that it will deal with chaps who work under the bonnets of lorries. Lexical ambiguity is the basis of much of what we think of as jokes.

However, the purpose of this chapter is to define, describe, and help in the practice of some basic concepts of English mechanics as they apply to professional writing in speech-language pathology and audiology.

The section includes information and practice on grammatical classes (parts of speech) and structure rules (syntax). We have devoted considerable attention to most parts of speech, but have given others a cursory review. Most writers have no difficulty using *conjunctions* (and, but, yet) to join two simple sentences to form a compound sentence, or to use them to join words, phrases, and clauses. Similarly, we don't need to teach you that *articles* (a, an, the) identify and specify nouns. Finally, *interjections* (ouch, ah, whoops) express emotion, and do not belong in professional writing. We have chosen to describe *particles* briefly, because the prepositional and adverbial forms they take may be somewhat confusing. Finally, we relate concepts of English mechanics to theories of language development and language disorders, and demonstrate how knowledge of syntax can apply to clinical intervention.

We have tried to answer the following questions: What are characteristics of nouns and verbs? How do we use pronouns? How do adjectives/attributes develop in typical children? What are the differences between adjectives and adverbs? What are content (lexical) and function (functor or helping) words? What is a noun phrase? What is a verb phrase? How do we put them together to form sentences? What kinds of sentences can we create?

Parts of Speech

(See Goldberg & Goldfarb, 2005)

Nouns

Acquired earlier than verbs

Processed more quickly

Have an identity independent of verbs

More typical stress patterns in English

More syllables and longer durations

Conceptually, mapped as things

Verbs

Verb relations often include nouns

More complex syntactically and morphologically

Greater range of meaning than nouns

Less typical stress patterns

Fewer syllables and shorter durations

Conceptually, mapped as relations

Limited number of verb forms convey a wide variety of meanings

Pronouns

There are nine types of pronouns, and some of them give professional writers considerable trouble. Let's look at the easier ones first.

1. An *indefinite pronoun* refers, in general terms, to a person or thing. Indefinite pronouns include *all*, *any*, *both*, *each*, *everyone*, *few*, *many*, *neither*, *none*, *nothing*, *several*, *some*, and *somebody*. Some examples of indefinite pronouns in sentences are:

   Several answers come to mind.

   Any exercise is usually better than none.

   Nothing good will come of this.

2. A *reflexive pronoun* refers back to the subject of a sentence. The reflexive pronouns are *herself*, *himself*, *itself*, *myself*, *ourselves*, *themselves*, and *yourselves*. These same words can also act as intensive pronouns (see C, below). Some examples of reflexive pronouns in sentences are:

   They should take better care of themselves.

You should make yourself scarce.

I learned much about myself in clinical practicum. (Note that *much* is preferable to *a lot*. In professional writing, try to avoid colloquial usage.)

3. An *intensive pronoun* strengthens or emphasizes the noun or pronoun that comes before it. Some examples of intensive pronouns in sentences are:

   Professor Serpanos herself told me to take this course.

   I myself would not have chosen to go.

4. A *demonstrative pronoun* points out a noun. The demonstrative pronouns are *that*, *these*, *this*, and *those*. Even though these pronouns may look like demonstrative adjectives, they are taking the place of a noun, as pronouns do. When *that*, *these*, *this*, and *those* are followed by nouns, they function as adjectives. If we say, "Take these before bedtime," then *these* functions as a demonstrative pronoun. However, if we say, "Take these pills before bedtime," then *these* functions as an adjective. Some examples of demonstrative pronouns in sentences are:

   That is what we should use.

   How can you handle all those?

5. An *interrogative pronoun* is used, as the reader has probably already guessed, when asking a question. Interrogative pronouns include *what*, *which*, *who*, and *whom*. They also attach to ever, as in the compound words *whatever*, *whichever*, *whoever*, and *whomever*. As with demonstrative pronouns, interrogative pronouns may look like interrogative adjectives, but these pronouns take the place of nouns. Note that *which*, *who*, *whose,* and *whom* may also be used as relative pronouns (see 6, below). Some examples of interrogative pronouns in sentences are:

   Which hat goes with this dress?

   What is the meaning of this?

   Whatever does Lola want? Note that in the song from the musical *Damn Yankees*, "Whatever Lola Wants (Lola Gets)," the word *whatever* is used as the object of a verb in a dependent clause.

6. A *relative pronoun* introduces a clause, or part of a sentence, that describes a noun. The relative pronouns are *that*, *which*, *who*, *whose,* and *whom*. Some examples of relative pronouns in sentences are:

   Use the test that you find most appropriate. *That* introduces "appropriate," which describes the test.

   Larry is a scientist who is familiar with the CSL. *Who* introduces "familiar with the CSL," which describes Larry.

7. A *subjective pronoun* acts as the subject of a sentence; a person or thing that performs the action of the verb. The subjective pronouns are *he*, *I*, *it*, *she*, *they*, *we*, and *you*. Some examples of two subjective pronouns in sentences are:

   She and I are assigned to the same client.

   We are never late, but they always are.

   It seems as if we'll never finish our 400 hours of practicum.

8. An *objective pronoun* acts as the object of a sentence; a person or thing receives the action of the verb. The objective pronouns are *her*, *him*, *it*, *me*, *them*, *us*, and *you*. Some examples of two objective pronouns in sentences are:

   Blame him for the mess, not us.

   Take her along with them.

9. A *possessive pronoun* indicates who owns something. The possessive pronouns are *hers*, *his*, *its*, *mine*, *ours*, *theirs*, and *yours*. As we note elsewhere, punctuation errors are the bane of professional writers who make errors when using possessive pronouns. We also note regional dialectal

variations for some possessive pronouns, especially *mines*. Some examples of possessive pronouns in sentences are:

The responsibility is mine, not hers.

When we get married, what was yours becomes ours.

Adjectives and Adverbs

Adjectives describe nouns or pronouns. It makes no difference if the description comes before (What a *cute* baby) or after the noun (That baby is so *cute*). Adverbs modify adjectives, verbs, and other adverbs, but not nouns or pronouns. *Adverbs* answer questions of how (where the adverb usually has the *-ly* ending), as well as when and where. The non-*ly* adverbs are called flat adverbs. If you are describing a careful worker, then you are using an adjective (to modify the noun, *worker*); but if you write about someone who works carefully, then you have used an adverb (to modify the verb, *works*).

Of course, as we are discussing English grammar, there are special rules regarding the *-ly* ending, which is not used when describing sense experiences of taste, smell, look, and feel. Then we drop the ending when using adverbs. Accordingly, a baby's head smells sweet, not sweetly; you look happy, not happily; a poor grade on an exam makes you feel bad, not badly; and chocolate tastes delicious, not deliciously. Another special rule applies to *good* and *well*. In general, good is an adjective (You did good work), and well is an adverb (You worked well). However, use well, and not good, when describing health. You may look good in your new clothes, but you will look well once you get over the flu. Elsewhere in this book we refer to comparatives (usually taking the ending *-er*) and superlatives (*-est*) in reference to adjectives and adverbs. However, we do not drop the *-ly* from an adverb when using the comparative form. That is, we do not speak *quieter*, but *quietly* in the audiology booth.

The use of certain classes of adjectives changes as children get older. Cognitive discrimination relates to stages of development in children, and reflects impairment related to brain damage in adults. According to Piaget's decentration theory (2001), the child develops the ability to move away from one system of classification to another. For some children, the ability to decenter from color to various aspects of form (that is, initially describing an object as blue, but then changing the description to big, round, and soft) begins in the preoperational period, between 2 to 7 years, and is usually completed during the concrete operational period of 7 to 11 years. Choosing color or form as the primary attribute in a controlled experiment has been shown (Goldfarb & Balant-Campbell, 1984) to differentiate neurotypical adults from those with left- and right-brain damage.

Prepositional Phrases

Most of us have heard (or even said), "Between you and I . . . " This prepositional phrase represents correct usage of *between*, because two elements are involved, but it is incorrect usage of the object of the preposition. That is, the sentence should start as, "Between you and me," because *between* is a preposition and *me* is the objective pronoun.

While (or, perhaps, *whilst*) it is appropriate to use the term *amongst* in British writing, the term *among* is preferred in American English usage. The same sentence that has the word *between* might also have the indefinite pronoun *both*; a sentence with *among* might also have the indefinite pronoun *all*.

Prepositions often refer to the position of one object in relation to another. One common clinical assignment for new SLP student clinicians is to work on basic spatial relations with young children who have a language delay. Therapy often begins with *in*, *on*, and *under*, which are used in grammar as prepositions. We remember taking an old shoebox, and cutting out a square in the lid to make a "preposition box." The clinician could put a toy "in" the box through the cutout; "on" the box, somewhere else on the lid; and, by lifting the shoebox, "under" the box.

Particles

Have you noticed that you can drink up and drink down, but you eat in only one direction (up, although you can chow down)? When a word that is usually a preposition or an adverb in another context joins with a verb to form a multi-word verb, that word is called a *particle*. An alphabetical list of the most commonly used particles are *along*, *away*, *back*, *by*, *down*, *forward*, *in*, *off*, *on*, *out*, *over*, *round*, *under*, *up*. The word *out* forms a phrasal verb in "look out," and the word *for* forms a prepositional verb in "care for."

Grammatical Morphemes

A morpheme is a minimal grammatical unit of a language that cannot be divided into smaller grammatical parts. The morpheme may be a word or a meaningful part of a word. How many morphemes are in the word "unconstitutional"? Your first job is to locate the free morpheme (also called a bound root) and then see which bound morphemes attach to it. If you said that the free morpheme was "constitution," nice try. Actually, "constitution" is a combination of the free morpheme "constitute," with the *-tion* ending needed to change a verb to a noun. The *-al* ending changes the word from a noun to an adjective, and the *un-* changes the word from affirmative to negative. So the correct answer is that there are four morphemes, one free and three bound.

In the Frank Loesser musical, *Guys and Dolls* (based on a story by Damon Runyon), the curtain rises to reveal a trio of men, one called Nicely-Nicely Johnson, singing, "Fugue for Tinhorns." Runyon and Loesser knew that an inappropriate adverbial form was required for the character's nickname. When asked how he was feeling, Johnson always replied, "Nicely-Nicely." Remember that we do not use the *-ly* ending for adverbs describing sense experience. Even though he was a morally sketchy character, Johnson's failed attempt at good grammar showed, paradoxically, that he was an upwardly mobile striver.

It is sometimes useful to have an operational definition of an utterance, especially when collecting pre-treatment data that will be compared to results of therapy. Our operational definition of an utterance is that it consists of two or more meaningfully related morphemes. Consider the following clinician–child interaction:

Clinician: Where do you live?
Child: New York

Clinician: What do you have?
Child: Toys

Even though "New York" has two words, it does not qualify as an utterance, because there is only one unit of meaning, or one morpheme. However, "Toys" does qualify as an utterance, because there is a free morpheme (toy) and a bound regular plural morpheme.

There are usually more morphemes than words in a series of utterances, but an individual utterance may have more words than morphemes. For example, consider the sentence, "Is the Empire State Building in New York City?" There are nine words, but only five morphemes, because "Empire State Building" and "New York City" have only one unit of meaning, even though there are three words. Much more frequently, bound morphemes tilt the imbalance in the other direction. For example, the sentence, "Nine miners were trapped irretrievably" has five words but 13 morphemes, as follows:

1. Nine: one word, one morpheme
2. Miners: one word, three morphemes (free morpheme "mine" and two bound morphemes of [er] for "one who" works in a mine, and the bound regular plural morpheme [s]).
3. Were: one word, three morphemes (present singular form of auxiliary verb "to be," plural form [is → are], and irregular past tense morpheme [are → were])
4. Trapped: one word, two morphemes (free morpheme "trap" and bound regular past tense morpheme)
5. Irretrievably: one word, four morphemes (free morpheme "retrieve" with negative morpheme [ir-], adjectival form [-able] and adverbial form [-ly]). It can even be argued that "retrieve" is composed of a prefix (re) and a bound root (trieve).

There are different ways to calculate mean length of utterance (*mlu*), which we hasten to add is a useful measure for baseline and baseline recovery, but much less useful as a therapy goal. Recursion rules, as noted below, can artificially inflate mlu without adding to syntactic complexity. Calculating mlu as number of words per utterance will usually yield a lower score than calculating by number of morphemes per utterance. We prefer to base mlu on a word-morpheme index. For example, if the average number of words in 100 consecutive utterances is 3.0 and the average number of morphemes in the same 100 utterances is 3.4, then the word–morpheme index will be 3.2.

Phrase Structure Rules

We don't read word by word, and we shouldn't think of writing in that way, either. If we consider the phrase to be the minimal unit for both reading and writing, then we need to learn some rules about phrases. Phrases are structured by *constituents*; that is, the word or group of words that function as a unit or can make up larger grammatical units. The property of language called *recursion* allows categories to be embedded (left-branching, right-branching, or center embedded). Recursion can theoretically produce infinitely long phrases. Some examples of recursion are in the increasingly longer, "This is the house that Jack built" and the Passover tale, "An only kid." In both cases, progressively longer sentences are constructed by appending right-branching dependent clauses beginning with the demonstrative pronoun *that.*

Here is an example of a simple sentence, followed by three dependent clauses. It comes from a song Sylvia Fine wrote for her husband, Danny Kaye to perform in the movie, "The Secret Life of Walter Mitty" (1947). Note that the first dependent clause makes the sentence syntactically correct, but preposterous. It is followed by the second of a pair of rhymed couplets that reveals the joke:

> I'll never forget the morning
> that Grandpa ate the awning
> to impress a pretty lady
> who went for men that were shady.

A sentence must contain a noun phrase (or a noun or pronoun) and a verb phrase. The minimal noun phrase consists of an article and a noun (e.g., *the student*; *a ball*). Other noun phrases can be created from a possessive pronoun + noun (e.g., *her mother*) or a possessive noun + noun (e.g., *John's house*). We can have an infinite number (theoretically, at least) of adjectives before the noun and still have a noun phrase (e.g., *the big red ball*). Look at our section (in the website) on building your vocabulary by using Shakespeare's insults to see some colorful examples of adjectives attached to nouns. The noun phrase can be the subject in a sentence, usually appearing at the beginning, or the object, usually appearing at the end.

Verb phrases are a bit more complicated. Transitive verbs require an object, whereas intransitive verbs do not. For example, *throwing* is usually a transitive verb, requiring a noun phrase, such as *the ball*, *a fit*, or *the game*. We can also combine *throwing* with a particle, as in *throwing up*, where *up* creates a phrasal verb, and the object of the phrase (*lunch* or *her food*) is understood. An intransitive verb does not take an object, either specified or understood. For example, the word *sleep* is intransitive, because you do not sleep anything (except, perhaps, a wink).

Sentences, in their basic form, are usually expressed in what is called *canonical order*, sometimes called *subject + verb + object* (or SVO), *agent-action-object*, or *who does what to whom* order. The construction is a noun phrase + a verb phrase, where the verb phrase includes a verb + a noun phrase. This becomes clearer when looking at tree diagrams (Figure 1–1), where S indicates a sentence, N is a noun, V is a verb, NP is a noun phrase, VP is a verb phrase, and T is an article (*the*, in the present example). We are using T here for clarity, instead of ART for article or DET for determiner, as is typically used in books on linguistics.

Tree diagrams are used principally in mathematics and linguistics. A parse tree represents an entire linguistic structure, from S (sentence) to leaf nodes (Singh + wrote + the + book). In the example above, the definite article ("the") is indicated by D for *determiner*. It can be a challenge to diagram ambiguous sentences. For example,

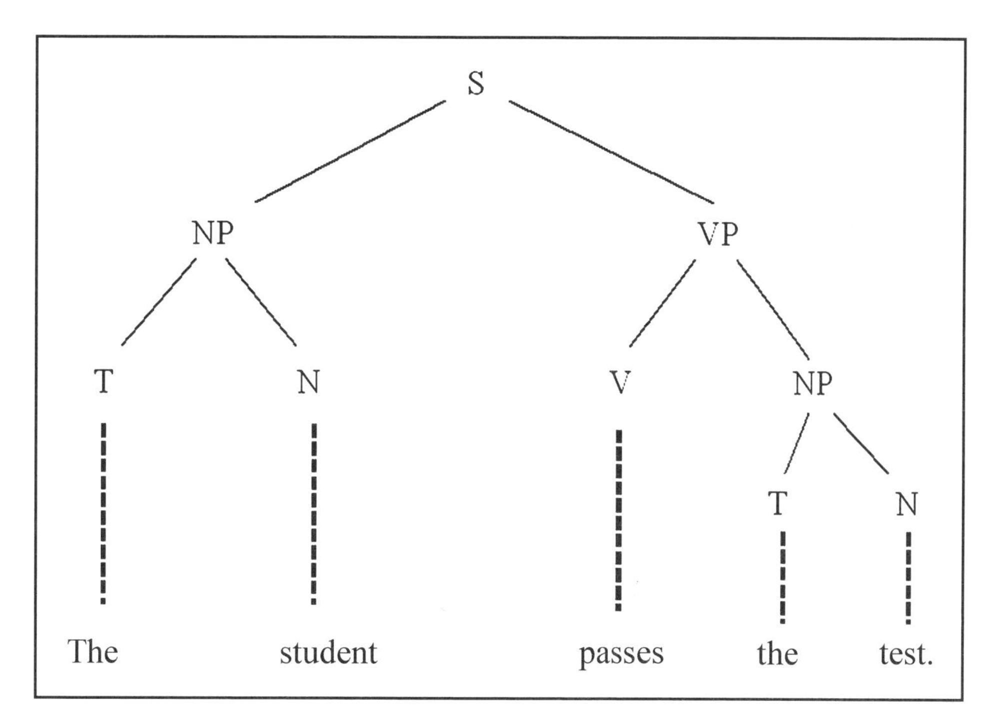

Figure 1–1. Example of a tree diagram, with a sentence in canonical order.

in the sentence, "Visiting relatives can be boring," the word *visiting* is an adjective if relatives have come to visit you, but a verb if you have gone to visit them. Try to create two parse trees for the sentence, "Flying airplanes can be dangerous."

The tree diagrams shown in Figures 1–1 and 1–2 represent examples of a simple sentence. They are also examples of *SAAD* (simple, active, affirmative, declarative) form, written in the present tense in Figure 1–1 and past tense in Figure 1–2. Now let's take out our language toy to play with each element.

We can change a simple sentence to one that is compound or complex. Using the example above, we can create a compound sentence by adding a conjunction (usually *and* and *but*, as well as others) and another simple sentence, such as, *The student passes the test, and the teacher is happy*. To create a complex sentence, add a phrase, not a sentence, and do not include a conjunction. We often add a prepositional phrase to a simple sentence to make it complex, as in, *The student who studied hard passes the test.*

The second part of SAAD is active, which we can change to passive. There are sentences that can become reversible passives, such as *The cow chased the sheep* where subject and object can switch places. In the passive form, both *The sheep was chased by the cow* (correct, given the active form above), and *The cow was chased by the sheep* (incorrect) are logical sentences. Errors occur when canonical order is assumed in a passive sentence. In non-reversible constructions, such as *The boy ate the ice cream cone*, S and O (or agent and object) cannot logically switch places. After all, cows can chase sheep and sheep can chase cows. Boys can eat ice cream cones, but ice cream cones cannot eat boys (except, perhaps, on Sesame Street). Not surprisingly, children and adults with language disorders have more comprehension problems when dealing with reversible passives than with non-reversible passives.

The opposite of affirmative is negative, and *The student does not pass the test* is an example of the negative transformation. Finally, there are three options for the last component, which can be declarative, interrogative, or imperative. An interrogative form might be, *Does the student pass the test?* and an imperative form might be, *Student, pass the test!* Of course, we can also change tense to past tense, as in, *The student passed the test*, or future tense, as in, *The student will pass the*

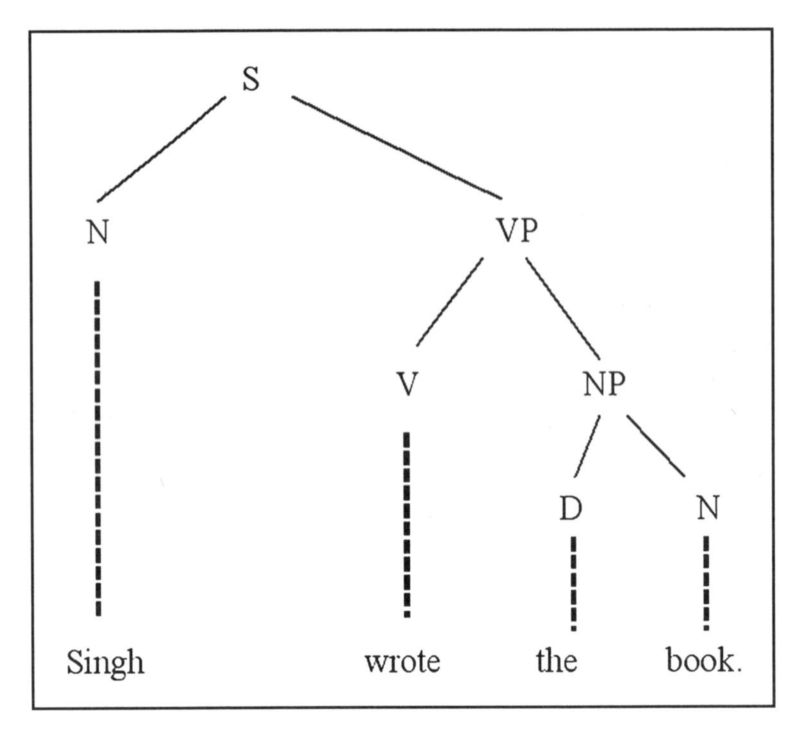

Figure 1–2. A parse tree.

test. We can combine transformations and make the sentence past tense, negative, and interrogative, for example, as in, *Didn't the student pass the test?*

Competence and Performance

The work you will do in the exercises that follow reflect what Chomsky (1957) called linguistic performance, which refers to actual acts of speaking, listening, reading, and writing, with temporal limitations (your instructor may have given you only five minutes to complete the exercise), and subject to a variety of distractions (stomach rumbling from hunger; noisy class next door). The task also requires linguistic competence, which refers to the underlying set of rules for syntax, meaning, and sound that make performance possible. We can't always infer competence from performance. The following is offered as an example of how a typical adult's syntactic competence may be challenged, even by a short sentence.

The cow the sheep chased jumped. We understand that the cow did the jumping and the sheep did the chasing. Look what happens when we add one more element: *The cow the sheep the dog chased jumped ran.* Now we're scratching our heads, even though the sentence is syntactically correct, if unusual. Adding the word "that" and changing the order helps: *The cow that the sheep chased, that the dog jumped, ran.* Does this give you a bit more empathy for children and adults with syntactic comprehension deficits?

Theoretically, we can insert an infinite number of relative clauses into a grammatically correct sentence. However, when we insert even two relative clauses instead of one, our comprehension is severely challenged. The advice given many years ago by Rolnick and Hoops (1969) to use short, simple sentences when speaking to adults with aphasia certainly makes sense in this context.

The three sentence types—simple, compound, and complex—are well named. Not surprisingly, most writers have greatest difficulty with complex sentences. Think of a complex sentence as an independent clause plus a dependent clause. It is fairly easy to write an independent clause, such as *The man ran up the stairs,* and a dependent clause (in this case, starting with a subordinating conjunction) such as *because he had to catch the train*. We then have three choices. The relative clause can be right-branching, as in, *The man ran up the stairs because he had to catch the train*; left-branching, as in, *Because he had to catch the train, the man ran up the stairs*; or center-imbedded, as in, *The man, because he had to catch the train, ran up the stairs*. All are correct, although, in the current example, right-branching seems most natural, and center-imbedded may feel forced. The sentence, *Throw the baby out the window a cookie*, seems not only a forced but a criminal version of the sentence, *Throw a cookie out the window for the baby*.

Apparent Regression

Young children may produce syntactic forms that confound their parents, if not the SLP who does the evaluation. The old ICP studies of Roger Brown (1973) indicate that, in typical language development in children, **I**mitation occurs before **C**omprehension of language, and both precede spontaneous **P**roduction. Accordingly, the child who recites the Pledge of Allegiance in first grade may have no idea what *pledge* or *allegiance* mean. Saying that the child is a little linguist who tries to write mental rules for a linguistic community is not the same as saying that the child is a little adult. Rules may be written and modified frequently during language acquisition. The 3-year-old child who had previously said, "I went out" and now says, "I goed out" might not need a referral for speech-language pathology services. This apparent regression may instead indicate that the child has now overgeneralized the regular bound morpheme representing past tense to a novel context, without understanding that "go" is an irregular verb. Not having heard adults say "goed," the child may be demonstrating linguistic competence for the regular past tense allomorph.

A Model of Syntax Training

In the website that accompanies this book, we provide a program of instruction for forms of "to be" (*is*, *are*, *am*), used as a verbal auxiliary (preceding a verb, as in, "He is running") and copula (preceding an adjective, as in, "We are hungry"). Our purpose here is to examine the four levels of programming, in terms of the degree of syntactic support that the clinician provides to the client. The following example refers to "to be" as a verbal auxiliary, not as a copula. We are using the structure: PN (pronoun) + Aux (auxiliary verb is/are/am) + V (verb) + ING (the gerund form).

Level I: Who is *verbing*? (Interrogative PN + Aux + V + ING) The target response requires only substituting the subjective pronoun "he," "she," or "it" for the interrogative pronoun "who." That is, if the clinician asks, "Who is sitting?" the client need provide only the target pronoun (let's say it's "she") to answer, "She is sitting."

Level II: What is *pronoun* doing? (Interrogative PN + Aux + PN + V + ING) The client now needs to delete the interrogative pronoun, move the subjective pronoun provided by the clinician to the beginning of the sentence, and substitute the specific verb for the word "doing" when responding, "She is sitting." The auxiliary verb (*is*) and the present participle form of the verb (*ing*) are provided by the clinician. *Sitting* may also be a gerund if it is used as a noun, as in "The photographer had a sitting for the wedding party" (Behrens, 2010).

Level III: What's happening? (Interrogative PN + contractible Aux + V + ING) The grammatical structure is provided, but the auxiliary verb now appears in its contracted form (*what's* instead of *what is*). The client substitutes a subjective pronoun for the interrogative pronoun, while maintaining pronoun position in the sentence. The auxiliary verb may be used in contracted (she's) or uncontracted (she is) (except in some instances, such as *There she's* for *There she is*) form, and the client substitutes the target verb for the verb "happen" before adding the present participle form (*ing*).

Level IV: Tell me about this picture. No contextual or grammatical support is provided.

Brain Mechanisms Underlying Syntax

Individuals with nonfluent (Broca's type) aphasia tend to have more difficulty retrieving verbs than nouns, whereas the reverse is true for those adults with fluent (Wernicke's type) aphasia. Nonfluent aphasia is associated with damage to the frontal lobe in the left hemisphere of the brain, and fluent aphasia with left temporal infarction. It is not surprising that Broca's area, located near the primary motor cortex, may be expected to influence action words (verbs); and that Wernicke's area, near what is sometimes called the "mental dictionary" in the fusiform gyrus, is more associated with nouns.

Some programs in communication sciences and disorders have a laboratory for research with a form of electroencephalography (EEG) called event-related potentials (ERP). An electrode net is placed on the head, and one-second EEG signal plots may be averaged over "easy," "difficult," and "control" trials from −100 ms to 900 ms. ERP signals are described in terms of positive and negative peaks and their latencies. Early components indicate intensity of the stimulus, and later components show attention to the stimulus. Brain responses may yield N400 signals (a negative peak occurring 400 milliseconds after presentation of the stimulus) for associative/semantic tasks. The response may be generated by having an individual engage in picture naming. A P600 signal may occur for syntactic processing, when individuals engage in a verb generation task.

Agrammatism and Paragrammatism

Individuals with nonfluent aphasia often have impaired expressive syntax, sometimes called agrammatism. There does not have to be an equivalent impairment (concordance) in receptive syntax, so some individuals who show the characteristic omission of function words (such as articles, auxiliary verbs, and prepositions) can recognize their absence in comprehension tasks. Agrammatic language is sometimes described as telegraphic, referring to pre-electronic communication days, when people would pay by the word to send a telegram. Accordingly, the lexical or content words were included, and the helping or function words were omitted. If you were robbed overseas, and could pay for only five words, "American Embassy Geneva Send Money" would probably work. Deleting the functors "[I am at the] American Embassy [in] Geneva" might not detract from your message, and you would have saved the cost of another five words. Where one notable characteristic of agrammatism is deletion of functors, individuals with paragrammatism (associated with fluent aphasia) may substitute one function word for another. One of our rules for writing diagnostic reports (see Chapter 8) is to say what the patient does, not what the patient is, so it is not appropriate to label an individual as having paragrammatism because of a substitution or two of a function word.

Typical Errors in Grammar

What about errors that people with typical brains (such as yours) might make? In our experience, they include run-on sentences and sentence fragments. We have addressed other frequent errors, including lack of agreement, as well as the misplaced apostrophe, in other sections of this book.

Run-on sentences: "Don't walk on the kitchen floor I just washed it." Does this sound like your mother, spoken in exasperation and haste? Run-on sentences can often be saved by a single strategic placement of a semicolon; in the present example, after the word "floor." Other sentences run on intentionally, as is apparent to anyone attempting to read James Joyce. We grant Joyce, one of the greatest writers in the English language, some leeway, but in professional writing, clarity, not literary merit, is paramount.

Sentence fragments: We have been told that the only people who insist on complete sentences in oral English are elementary school principals and speech-language pathologists. Most people would agree, though, that written sentences should be complete. A sentence fragment is not necessarily a short one. In fact, some writers lose control of their long sentences and don't realize they have not included a subject.

A *run-on sentence* is a sentence with at least two independent clauses and insufficient punctuation to separate them. Another way to view this is to think of a sentence with at least two complete thoughts that are forced together instead of connected properly.

To correct these sentences, you may use one or more of the following three options:

1. Separate clauses using punctuation.
2. Separate clauses using a conjunction.
3. Rearrange the sentence by adding or removing words.

Run-on sentence: *She wanted to do a pure-tone screening, the audiometer wasn't working properly, and she thought she should tell her supervisor.*

1st clause: *"She wanted to do a pure-tone screening"*

2nd clause: *"the audiometer wasn't working properly"*

3rd clause: *"she thought she should tell her supervisor"*

Corrected sentence: *She wanted to do a pure-tone screening, but the audiometer wasn't working properly. She thought she should tell her supervisor.* In the corrected sentence, we separated the first and second clauses using the conjunction "but." We also separated the second and third clauses using a period, and deleted the conjunction "and."

A long sentence is not necessarily a run-on. Some long sentences are grammatically correct, whereas some short sentences are run-ons. In clinical file writing, we tend to use simple, short sentences because they are easier to read and understand.

A *sentence fragment* cannot stand by itself because it does not contain even one independent clause. There are four reasons why a group of words may seem to act like a sentence but lack the components of a complete thought. Note that the word *phrase* means a group of words that does not contain a subject-verb pair. Also note that that the auxiliary verb *to do* is written in its singular form (*does*) and not the plural form (*do*) because it refers to the single *group,* not the plural *words.*

1. A prepositional phrase locates a noun in time and place, but does not have a subject-verb relationship within an independent clause. Example: *In our clinic, after registration, but before midterms.* We know the time and place, but there is no subject or verb.
2. A verbal phrase describes a noun or verb, but does not have a subject. Example: *Thrilled to be accepted into the graduate program of such a prestigious institution.* The subject of the sentence, probably a student, has not been identified.
3. The phrase uses the gerund (*-ing*) form of a verb without an auxiliary verb. *Most of the people receiving aural rehabilitation after their cochlear implants.* The gerund form can never function as a verb without an auxiliary verb (e.g., *are receiving*).
4. There is a dependent clause without an independent clause. *For the applicant to earn the Certificate of Clinical Competence awarded by ASHA.* The dependent word "for" is a subordinating conjunction. Even though there is a subject (*applicant*) and verb (*earn*), we need an independent clause (e.g., *Have the program director sign the form.*) to be included in the sentence. Note that the dependent clause can come before (*For the applicant to earn the Certificate of Clinical Competence awarded by ASHA, have the program director sign the form.*), after (*Have the program director sign the form for the applicant to earn the Certificate of Clinical Competence awarded by ASHA.*), or sometimes in the middle of the independent clause.

EXERCISES

Exercise 1–1. Pronouns

1. In the song, "I Feel Pretty" from the musical *West Side Story*, Maria's tormenters ask, "Which, what, where, whom?" Identify the wh- word that is not an interrogative pronoun.

 ____

2. Which words can never take an apostrophe, no matter what the context? Our's, it's, her's, their's, your's.

 ____

Identify the type of pronoun used in the following sentences:

3. Please assign the client to the student who comes in first.

 ____

4. Before intersession, take home everything that is yours.

 ____

5. Give these to the client on the first day.

 ____

6. Who knows what will happen this semester?

 ____

7. I was also nervous on the first day of practicum.

 ____

8. You will know yourself if therapy is effective.

 ____

9. Any standardized test is not useful without skilled interpretation.

____

10. Give them the results next week.

____

Exercise 1–2. Adjectives and Adverbs

1. How is the weather today? (hot, hotly)

____

2. What is her reputation as a student clinician? (bad, badly)

____

3. How did she perform in her audiologic evaluation? (bad, badly)

____

4. Did he do it by accident or on purpose? (purposeful, purposefully)

____

5. Were you late or on time? (late, lately)

____

6. Is the rain coming down hard or soft? (hard, hardly)

____

7. How did he eat his food? (greedy, greedily)

____

8. How did she play the piano? (perfect, perfectly)

____

9. What score did you get on the quiz? (perfect, perfectly)

____

10. How do you feel about learning grammar? (delighted, delightedly)

____

Exercise 1–3. Between–Among/Object of the Preposition

Between–Among

1. Divide the candy between the three of you.

2. The choice for NSSLHA President was between Reem, Renee, and Dana.

3. Graduate students need to decide among speech-language pathology and audiology as a major.

4. When you are presented with all the choices, you have to decide between them.

5. Make up your mind among both of them, whichever you want.

Object of the Preposition

6. Her and Elizabeth were both accepted.

7. Give the books to he and I.

8. The best judge of his errors is him.

9. Us and the professors are going to ASHA.

10. A hospital is the best placement for you and I.

Exercise 1–4. Sentence Structure

Beginner

1. *Elizabeth failed a pure-tone screening*. Change the sentence . . .
   a. from simple to complex

   ____

   b. from past to present tense

   ____

   c. from declarative to interrogative

   ____

2. *The toddler was scheduled for Tot Talk twice a week*. Change the sentence . . .
   a. from complex to compound

   ____

   b. from active to passive

   ____

   c. from declarative to interrogative

   ____

3. *Give the Goldman-Fristoe to Billy*. Change the sentence . . .
   a. from imperative to interrogative

   ____

   b. from affirmative to negative

   ____

   c. from present to future tense

   ____

4. *The Praxis II exam, which was taken twice, wasn't a good indicator of John's ability*. Change the sentence . . .
   a. from negative to affirmative

   ____

b. from passive to active

____

c. from complex to compound

____

5. *Have you seen my book?* Change the sentence . . .
   a. from past to present tense

   ____

   b. from simple to complex

   ____

   c. from affirmative to negative

   ____

Advanced

6. *Joe drinks warm beer*. Change the sentence . . .
   a. to negative interrogative

   ____

   b. to complex past tense

   ____

   c. to compound future tense

   ____

7. *Janet doesn't wear her hearing aids in church*. Change the sentence . . .
   a. to simple affirmative

   ____

   b. to compound interrogative

   ____

   c. to affirmative future tense

   ____

8. *Bill helped George in therapy.* Change the sentence . . .
   a. to complex passive

   ____

   b. to interrogative future tense

   ____

   c. to imperative present tense

   ____

9. *Suzy wants a preschool externship placement.* Change the sentence . . .
   a. to negative interrogative future tense

   ____

   b. to complex interrogative past tense

   ____

   c. to compound negative interrogative

   ____

10. *Cindy saw Fran in the clinic.* Change the sentence . . .
    a. to negative imperative present tense

    ____

    b. to compound future interrogative

    ____

    c. to simple passive negative interrogative future tense

    ____

Exercise 1–5. Agrammatism/Paragrammatism

1. *John brain tumor.* Agrammatism or paragrammatism? Why?

2. *John was a brain tumor.* Agrammatism or paragrammatism? Why?

Exercise 1–6. Analyze the Grammatical Errors

Here is an example (from Halpern & Goldfarb, 2013) of the spontaneous speech of an individual with mild-moderate nonfluent aphasia and agrammatism. Try to do a bit of detective work to analyze and correct RM's grammatical errors.

> "Good morning. My name is RM. I am Forest Hills Gardens with a house. Normally I started September 1st. I was working Irving Trust Company at night. Four hundred people. I was the boss. Data processing. A lot of girls, like a hundred girls, clean up. These are things I can't say exactly. Clean up, more or less. Wall Street."

____

____

____

____

Exercise 1–7. Correct the Following Run-On Sentences

1. The Goldman-Fristoe and the PLS and the CELF test articulation and language.

2. I used to give the WAB now I give the BDAE to examine for aphasia.

3. Renee is an expert in fluency disorders she specializes in stuttering.

4. I study speech, I study language, my teachers are great.

5. Audiology is my favorite subject it lets me help people and I want to have a private practice after I graduate.

6. John didn't say much at his evaluation just a few one-word answers and one three-word spontaneous utterance.

7. For a complete audiological evaluation, give a speech discrimination test, it's important to find out how speech is understood.

8. I like my classes on Mondays and Wednesdays and I don't like Fridays, the weekend starts on Friday.

9. We need to test babies early if we wait to test their hearing it may be too late.

10. The hard part of speech science is acoustics, you have to learn formulas, and math and physics weren't my strongest undergraduate subjects.

____

Exercise 1–8. Correct the Sentence Fragments in the Following Paragraph

Although, the number of required credits is increasing for a graduate degree in communication sciences and disorders. Some of the older professors remember. When it was possible to earn a graduate degree in one year as a full-time student. Which is hard to believe. It seems unreasonable that my teachers to get a graduate degree with only 33 credits. And only 300 hours of clinical practicum. Especially with so much complicated information to absorb. Of course, such courses as dysphagia that weren't required a generation ago. More clinical privileges and responsibilities in speech-language pathology. Cochlear implants on clinical practice in audiology. All in all, students learning more now.

Exercise 1–9. Change these complex sentences with center-imbedded relative clauses to two simple sentences and then to sentences that are left-branching, right-branching, and compound.

1. The audiologist, because she did a complete audiological evaluation, tested air conduction, bone conduction, and speech recognition thresholds.

   a. Two simple sentences ______________________________

   ____

   ____

   ____

   b. Left-branching complex sentence ______________________________

   ____

   ____

   ____

   c. Right-branching complex sentence ______________________________

   ____

   ____

   ____

   d. Compound sentence ______________________________

   ____

   ____

   ____

2. Brainstem evoked response audiometry, which is used to search for retrocochlear lesions, evaluates auditory function from the eighth nerve through the brainstem.

   a. Two simple sentences ______________________________

   ____

   ____

   ____

b. Left-branching complex sentence ____

____

____

____

c. Right-branching complex sentence ____

____

____

____

d. Compound sentence ____

____

____

____

3. The smallest bone in the body, which is one of three bones in the ossicular chain, is the stapes.

a. Two simple sentences ____

____

____

____

b. Left-branching complex sentence ____

____

____

____

c. Right-branching complex sentence ____

____

____

____

d. Compound sentence ______________________________

____

____

____

4. The new student clinician, who is to assess articulation, used a developmental model.

a. Two simple sentences ______________________________

____

____

____

b. Left-branching complex sentence ______________________________

____

____

____

c. Right-branching complex sentence ______________________________

____

____

____

d. Compound sentence ______________________________

____

____

____

5. The term "stammering," that is used in the United Kingdom, is sometimes used interchangeably with the term "stuttering."

   a. Two simple sentences ______________________________

   ____

   ____

   ____

   b. Left-branching complex sentence ______________________________

   ____

   ____

   ____

   c. Right-branching complex sentence ______________________________

   ____

   ____

   ____

   d. Compound sentence ______________________________

   ____

   ____

   ____

Exercise 1–10. Identify the number of morphemes in the following highlighted words, and explain why you found that number.

1. I had to do 10 hours of observation for my **audiological** practicum.

   a. How many morphemes? _______________

   b. Why?

   ____

   ____

2. Stuttering is an **atheoretical** discipline.

   a. How many morphemes? _______________

   b. Why?

   ____

   ____

3. Should auditory processing disorders be treated by a speech-language **pathologist**?

   a. How many morphemes? _______________

   b. Why?

   ____

   ____

4. Why is a clinical **doctorate** required for audiology but not for speech-language pathology?

   a. How many morphemes? _______________

   b. Why?

   ____

   ____

5. How many undergraduate observation hours are credited to the graduate clinical **practicum** requirement?

   a. How many morphemes? ______________

   b. Why?

   ____

   ____

We now move on to Chapter 2 "Writing Rules," where the professional writer can practice identifying and correcting some of the more common mistakes.

References

American Academy of Audiology. (2018). *Academy information*. Retrieved from http://www.audiology.org/about/information/Pages/default.aspx

American Speech-Language-Hearing Association. (2018a). *About the American Speech-Language-Hearing Association (ASHA)*. Retrieved from http://asha.org/about/

American Speech-Language-Hearing Association. (2018b). *ASHA summary membership and affiliation counts, year-end 2017*. Retrieved from https://www.asha.org/uploadedFiles/2017-Member-Counts.pdf

Behrens, S. J. (2010). *Grammar: A pocket guide*. New York, NY: Routledge.

Bess, F. H., & Humes, L. (2003). *Audiology: The fundamentals* (4th ed.). Philadelphia, PA: Lippincott Williams & Wilkins.

Brown, R. (1973). *A first language: The early stages*. Cambridge, MA: Harvard University Press

Chomsky, N. (1957). *Syntactic structures*. The Hague, Netherlands: Mouton.

DeBonis, D. A., & Donohue, C. L. (2008). *Survey of audiology* (2nd ed.). Boston, MA: Pearson Education.

Goldberg, E., & Goldfarb, R. (2005). Grammatical category ambiguity in aphasia. *Brain and Language, 95*, 293–303.

Goldfarb, R. (1985). Speech handicaps/communication disorders. In T. Husen & T. N. Postlethwaite (Eds.), *The international encyclopedia of education* (pp. 4760–4766). Oxford, UK: Pergamon.

Goldfarb, R., & Balant-Campbell, A. (1984). Cognitive discrimination in brain-damaged adults: Color vs. form preference. *Perceptual and Motor Skills, 58*, 63–71.

Halpern, H., & Goldfarb, R. (2013). *Language and motor speech disorders in adults* (3rd ed.). Burlington, MA: Jones & Bartlett Learning.

Jones, J. E., Obler, L. K., Gitterman, M., & Goldfarb, R. (2002). The interface of phonology and morphology in agrammatism: Negation in African American vernacular English. *Brain and Language, 83*, 164–166.

Martin, F., & Clark, J. (2012). *Introduction to audiology* (11th ed.). Needham Heights, MA: Allyn & Bacon.

Paden, E. (1975). ASHA in retrospect: Fiftieth anniversary reflections. *ASHA*, 571–572.

Piaget, J. (2001). *The language and thought of the child* (3rd ed.). London, UK: Taylor & Francis.

Rolnick, M., & Hoops, H. R. (1969). Aphasia as seen by the aphasic. *Journal of Speech and Hearing Disorders, 34*, 48–53.

Writing Rules

The following may look like the drill portion of the book, but, before you have a MEGO (my eyes glaze over) moment, remember that we are playing with our language toy. It probably will take less time to learn the skills in this chapter than to learn the intricacies of a new website or video game, and it will pay off handsomely in terms of your credibility as a professional writer.

In this chapter, you will be required to edit worksheets on basic rules of form (punctuation, spelling, grammatical morphemes), as well as content and composition (semantics, sentence structure).

1. Identify errors on the worksheets.
2. Correct the errors.

Many of the examples in the worksheets are composites of student writing. That is, we have attempted to combine examples from thousands of students and decades of courses. If we have taught you at some level, graduate or undergraduate, don't worry that your most egregious errors will be included for all to see. In fact, we are grateful to you for showing us what aspects of professional writing are most likely to cause errors.

There are 33 exercises in this chapter, beginning with basic rules of form and ending with general problems of content and composition. Work on specific issues related to form in Worksheets 1 to 20. Then try to correct the errors of form, content, and composition in Review Worksheets 21 to 33. In all cases, indicate which errors you have found. Even if you are not sure how to correct these errors, it is important to identify them. An important goal of speech-language or hearing intervention is improving the client's self-correction, but success depends first on sharpening self-monitoring skills. Similarly, noticing writing errors is a prerequisite to correcting them.

Errors in Form

Errors in form may often be detected by judicious proofreading. It is helpful to have a second set of eyes proofread your professional writing before you submit it (that's what roommates and loved ones are for). Be on the lookout for spelling and punctuation errors, as well as more hard-to-find errors involving grammatical morphemes and abbreviations. For example, consider expanding an abbreviation as a plural: Similar to the rule of plural usage (see Apostrophes, Possessives, and Plurals below), when referring to more than one item that has been abbreviated, no apostrophe is required, for example:

Auditory brainstem responses (ABRs),
Electroencephalograms (EEGs)

Writing Form (punctuation, spelling, grammatical morphemes)

Punctuation

Our Pet, Peeve

For those whose eyes glaze over at the thought of punctuation and cannot imagine anyone using a comma, dash, semicolon, or colon as a toy, please avail yourselves of a recording of the legendary Victor Borge performing "phonetic punctuation." You may laugh yourself off your seat.

Target Skill: Commas

Rules of punctuation seem to be guided by the notion that every generalization is false, including this one. Regarding commas, high school English teachers may invoke the *when in doubt, leave it out* rule, based on student compositions with commas appearing after rather than before conjunctions. Beyond the accepted convention that commas are needed between every three numbers in a group (e.g., 1,000,000 to represent one million; note the comma after *e.g.*; there would also be a comma after *i.e.*; see Latin Abbreviations below for rules on those), there are other situations where writers tend to have more trouble (Shipley, 1982).

Most references on punctuation insist on a comma before the *and* to separate items of a series of three or more (e.g., parsley, sage, rosemary, and thyme), which is called "closed punctuation." Shipley (1982) agrees, rejecting the "open punctuation" model of no comma before the *and*, and so do we.

As noted in Out-of-Control Sentences below, commas are needed in sentences with relative or nonessential clauses. However, we do not use a comma after *relative* in the sentence above, because *relative or nonessential* describes and identifies the clause. A comma is also not used between two parts of a compound predicate (e.g., *The client progressed well and was discharged from therapy.*) Finally, there is a comma after *however* (and *finally* in this sentence) when used alone to begin a phrase or sentence, but not when used as part of a phrase (e.g., *However you go, don't take the train*). Our colleague (Behrens, 2010) notes that the #1 hotspot for comma splices resulting in run-on sentences is the independent clause-comma-however-comma-independent clause, e.g., *The client arrived early, however, the clinician was running late.* If the punctuation is revised by substituting a semicolon for the comma after *early*, then the sentence is correct, e.g., *The client arrived early; however, the clinician was running late.*

Target Skill: Hyphens and Dashes

Both hyphens and dashes are made with the lowercase key to the right of the zero, one press for hyphen and two for dash. Microsoft Word will automatically reformat the double dash into a single longer "em" dash. Dashes are to be used sparingly, and only when interrupting the flow of a sentence. The em dash is used to set off an element added to amplify or to digress from the main clause. Most sentences can be changed to avoid the use of dashes, without any obvious loss of clarity. The single dash or hyphen, also called "en" dash in different contexts, is used much more frequently, and is used between words of equal weight in a compound adjective; use no space before or after. The en dash is different from a hyphen. For example, number ranges are separated with en dashes in this book, not hyphens. The *Publication Manual of the American Psychological Association* (6th ed.; American Psychological Association, 2010) notes that, with some exceptions, hyphens are not used after the following prefixes:

after	intra	semi
anti	multi	sub
bi	non	super
co	over	supra
counter	post	ultra
extra	pre	un
infra	pseudo	under
inter	re	

Some words that do not use a hyphen include bilateral, interjudge, and posttest. The hyphen is always used when the same vowel is doubled, such as re-elect, and co-occur. An important qualification (Hegde, 2010) is that some words lose their hyphen and become solid words, so make sure to check current usage with an up-to-date dictionary. We note that email (hyphen was in current use in the second edition of this book) is now email. Finally, some compounds take the hyphen only when they precede, but not when they follow, the terms they modify (e.g., first-generation male relatives/male relatives in the first generation), or when used as an adjective, but not as a verb (follow-up activities/no need to follow up).

Target Skill: Colons and Semicolons

Most of us know that we use a colon before a series of items in a list, with the colon frequently preceded by the phrase, the following. For example, ASHA certification requires evidence of coursework in the following disciplines: biological sciences, including biology and other life sciences; physical sciences, including physics, earth science, and astronomy; social sciences, including sociology and psychology; and mathematics. Note that the items in the series of biological, physical, and social sciences are separated by semicolons, and descriptors of these items are separated by commas.

We also use colons to represent ratios, either with numerals, such as 10:1, or with words, such as male: female. For example, most authors estimate the male: female ratio of individuals who stutter as 3:1.

There remains some confusion about punctuation in notation of years and months of age in describing participants in an experiment. Generally agreed upon is the notion that a period separating years and months may be misleading. An individual who is 7 years 6 months of age is not 7.6 years; the correct notation is 7.5, because that person is 7½ years old. If it is better to avoid the confusion of the period between years and months, should there be a colon or semicolon separating them? Both have been used, with colons having more frequent use. That is, our 7½-year-old individual would be 7:6, representing 7 years and 6 months.

Finally, colons are used after the place of publication in book citations. An example, using the present publisher, is San Diego, CA: Plural.

We have seen semicolons used above, where there are items already separated by commas. Semicolons often take the place of a conjunction, when the two independent clauses are related. For example, we may write about two sets of scores with a semicolon separating the clauses instead of the conjunction and. Thus, JK's bone conduction thresholds were within normal limits; his air conduction thresholds were 40 dB in the right ear.

Semicolons are also used in referencing, using the separation by comma rule, when multiple citations are listed. For example, we might indicate that Nursery rhymes are useful in child language development (Horner, 2006; Winkin, Blinkin, & Nod, 2007).

Colon or Semicolon? (see Shipley, 1982, p. 54)

For ratios or proportions (colon, as in 10:1)

Before listing a series (colon, as in, We evaluated the following clients:)

When items are already separated by commas (semicolon, as in, ASHA conventions were held in Philadelphia, PA, in 2010; San Diego, CA, in 2011; and Atlanta, GA, in 2012.)

When independent clauses are not separated by a conjunction (semicolon, as in, Our meeting will be held at 12:00; pizza will be served.)

When indicating discontinuous pages (semicolon, as in pp. 14; 23–27)

Spelling

Target Skills: Archaic and Stilted Usage; American Spelling

Ye Olde Antique Shoppe

Driving through some of the beautiful small towns of New England is an antique-lover's paradise. Some of the shops have adopted pseudo-old-fashioned spelling as a way of highlighting the antiques they sell. Unfortunately, the titles often make an unintentionally humorous mistake. The word *ye* in Ye Olde Antique Shoppe, combined with the spelling of *olde*, suggests Middle English (Remember when you read Chaucer's *Canterbury Tales*?), whereas a more recent definition of *ye* is "you." Of the many, varied, and ingenious insults created in American English, no one has ever hurled the epithet, *You old antique shop* at a transgressor. In fact, the *y* in *ye* was a variation of the thorn (/ð/, or voiced *th* sound) in Middle English, so that *ye* was pronounced as "the." The message of this anecdote is to avoid archaic usage.

American spelling does not permit the use of European English forms, such as *colour, centre*, and *programme*, even if Spell-Check™ does not highlight *centre*. European journals will accept manuscripts with American spelling, although some will change it to the forms noted above. The European notation of calendar dates is probably clearer than the American version. For example, in the section Beginnings of Speech-Language Pathology, writing the dates of the first meeting of the ICLP as 3–5 July 1924 avoids a comma, and nicely separates the days of the month from the year. However, American writers should continue to use the less clear version of July 3–5, 1924.

More than 20 years ago, RG had a meeting with his daughter's first-grade teacher on Open School Night. The teacher gave a very positive report, but expressed concern about the topic of inventive spelling. It seems Elizabeth was insisting on spelling words correctly, rather than the way she thought they should be spelled, based on the way the words sounded. In an odd way, the teacher was making an interesting point. Communication through the Internet, in chat rooms, and in emails has resulted in a fascinating and inventive spelling system. Similarly, new terms and new forms of familiar terms seem to go through a period of natural selection where only the fittest ones survive. In the 1980s the adverbial form of the word *auditory* was written as *auditorily, auditorally*, and *auditorially*. Spell-Check doesn't have a reasonable substitution for any of these terms. The *auditorily* form seems to have survived, probably because it follows a rule (e.g., happy → happily; hungry → hungrily) accepted for other words.

Finally, professors and supervisors will not be impressed if their students use stilted vocabulary. There are places for stilted words, or they would not exist, but clinical and professional reports are generally not such places.

Grammatical Morphemes and Common Confusions

Target Skills: Apostrophes, Possessives, and Plurals

Apple's and Orange's

> He who sells what isn't his'n
> Must buy it back or go to prison.
>
> (Daniel Drew, July 29, 1797–September 18, 1879)

Most of us have been to markets where *apple's* and *orange's* are for sale. If we learn the rule that the apostrophe is used only for possession and abbreviation, but never for plurals, we will not make this mistake. We may make another mistake with possessive pronouns, though, writing *their's, our's, her's*, and especially *it's* (curiously never *hi's*; it must have to do with the placement of a vowel before the *s*), where the apostrophe should not appear. On the other hand, slavish devotion to correcting "mistakes" may interfere with our appreciation of diversity in English usage. For example, 19th-century American English included such pronouns as *your'n, our'n*, and *his'n*. Indeed, Drew's aphorism above works only because of the rhyme enabled by the use of *his'n*. Current usage of *dem* ("them," with the phonological rule of prevocalic /ð/ → /d/) as a plural allomorph in rural areas of the West Indian island of Jamaica differs from the [s] morpheme applied to the ends of words to represent plural in urban areas of Jamaica, but is not a mistake. In a way, it may be seen as an improvement. Saying *gimme dem book* refers to a request for generic books, whereas *gimme de book dem* refers to a request for specific books.

With the *caveat* (Latin for "warning," as in *caveat emptor*, or, "Let the buyer beware") about diversity understood, some examples and exercises for apostrophes, possessives, and plurals follow. We also note that, in current professional and scholarly usage, it is no longer appropriate to use *apostrophe + s* after the name of the scientist associated with a disease. That is, *Alzheimer disease* and *Parkinson disease* are used, rather than Alzheimer's and Parkinson's. For more examples and exercises in this and other writing topics, see Hegde (2010).

Just as we exercise care to avoid using an apostrophe to turn a plural into a possessive (e.g., I bought two delicious *apple's*), we must also avoid turning a possessive into a plural (e.g., The *supervisors* desk is down the hall). Remember that the apostrophe may also be used to mark a missing letter or letters (e.g., I *can't* [cannot] do it. *That's* [that is] mine.).

Evaluate the following as correct or incorrect and explain why or why not. Try adding your own examples.

> Supervisor: Which students therapy plan is this?
>
> Student: Its not mine; its her's. Mine already received its grade.

The supervisor above may be referring to one or more students. If the therapy plan represented individual effort, it would be the *student's* therapy plan; if it was a group project, it would be the *students'* work. The answer by the student indicated that the therapy plan was individual work, but used an unnecessary apostrophe in the pronoun *hers*. Finally, there are different uses of the pronoun *it*. The first two uses represent an abbreviation of *it is*, and should be written as *it's*; the last usage, indicating that the therapy plan already possessed a grade, was correct. A good strategy for deciding if an apostrophe belongs with a pronoun is to use the word *is*, and then decide if an abbreviation is appropriate. In the example above, we can reasonably write, *It is not mine*, so *It's not mine* would also be correct. There is never a time that *her is* would be correct, so there can be no apostrophe in *hers*. The interaction, written correctly, follows.

> Supervisor: Which student's therapy plan is this?
>
> Student: It's not mine; it's hers. Mine already received its grade.

The owner of a diner is pleased with his new line cook and decides to send a text of congratulations. Instead of writing "You know your toast," the owner writes, "You know you're toast." Errors in punctuation (and grammar in the present case) can cause anxiety.

Students tend to have problems with your/you're, its/it's, and their/they're, because they are homonyms; they sound the same. In addition, the apostrophe is used for the possessive form of proper nouns or names, so the extension of the apostrophe to the possessive form of the pronoun "its" may seem logical in a way. Word order doesn't always help; here are some examples:

> Show the dog its bone. Show the dog it's wrong.
>
> Imagine their reaction. Imagine they're coming.

The confusion doesn't affect were/we're, because they're pronounced differently, unless you're confusing "We're wolves" with "werewolves."

The simple solution is to use the noncontracted forms—*I am, you are, it is*—until you reach a comfort level with the contractible form. In other words, if you write, "Show the dog it is wrong," you won't (or will not) have a problem with a misplaced apostrophe. If you write, "Show the dog it is bone," you will likely realize that the contraction "it's" does not apply, and that the sentence requires "its" as a possessive pronoun.

Target Skills: Correct Use of Upper- and Lowercase Letters

A Capital Offense

Some school districts have taken cursive writing out of the elementary school curriculum. We never much liked the cursive uppercase "Q," which looks like an overgrown number 2. At the same time, we grieve for the future pharmacists who will have to read handwritten prescriptions written by these children who may grow up to become medical doctors. When inkwells are replaced by modems, that is progress, but when professional writers don't know up (capital letter) from down (lowercase), then that is regression.

Later in this book we will show how to go up and down in the Harvard Outline.

Most writers are familiar with basic rules of capitalization relating to first words and proper nouns. Frequent errors occur when capital letters are sometimes used, and sometimes not, in the same word. For example, there is a lowercase *p* in *the professor*, but a capital letter in *Professor Singh*. Another inconsistency relates to hyphenated terms. We capitalize all first letters in hyphenated titles of organizations (e.g., American Speech-Language-Hearing Association) or volumes (e.g., *Models of Short-Term Memory*), but not in titles of articles or books appearing in a reference list (e.g., *Smith, J., 2006. Noun-verb ambiguity in aging*). We also capitalize the first letter of a noun when it is followed by a numeral or a letter, such as Section 1.3 or Exhibit A. There is no universal use of the convention of using a capital letter after a colon in the title of a book or article. We agree there should be a capital *A* in such a title as, *Neurolinguistics: A book of readings*, when cited in the reference section of a journal article.

The poet e. e. cummings distinguished himself not only by his writing, but also by his signature, which he insisted be in the lower case. Users of social media, such as Twitter, may try to subvert the 140-character limit by abbreviating, with capital letters substituting for words typically written in lower case. Twitter officially expanded its character count to 280 on November 7, 2017. And yes, we old folks know that POMS means, "parent over my shoulder." There is no claim here that individual expression should be suppressed on social media. It's hard to stand out if everyone writes the same way, and who is harmed if the individual refers to herself as *i* in the lower case? Problems arise when these adopted quirks generalize to email correspondence to professors, employers, or professional colleagues. Not all electronic media or written communicative interactions are appropriate for rule bending.

When she is out of town, and a student needs the signature of the AuD coordinator (YCS), our office administrator, Jill Wishney, will (with permission of Prof. Serpanos) sign her name and add her initials in parentheses and in lowercase. In other words, she will sign Yula C. Serpanos, PhD (jw). This shows that someone else has signed the form. Adhering to this notation might have prevented an enormous amount of suffering caused in part by the use of unauthorized electronic signatures, when banks automatically approved balloon payment mortgage loans that should not have been offered. Both the authorized individual and the person who has been given permission to sign in the signatory's absence (and add lowercase initials) are accountable for the approval of the document.

Target Skills: Noun–Pronoun, Subject–Verb, and Tense Agreement

Are We in Agreement?

Many errors of agreement represent the writer's effort to avoid gender bias by using a plural pronoun, such as *them* or *their*. For the past few years, it has been accepted that a person who prefers *they* can use it as *their* pronoun. Although gender neutrality is a laudable goal (see Put Your Gender in Neutral below), it is no excuse for poor grammar. The most common error of agreement is lack of correspondence between the noun and pronoun (e.g., *A student wishing to receive a change of grade must speak to their instructor first.*). The error here is lack of agreement between the singular noun, *student*, and the plural pronoun, *their*. The two easiest ways of correcting agreement are to change the subject of the sentence to a plural, (*students*), or to substitute an article for a pronoun before the object of the sentence, (*an instructor* or *the instructor*).

EXAMPLE:
Correct versions, without gender bias:

1. Students wishing to receive a change of grade must speak to their instructor first.
2. A student wishing to receive a change of grade must speak to an instructor first.
3. A student wishing to receive a change of grade must speak to the instructor first.

Subject and Verb Must Agree in Number

That is, if the subject of the sentence (which may or may not be the first noun or pronoun in the sentence) is a plural, then use the plural form of the verb. Here are some tricky examples:

EXAMPLE:

No model, whether organismic, environmental, or interactive, *is/are* adequate to explain the onset of stuttering.

Answer: *is*, because the singular form of *to be* corresponds with the singular form of *model*.

EXAMPLE:

Schuell is among the aphasiologists who *propose/proposes* a reduction-of-efficiency model.

Answer: *propose*, because the verb relates to the plural *aphasiologists*, not the singular *Schuell*.

Another Error in Agreement Involves Tense Markers

This error occurs when the writer loses control of the sentence or paragraph, usually by creating sentences that are unnecessarily complex. Consider the following:

EXAMPLE:

When he discussed whether or not conductive hearing loss led to delayed language development or other language disorders, Ventry shows that we must study the literature carefully.

The agreement error in the sentence above relates to the verbs *discussed* and *led* (past tense) and *shows* (present tense). The injunction *to study* (present tense) the literature carefully does not violate agreement, even if the other verbs are past tense, because it is advice for us to take now.

Target Skills: Imply/Infer; Creeping/Crawling; Home/Hone; Eager/Anxious; Regard/Regards

Confused Pairs (and Other Dazed Fruit)

Understanding inferences requires decoding of implied meanings of spoken words, sentences, and discourse. Both speaker and hearer must have prior knowledge of the world, of lexical items, and of grammatical rules. Adults with aphasia, traumatic brain injury, and right hemisphere damage may have impaired ability to construct inferred meanings from given linguistic stimuli. The clinician who describes such behavior needs to know the difference between *imply* and *infer*.

An old doctoral dissertation (Fuchs, 1981, cited in Santo Pietro & Goldfarb, 1995, p. 124) examined the following four categories of inferences.

Implied instruments are tools, containers, vehicles, or other objects conceptually necessitated by the function or operation of certain verbs. For example, the statement, "She cut out paper dolls," strongly suggests that a pair of scissors was used.

Semantic entailments are lexical items that can be conceptually subsumed within superordinate classes. The listener knows that statements valid for the member element may also be valid for the class in general. For example, for the statement, "I ate an apple," a valid inference would be that a piece of fruit was eaten.

Presuppositions refer to prior actions or states of being suggested by an event or series of events. For example, from the statement, "I drank a quart of water after football practice," one can infer that the speaker was thirsty.

Consequences are subsequent actions or states of being suggested by an event or series of events. For example, "He watched in horror as the baseball headed toward Mrs. Jones' living room window," one could infer with a high probability that the window was about to break.

Imply/infer errors almost always go in only one direction. The speaker implies and the hearer infers. The confusion relates to incorrectly saying that the speaker inferred, and not that the hearer implied.

Was he creeping or crawling? Gilbert and Sullivan's "The Yeoman of the Guard" opened at the Savoy Theatre in London on October 3, 1888. Fun fact: Did you know that someone actually invented the line (called "queue" in England)?

Richard D'Oyly Carte instituted the queue to ease entry into the pit and gallery of his Savoy Theatre, where Gilbert and Sullivan's enormously popular operettas were performed.

From Act 2 of "The Yeoman of the Guard"

Like a ghost his vigil keeping —

Or a spectre all-appalling —
I beheld a figure creeping —

I should rather call it crawling —
He was creeping —

He was crawling —
He was creeping, creeping —

Crawling!
He was creeping —

He was crawling —
He was creeping, creeping —

Crawling!
Not a moment's hesitation —

I myself upon him flung.
With a hurried exclamation

Creeping and crawling are different, and need to be observed and documented correctly, especially for infants and young children with movement disorders. In creeping, the stomach makes contact with the floor; not so in crawling. Early locomotion may start as creeping, or pushing around on the stomach. Crawling may follow, and there may even be an intermediate stage of scooting, where the youngster crawls on one leg and drags the other. Various combinations on the stomach, side, and back are also possible in early movement.

The other confused pairs in this exercise result from lack of a clear definition. For example, an individual who says she is "honing in" on the appropriate therapy to use (rather than the correct form of "homing in" or "zeroing in") needs to understand that "to hone" means to sharpen. She can hone her clinical skills, so that she will be better at homing in on the solution to the problem.

Anxiety is a troubled mental state, but it is often used instead of the positive mental state of eagerness. You can be *eager to* (but not anxious to) do something or *anxious about* something. You may also have both feelings at once, where you are eager to start a private practice, but anxious about the financial commitment that a private practice entails.

Finally, if you think of regards as meaning best wishes, you will not write, "In regards to the memo you sent last Monday . . . " The word *regard* means consider or look (as it also does in French). Think of "in re" used in memos to be an abbreviation of "in regard to . . . " So feel free to send regards, in regard to a certain situation or event.

Target Skills: Euphemisms, Political Correctness, Use of Adjectives as Nouns

Corporeally Challenged

How far is too far to go in terms of political correctness? Clearly, to describe an individual as "dead" instead of the example of "corporeally challenged" used above will not offend the decedent. Should a wheelchair-borne individual see a staircase as a "physical challenge" when it is actually an impossibility?

The concept of referring to challenges stems from an important concept in rehabilitation, which is expressed as the ratio of challenge to assistance. In speech-language rehabilitation, we work to increase the client's challenge, in terms of communicative responsibility, while decreasing assistance in the form of prompts or cues. In audiology, we challenge the consumer of hearing aids to assume responsibility for maintenance and use. The philosophy is to maximize therapeutic challenge while minimizing therapeutic assistance; the more we assist, the more we have to assist, until we are figuratively killing our clients with kindness.

Euphemisms, including the family of "challenges," are created for noble reasons. We want to include people with differences, impairments, disabilities, disorders, and handicaps in the great sea of humanity; we want to focus on what makes us one, not what separates us. Accordingly, in the early 1980s, our national organization (ASHA) took a first step when it stopped using the term *aphasic* as a noun (e.g., separating *aphasics* from *controls* in experimental research) in its professional journals. The term *aphasic*, an adjective, never made much sense when used as a noun. It probably should have been *an aphasiac*, to correspond with the politically (and diagnostically) incorrect use of *maniac* to describe an individual with schizoaffective disorder. Recent use of the term *an aphasiac* in a television program about a neuroscientist with schizophrenia suggested that the show could have benefited from an expert consultant. We currently prefer to think of an individual who is "wearing" a disorder, rather than the other way around. We also refer to unimpaired individuals as *typical* rather than *normal*, and to individuals in experimental research as *participants* rather than *subjects*.

Here are some examples of correct usage.

1. Change *stutterer* to *individual who stutters*.
2. Change *autistic child* to *child with autism*.
3. Change *cleft-palate child* to *child with orofacial anomaly*.

There continues to be controversy in the use of such terms as *hearing impaired* versus *hard of hearing* and *deaf*, depending on the community using the terms (see About the Deaf Community and "Hearing Impairment" in Chapter 1).

Target Skill: However

"Professor" Irwin Corey, who was self-titled "The World's Foremost Authority," had a comedy routine that frequently included a discourse in (not on) gibberish. He would ramble on about such topics as the barometric pressure of the knee, until the audience was roaring. His next sentence would consist only of the word, "however," punctuated by a raised index finger, which would set the audience off again.

We single out the word "however" as an example of particular difficulty for professional writers. It usually is used to signify contrast, as a synonym for the following:

1. on the other hand;
2. despite anything to the contrary;
3. nevertheless;
4. nonetheless;
5. even so;
6. by contrast;
7. that said;
8. in spite of this;
9. although;
10. though;
11. but;
12. yet.

For the above uses, "however" starts a sentence or a phrase. Accordingly, we must use a period or a semicolon, *not a comma*, before it. Note that when you use "however" to substitute for numbers 1 to 12 above, you must write a comma after the word. If you write the words in numbers 9 to 12 above instead of "however" ("although," "though," "but," and "yet"), do not write commas following their use. As conjunctions, numbers 9 to 12 require a comma before usage, but not after (e.g., I emailed five times, yet he didn't get back to me). If numbers 10 and 12 are not used as conjunctions, there are different rules. For some constructions, there is a comma before usage (e.g., I'm pretty satisfied, though), and for others, there is no comma at all (e.g., She didn't get home yet).

In the examples below, the odd numbers have correct punctuation, and the even numbers do not.

EXAMPLES:

1. Correct: I could not get through to Professor Smith; however, I left a message.
2. Incorrect: Jane was not home, however, I'll call her tomorrow.
3. Correct: My driveway was snowed in. However, I managed to get to school by bus.
4. Incorrect: The icy roads were tricky, however, I have snow tires.

We also use "however" to indicate degree, as in the following synonyms:

1. to whatever degree;
2. to whatever extent;

3. in whatever way;
4. in whatever manner.

We do not use a comma after "however" when we use the word to indicate degree.

Here are some examples of common "however" errors, with explanations, followed by examples to be corrected by the student.

EXAMPLES:

Correct: However you decided to go to school, don't take the bus.

Incorrect: However, often he asks, don't go out with him.

Correct: Make sure you come to class however you can.

Incorrect: Finish your assignment, however, long it takes.

Target Skill: Past Participle

How many fathers you got: A tale of participles passed down.

William Stewart was a linguist who studied Ebonics, and was particularly interested in the creole language of Gullah. Based on West African languages, Gullah is spoken in the Sea Islands off South Carolina and Georgia. Bill told the following story about a conversation between two 9-year-olds, one of whom was showing off the bike he had received for his birthday. The boy with the bike spoke a dialect that was more closely associated with Gullah than the dialect spoken by the other lad, one which differentiated a less recent performance (*has did*) from a more recent one (*did*). Temporal distinctions are also expressed in the South African Ndebele and Zulu dialects of English, where *now* means in the next day or so, *just now* means probably today, and *now now* means right away. Back to Gullah, the fellow without the wheels asked his friend, "Who got you the bike?" The kid replied, "My father's did" (an abbreviation of *My father has did*), and his friend asked, "How many fathers you got?"

Dialectal variations, fascinating as they are, can result in confusion of a message. For this reason, they are not accepted in professional writing. A descriptive linguist (Behrens, 2010) thinks that biases against non-standard English run deep enough that even with an unambiguous utterance, a listener might still reject the message. In this section we turn our attention to past and present participles. The past participle occurs in five verb forms and one form as an adjective. We use past participles for all perfect tense forms of a verb as well as for the passive voice. Regular verbs take the typical *-ed* ending to form its past participle, but irregular verbs, by definition, do not adhere to rules.

The highlighted words below are examples of past participles:

1. **Present perfect**
   A. Regular verb forms

      She hasn't **finished** her homework yet.

      They haven't **tested** his hearing through bone conduction.

   B. Irregular verb forms

      I still haven't **found** my keys.

      We haven't **gone** to the movies in ages.

2. **Past perfect**
   A. Regular verb forms

      The surgeon's wide cannula had **traumatized** the patient's vocal folds.

      Janet came back for a complete audiologic evaluation because she had **failed** the initial screening.

   B. Irregular verb forms

      John was aspirating because he had **eaten** chocolate.

      She missed her first class because she hadn't **set** the alarm.

3. **Future perfect**
   A. Regular verb forms

      Dana will have **completed** her PhD in June.

If you come after 5:00, I will have **finished** my office hours.

B. Irregular verb forms

Kristen will have **given** birth by the end of the summer.

Elaine will have **been** an associate professor for 20 years by the time she is promoted to professor.

4. **Conditional perfect**

A. Regular verb forms

"If it had not been for these things, I might have **lived** out my life talking at street corners to scorning men." (This was part of a statement made by Bartolomeo Vanzetti in 1927, shortly before he was executed.)

If I were a carpenter and you were a lady, would you have **married** me anyway?

B. Irregular verb forms

If you couldn't stand the heat, you shouldn't have **gone** into the kitchen.

Would you have **told** me if I had been home?

5. **Passive Voice**

A. Regular verb forms

We were **amazed** by the positive response to our petition.

Dr. Singh was **satisfied** that the revised book was better than the original one.

B. Irregular verb forms

We were **given** two hours to complete the Praxis II examination.

The entire class was **brought** low by the sad news.

Past participles as adjectives

A past participle may serve as an adjective when it appears before a noun.

1. Regular forms

The **famished** student couldn't wait for his class to end.

If you bring your **completed** assignment in by Friday, you will get full credit.

2. Irregular forms

Bob was walking around as if in a **drunken** stupor.

Mariano Rivera rarely had a **blown** save.

A classic example: Use punctuation to make sense of this statement about past participles.

John where Mary had had had had had had had had had had had the teacher's approval.

Present participles use the *ing* ending after a verb in several ways. However, when a verb + *ing* functions as a noun, it is called a **gerund**, as in, John decided that *stuttering* was something he could change.

1. The present action is continuous, as in, I'm *wondering* what to do with the client in therapy.
2. The present participle follows movement and position and is used with forms of *to go*, as in, She goes *shopping* as a reward for a grade of A.
3. The present participle follows verbs of perception (see, hear, touch, taste, smell), as in, I saw my supervisor *testing* a new client. The present participle indicates that the action is ongoing, as opposed to a complete action (I saw my supervisor *test* a new client).
4. The present participle is used as an adjective, as in, The research on cochlear implants yielded *stunning* results.
5. The present participle explains a reason, as in, *Knowing* that her next client stuttered, she reviewed her course notes. This construction can substitute for a phrase that starts with *as*, *because*, or *since*.

6. The present participle may be used when the same person or thing does two actions at the same time, as in, *Testing* for air conduction of sound, the audiologist put the earphone with the red dot over the patient's right ear.
7. The present participle may be used with specific words.
   a. With the verbs *spend* or *waste*, an example is, We spend too much time in class *reviewing* basic concepts.
   b. With the verbs *catch* or *find*, an example is, I caught him *copying* his neighbor's answers.

Target Skills: Numbers and Numerals, Arabic and Roman Numerals

Let Me Count the Ways

Numbers Versus Numerals

As a general rule, write numbers below 10 as words, and numbers 10 and above as numerals. Never start a sentence with a numeral.

Some applications of the rule follow.

EXAMPLES:

1. *Correct*

   There were 33 children with sensorineural hearing loss in the study.

   Incorrect

   33 children with sensorineural hearing loss participated in the study.

2. *Correct*

   I saw nine clients in the clinic today.
   Nine clients came to the clinic today.

   Incorrect

   The # one reason for absence in the speech and hearing center is illness.

   (Use the numeral 1, because it follows the # sign).

Even if the number is less than 10, use numerals to represent time, date, age, as well as mathematical and statistical functions or units of measurement (e.g., Figure 3, 5%, 4 weeks, 8-channel). Recall that punctuation for age in years and months requires a colon or semicolon (preferred), and not a decimal point. Writing that "The child we tested was 4;5 years" means that the child was 4 years and 6 months or 4½ years old.

Roman Numerals

Convention dictates that Roman numerals are used for cranial nerves, statistical errors, and three or more generations of males with the same name (except for royalty, which is not gender-biased, and begins with the first generation).

EXAMPLES:

1. *Correct*

   The son of John Smith is John Smith, Jr., and his son is John Smith III.

   Incorrect

   Shakespeare wrote Hamlet during the reign of Queen Elizabeth (should be *Queen Elizabeth I*).

   Queen Elizabeth, Jr. (should be *Queen Elizabeth II*) did not abdicate the throne in favor of her son, Prince Charles.

2. *Correct*

   The cricothyroid muscle is the only intrinsic muscle of the larynx innervated by the superior laryngeal nerve, a branch of Cranial Nerve X, the vagus.

   Incorrect

   There are three branches of the 5th cranial nerve (should be Cranial Nerve V or CN V).

3. *Correct*

   Assuming an effect or relationship exists when it does not is an example of a Type I error.

   Incorrect

   A type 2 error (should be Type II) accepts the null hypothesis when it should have been the rejected alternative.

Target Skills: Amount Versus Number, Less Versus Fewer

Use "number" and "fewer" when describing a complete unit; use "amount" and "less" when using a portion of the unit. Although it is unlikely that you would write, "number of milk" instead of "amount of milk," it is entirely possible that you might have written, "amount of ounces of milk," instead of "number of ounces of milk." Similarly, you would not claim to "weigh fewer than she does," but you might have noted that you have "less classes than he does." So do the assignments carefully, or you won't amount to anything, and your number will be up. By the way, the "tastes great, less filling" beer commercial is grammatically correct ("fewer filling" doesn't make sense). Another way to remember the differences above is to think of nouns that indicate mass, such as *weight* (less, not fewer) versus nouns that count something, such as *calories* (fewer). You can also think of the count noun, *courses* (number), versus the mass noun, *information* (amount).

Your first job is to find the noun in the sentence and then ask if it is a complete unit. For example, the word "dollar" is used to describe something that is always 100 cents. If it is more or less than 100 cents, it no longer amounts to a dollar. Therefore, it is wrong to talk about "amount of dollars," but fine to say "number of dollars." Money can fluctuate (Don't we know it!), and still be appropriately defined as "money." We can lose some of it (and have a smaller amount of money), and it will still be money. When cooking pasta for a campus event, remember that a large *amount* of sauce calls for a good *number* of tomatoes.

Target Skill: Forms of Address

Meet You at the Convention

This does not refer to A-line or Empire-style, which are forms of a dress. There goes our language toy again.

Academic degrees

Many years ago, a striving externship student offered written congratulations to one of us "on your P.H.D." In the past, the Doctor of Philosophy degree was abbreviated as Ph.D., with no spaces between letters; currently, the periods are often deleted. Notation for the AuD, an abbreviation for Doctor of Audiology, does not use periods. These rules are apt to change and may also vary according to journal style (e. g., Chicago Manual versus APA).

Miss, Mrs. or Ms.?

In 1972, Gloria Steinem became editor of *Ms.*, a magazine devoted to the Women's Movement. The title reflected the two terms (Miss and Mrs.) used to refer to single and married females, compared to only one (Mr.) that referred to both single and married males. There was some tongue-in-cheek blowback at the time to refer to single males as Smr. (to be pronounced "smur") and married males as Mrm. (to be pronounced "murm"), in order to parallel Miss and Mrs. To complicate the matter, a popular British television program that started in 1971, "Upstairs, Downstairs," referred to the cook as "Mrs. Bridges," even though she was unmarried. This reflected conventional Edwardian British usage, in the years just before World War I, of "Mrs." as an honorific for any older woman. If you adopt the newer usage, then you cannot write "Ms." only for single females and "Mrs." for married women.

What's up, Doc?

There is a story about a deputy sheriff in a small town in the southern United States who stopped a late-model Lexus bearing Massachusetts license plates. The deputy, noting the driver to be African-American, requests driving documents and asks, "What's your name, boy?" The driver responds, "Dr. Johnson," and the deputy rephrases, "What's your first name, boy?" The power differential and racial discrimination could not be maintained if the deputy used the title "Doctor" while trying to infantilize the driver.

In England, a general medical practitioner would be called "Doctor Higgins" while a medical specialist would be addressed as "Mister Higgins." Not all doctors are professors, and not all professors have doctoral degrees. In addition, there are assistant, associate, and full professors, as well as some named, distinguished, and presidential professors. In some countries in South America, individuals with a masters (or master's; the jury is still out on which form is preferred) degree are called "doctor," and in France, a *doctorat ès lettres* is not equivalent to a PhD. Finally, in some European countries, a speaker at a convention was introduced as Professor Doctor Goldfarb, but only because the individual held the rank of (full) professor.

So what is a student to do? Of course, spelling counts, so writing "Hi Proffesor" in an email is never correct. We recommend that you ask your adviser about the conventional forms of address at your college or university. At some institutions, the term "Professor" applies to anyone with any professorial rank, and even to adjunct lecturers. At others, the title of *Professor* supersedes that of *Doctor* on campus. Still others will insist that faculty be addressed by first names, especially by doctoral students. Once you know how to address your teachers, use that form, even in emails. However, it is never appropriate to use slang, such as "Hey, Prof," even in electronic communications. Here is a recent example of an email gone astray.

Student's Email

Hell Dr. Goldfarb,

I have been accepted at the Manhattan Center campus for my CSD graduate study.

Professor's reply

Ms. R____: First, please proofread your emails. It seems you're very angry with me, based on your salutation, but I'll assume it's just a typo.

Student's response

Dr. Goldfarb,

I am so very sorry about that salutation. It was an awful typing error to make and not my intended greeting. I will of course be sure to proofread so this mistake does not happen again.

Sincerely,

R____

There is one form of address that is completely your decision. You are the final authority on the pronunciation of your own name. I your name is Michaela, and you choose to call yourself "Mick Ayla," "Me Shella," or "My Sheila," that is your choice. The rap artist and entrepreneur Sean Combs has decided to refer to himself professionally as Sean "Puffy" Combs; that is, Puff Daddy; or rather, P. Diddy; we mean, Diddy. He has every right to do so, and to make as many changes as he wants that are not illegal, scatological, or obscene.

Target Skills: s/he and [s]he; Gender Neutral; Agreement

Put Your Gender in Neutral

Most audiology students and practicing audiologists are female; the overwhelming majority in speech-language pathology is female. Some reasons for the large proportion of women in communication sciences and disorders may be the tendency to practice in schools (where the majority of teachers are female), and the ability to maintain flexible schedules in private practice and agency work, which is attractive to mothers of young children. Therefore, the default position of using the male pronoun to represent both genders seems inappropriate for our professions. Some attempts at gender neutrality in English seem natural, graceful, and effortless, whereas other formulations are awkward, clunky, and reeking of political correctness. In many instances the efforts to avoid gender bias result in grammatical errors. Consider the following example, and try adding some of your own:

EXAMPLE:

A new graduate undertaking a clinical fellowship (CF) has questions about the ASHA Certificate of Clinical Competence. The Clinical Fellow is advised to call the toll-free ASHA hotline for clarification.

1. Standard construction, with gender bias: *When the Clinical Fellow had questions about certification, he was told to call the ASHA hotline.*

2. Politically correct, but awkward construction: *When the Clinical Fellow (Clinical Gal?) had questions about certification, she was told to call the ASHA hotline.*
3. Gender-neutral construction with grammatical error (lack of agreement between noun, *Clinical Fellow*, a singular form, and pronoun, *they*, a plural form): *When the Clinical Fellow had questions about certification, they were told to call the ASHA hotline.*
4. More graceful construction, avoiding gender, active voice: *Tell the Clinical Fellow with questions about certification to call the ASHA hotline.*
5. More graceful construction, avoiding gender, passive voice: *The Clinical Fellow with questions about certification was told to call the ASHA hotline.*

As noted above, the best way to cope with potential gender bias is to avoid using gender-specific terms. Writing *s/he* or *[s]he* is clumsy and is not accepted in professional publications. See Battistella (1990) for guidelines for nonsexist usage. Gender identity is a protected class in many institutions, along with race, disability, and many other classes. If you are a student who identifies as gender fluid and does not want to be referred to by the pronoun he or she or any of the inelegant forms such as hir (combining his and her), then that is your right. The National Council on Teachers of English (2002) indicate strategies for avoiding exclusionary forms, such as the pseudo-generic *he* and *man*, and adopting the following inclusionary strategies:

Substitute a plural noun for a singular noun.

Substitute an article for a pronoun.

Substitute the first-person (*we*) or second-person (*you*) pronoun for the third-person singular pronoun of *he* or *she*.

Use *one* or *one's* instead of pseudo-generic *he* or *his*, but use it sparingly to avoid changes in the tone of writing.

Recast the sentence in the passive voice, although some editors malign this usage.

Substitute a participial phrase for a clause, such as, "Help the child who is speaking with a lisp," instead of "Help the child when he speaks with a lisp."

Use the singular *they* or *their*, such as, "Does each student have their assignment?" The NCTE warns that some state or national assessments may regard this form as incorrect.

EXAMPLE:
Avoid using s/he or [s]he by changing syntax.

1. Clumsy avoidance of gender bias: If a student arrives late to class, he or she will be penalized.
2. Better construction: A student arriving late to class will be penalized.

Change these constructions:

1. A student will become a successful audiologist if s/he excels in science.
2. Everyone should accept his or her responsibilities in clinic.
3. Completing all exercises in this book will make him or her a better writer.

In a study comparing comprehension in nonfluent aphasia (where verbs are more impaired) and fluent aphasia (where nouns are more impaired; Goldberg & Goldfarb, 2005), one task involved ambiguous sentences. The female pronoun, *her*, was needed; the sentence could not be ambiguous with male pronouns. In the sentence, *He saw her slip on the floor*, the word *slip* could be interpreted as a noun (i.e., he saw her petticoat) or a verb (he saw her fall). However, it would take two forms of the male pronoun to make the word *crash* appear as both noun and verb.

1. She saw *him* crash at the corner (verb), and,
2. She saw *his* crash at the corner (noun).

There are times when experimental design and English syntax do not permit gender neutrality.

Gender neutrality in professional titles results in constructions that range from elegant to laughable. Some waiters and waitresses are now *waitrons*, *waitstaff*, or *servers*. The mailman has become the *letter carrier* or the *postal worker* (better than *mailperson*, *femailperson*, or *personperson* —excuse us, we're playing with our language toy again). Employment titles are an important part of an adult's case history. The following examples show gender-biased and gender-neutral names for occupations.

Occupations and places (try adding some of your own examples).

Gender-biased	*Gender-neutral*
Steward/stewardess	Flight attendant
Policeman/ policewoman	Police officer
Fireman/firewoman	Firefighter
Actor/actress	*Acter* would work, but is not used; some female theatre majors choose to be called actor
Singer/songstress	Male version is accepted for both
Ballerina/danseur	Gender-biased foreign language terms are accepted
Bachelor/bachelorette (or worse, spinster)	?
Men working	?
Cameraman	?
YMCA/YWCA	?
Men's/women's room	?

Most instances of lack of agreement, especially where a singular noun in a sentence is followed by a plural pronoun, stem from the writer's attempt to maintain gender neutrality. This is laudable, but incorrect. As you will see in the examples below, there are ways to maintain both gender neutrality (without resorting to the dreaded s/he, [s]he, or he/she) and noun–pronoun (or N–PN) agreement.

EXAMPLES:

1. Record a speech sample of the child speaking in their natural environment.
   Easy fix: change "their" to "the."
2. Consider the entire person, their communication partners, and environment in order to form a thorough diagnosis.
   Easy fix: delete "their."
3. At the start of the parent interview, the clinician lets them know what they will be doing with them and their child during the evaluation.
   No easy fix here: Try including both parents at the interview, among the other required changes.

The final comment is an injunction for all audiologists and speech-language pathologists to earn doctoral degrees (already required for audiologists), to avoid gender bias. The doctorate is the ultimate "Ms." No one will have to decide whether or not you are to be addressed as "Mrs." or "Miss" if you are called *Doctor*. On the other hand, we recall an instructor who wrote the following on the board: *Mrs. Smith*, *Dr. Smith*, *Prof. Smith*. She said, "You may call me by any of these titles. I worked hard for all of them." Please remember that you may not be called "the doctor," which is reserved for medical practitioners.

Target Skill: Superlatives

The slain hero in *The Princess Bride* is taken to Miracle Max, who says, "I've seen worse. He's only mostly dead." In general, we form the superlative by adding *-est* to the ends of adjectives, as in smartest, cleanest, and strongest. When an adjective of one syllable ends with one vowel and one consonant, then we double the consonant before adding *-est*, as in biggest, fattest, and drabbest (but be careful of words such as honest, where the *-est* does not signify superlative). A one-syllable word ending in "e" requires only *-st* to become a superlative (e.g., wise–wisest). When a two-syllable adjective ends in a "y," we change the last letter to "i" before adding *-est* (e.g., prettiest). Words of two or more syllables that do not end in "y" do not take *-est*; instead, use most before the adjective (e.g., most beneficial). Of course, there are exceptions to these rules, such as the superlative of good, which is best. Some language users intentionally change the rules, either for emphasis or for reasons of regional dialect. In a song by Jim Croce, Leroy Brown was the baddest man in town. Some adjectives, such as dead, are superlatives on their own, and degrees or levels do not apply.

Target Skills: Abbreviations

We Saw the FLK with SOB

Not long ago, an obstetrician who noted something wrong with a newborn would note *FLK*, for *funny-looking kid*, in the baby's chart. This practice has, thankfully, stopped, but the avalanche of abbreviations has not. Students and practitioners in communication sciences and disorders must become familiar with a large body of abbreviations and must be able to differentiate CAPD (central auditory processing disorder) from COPD (chronic obstructive pulmonary disease). The following noninclusive list includes abbreviations and their meanings related to imaging, testing, and diagnosis. Try adding some of your own examples. By the way, SOB means *shortness of breath*.

Our preferred strategy for abbreviations is to write the complete version followed by the abbreviation in parentheses, when used for the first time. Accordingly, write above the knee (A/K) the first time, and A/K after that. However, many professionals in medical settings assume the reader understands the abbreviations and write the shortened form the first time and every time.

ABBREVIATION LIST

(C)APD	(central) auditory processing disorder
a.c.	before meals
A.H.	adult home
a/b	antibiotic
A/E	above the elbow
A/K	above the knee
aa	equal parts of each
AAA	American Academy of Audiology
aaa	abdominal aortic aneurysm
abd	abduction
Abd.	abdomen
ABE	acute bacterial endocarditis
ABG	arterial blood gases
ABN	abnormal
ABR	auditory brainstem response
abs	absent
Act	activities
ad lib	as desired/as needed
AD	right ear
ADA	American Diabetes Association
add	adduction
ADL	activities of daily living
adm	admission, admitted
admin	administration
AF, AFIB	atrial fibrillation
AKA	above knee amputation; also known as
Alz	Alzheimer disease
AM	morning
AMA	against medical advice
amb	ambulation
AMB	ambulance
A–P	anterior and posterior
APAP	Tylenol (acetaminophen)
APE	acute pulmonary embolism
aq	water
AROM	active range of motion
ART	acoustic reflex threshold
AS	left ear
ASA	aspirin
ASHA	American Speech-Language-Hearing Association

ASHD	arteriosclerotic heart disease
AU	bilaterally; both ears
Aud	audiology/audiologist
A-V	atrio-ventricular
B/R	bathroom
BDAE	Boston Diagnostic Aphasia Examination
BE, B/E	below elbow
Bid	twice a day
BIM	twice a month
BIW	two times weekly
BK, B/K	below knee
BKA	below knee amputation
BM	bowel movement
BP	blood pressure
BRP	bathroom privileges
BS	blood sugar/bowel sounds/breath sounds
BSL	blood sugar level
C.P.	chest pain
c/o	complains of
CA	carcinoma, cancer
CAE	complete audiologic evaluation
CELF	Clinical Evaluation of Language Fundamentals
CHL	conductive hearing loss
COPD	central obstructive pulmonary disease
CP	cerebral palsy
CPR	cardiopulmonary resuscitation
CR	correct responses
CRF	chronic renal failure
CSF	cerebrospinal fluid
CT, CAT	scancomputerized (axial) tomography
CVA	cerebrovascular accident
CVD	cardiovascular disease
CW	case worker
D.P.	discharge plan
D/C	discharge/discontinue
DCP	dietary care plan
decub	decubitus
dep/depr	depression
DM	diabetes mellitus
DOB	date of birth
DSS	Department of Social Service
dx	diagnosis
E	extremity
e.g.	for example
E.R.	emergency room
ECT	electroconvulsive therapy
EEG	electroencephalogram
EKG/ECG	electrocardiogram
EMG	electromyogram
ENT	ear, nose, throat
ERP	event- (or evoke-) related potential
ETOH	alcohol
eval	evaluation
F/f	female/Fahrenheit
F/U	follow up
FBS	fasting blood sugar
Fe	iron
FH	family history
fMRI	functional magnetic resonance imaging
FUO	fever of unknown origin
fx	fracture
GC	geri(atric) chair
GCE	general conditioning exercises
GI	gastrointestinal
gm	gram
GSS	general social service
GT	gastrostomy tube
gtt(s)	drop(s)
G-U	genitourinary

gyn	gynecology
h.s.	at bedtime
H/O	history of
hx	history
hct	hematocrit
HD	Huntington disease
HEENT	head, eyes, ears, nose, throat
hemi	hemiplegia/half
hgb	hemoglobin
HH/hh/HOH	hard of hearing
hr	hour
HRF	health-related facility
HTN	hypertension
Hx	history
Hz	hertz (cycles per second)
I + D	incision and drainage
I + O	intake and output
I	independence
i.e.	that is
IBW	ideal body weight
IDDM	insulin-dependent diabetes mellitus
IM	intramuscular
imp	impaired
inj	injection
ITPA	Illinois Test of Psycholinguistic Abilities
IV	intravenous
JVP	jugular venous pressure
K	potassium
KCL	potassium chloride
kg	kilogram
L	liter
lb	pound
LE	lower extremity
liq	liquid
LLE	left lower extremity
LPN	licensed practical nurse
LTC	long-term care
LUE	left upper extremity
M	murmur/male/man
MA(P)	medical assistance (program)
MC	Medicare
MCE	medical care evaluation
MD	muscular dystrophy/medical doctor
met	metastatic/metastasis
mg/mgm	milligram
MI	myocardial infarction
mL	milliliter
mod	moderate
MOM	milk of magnesium
MP	muscle power
MRI	magnetic resonance imaging
MS	multiple sclerosis/mental status
M-S	muscular-skeletal
MTDDA	Minnesota Test for Differential Diagnosis of Aphasia
NA	no answer; not applicable
Na	sodium
NAD	no acute distress
NCP	nursing care plan
NGT	nasogastric tube
NH	nursing home
NL	normal
NMR	nuclear magnetic resonance (largely replaced by MRI)
NPO	nothing by mouth
NWB	non-weight-bearing
O.R.	operating room
O_2	oxygen
OA	osteoarthritis
OBS	organic brain syndrome
OD	right eye/every day
OM	otitis media
OME	otitis media with effusion

OMS	organic mental syndrome
OOB	out of bed
OPD	outpatient department
OS	left eye
OT	occupational therapy
OU	both eyes
oz.	ounce
P	post/after/pulse
p.c.	after meals
P.Op	postoperative
P/A	percussion and auscultation
P-A	posterior-anterior
PA	physician assistant
PD	Parkinson disease
PE/px	physical examination
PECS	Picture Exchange Communication System
per	by
PET (scan)	positron emission tomography
PICA	Porch Index of Communicative Ability
PLS	Preschool Language Scale
PMH/PMHx	past medical history
PN	progress notes
PO	by mouth
PPVT	Peabody Picture Vocabulary Test
PRE	progressive resistive exercises
prn	as necessary
PROM	passive range of motion
PT	physical therapy
Pt	patient
PTA	physical therapy assistant/prior to admission
PVD	peripheral vascular disease
q	every
q2h	every two hours
qd	every day
qh	every hour
qid	four times a day
quad	quadriplegia
R	right/respiration
r/o	rule out/reality orientation
RA	rheumatoid arthritis
RBC	red blood cell
re	about
Rec	recommendation
RLE	right lower extremity
RN	registered nurse
ROM	range of motion
RUE	right upper extremity
Rx	treatment
s	without
s.c.	subcutaneous
s/p	status post
S1S2	first heart sound, second heart sound
SD	seizure disorder
sec	seconds
sig.	label as/give as
SLB	short leg brace
SLE	systemic lupus erythematosus
SLP	speech-language pathologist
SNF	skilled nursing facility
SNHL	sensorineural hearing loss
SOB	shortness of breath
SPECT	single photon emission computed tomography
ss	one-half
SSA	Social Security Administration
STAT	immediately
SW	social worker
Sx	symptoms
T	temperature/thoracic
T & A	tonsillectomy and adenoidectomy
tab	tablet
TM	tympanic membrane
URI	upper respiratory infection
VA	Veteran's Administration

VNS	Visiting Nurse Service
VS, V/S	vital signs
w/o	well oriented, without
w/u	work up
WAB	Western Aphasia Battery
wbc	white blood cells, white blood count
WC (w/c)	wheelchair
wfl	within functional limits
wn	well nourished
wnl	within normal limits
wt	weight
x, X	times
xs	excess
yo	year old

Latin Abbreviations

In samples of students' writing, we have found considerable evidence of confusion in the use of Latin abbreviations. Here are some of the most common of them.

The abbreviation *e.g.*, for *exempli gratia*, means "for example." If you are not sure about the use of *e.g.*, then by all means write "for example," but never write *ex-*, unless you are referring to a former partner or spouse.

The abbreviation *i.e.*, for *id est*, means "that is." Be careful not to use *i.e.* and *e.g.* interchangeably.

The abbreviation *etc.* may be confusing, because it is an abbreviation for two words, *et cetera*, which means, "and others" (usually other things). Compare *etc.* with *et al.*, which we discuss further in our chapter on using library resources. The abbreviation *et al.* also means, "and others," but refers to other people, usually authors of a publication. Note that the Latin et is a whole word, meaning "and." Accordingly, there is no period after *et*, but there is a period after *al.*, which is an abbreviation for the Latin *alii* (others).

Writing Content and Composition (Semantics, Sentence Structure)

Target Skill: Say What the Client Does, Not What the Client Is

Eschew Obfuscation

See Chapter 8 on The Diagnostic Report for more information about this rule. Consider the following interaction:

Doctor: You are suffering from reflux esophagitis. Go to the hospital pharmacy and fill this prescription for 700 mg of calcium carbonate and 300 mg of magnesium hydroxide.

Patient: Gosh, I thought I had heartburn. I was going to go to the drug store and get some Mylanta.

Doctor: That's what I just said.

Why do professionals of every stripe insist on using so much professional jargon? The jaded answer is so we can charge more. Under the title of "Loose, baggy sentences," Cook (1985) skewers "officialese, prolixity, verbiage, periphrasis, windfoggery, and jargon" (pp. 1–17). Graff (2003, p. 1) argues that academia makes ideas, problems, and ways of thinking look more opaque, narrowly specialized, and beyond normal learning capacities than they are or need to be.

However, there is improved clarity in using precise terms. A careful examination of the interaction between the doctor and patient above shows that professional terminology, properly used, yields more accurate descriptions. For example, the term *heartburn* does not refer to the heart; it is more likely a stomachache. The common use of the term *stomachache*, though, generally refers to intestinal pain. Our general rule is that the first use of a professional term that may not be universally understood should be followed by an explanatory phrase beginning with *characterized by*, or by a commonly understood synonym.

EXAMPLES:

1. *Speech-language pathology example:*

   JR presented with Broca's aphasia, flaccid dysarthria, and right hemiparesis.

   Expand as follows:

   JR presented with Broca's aphasia, characterized by reduction of available vocabulary (especially verbs), impaired expressive syntax, and reduced speech fluency; flaccid dysarthria, characterized by reduction of speech rate, imprecise consonant formation, and hypernasality; and right hemiparesis, characterized by inability to grasp a pen to write with his dominant hand.

2. *Audiology example:*

   ST presented with bilateral otitis media, mild conductive hearing loss, and tinnitus.

   Expand as follows:

   ST presented with bilateral otitis media, characterized by redness and retraction of the tympanic membranes; mild conductive hearing loss, characterized by normal bone conduction thresholds and elevated air conduction thresholds; and tinnitus, characterized by an intermittent ringing sound.

Target Skills: Redundancy; Modifying Prepositional Phrases; Hyperbole; Parallelism

Out-of-Control Sentences

Catching Redundancy with the Squad Squad

William Safire, the former presidential speechwriter and late newspaper columnist, deputized his readers as members of "The Squad Squad" if they provided examples of redundancies. "The Squad Squad" is a pun on the old TV series "Mod Squad" and a reference to unnecessary repetition in words or meanings. One of his deputies found three consecutive examples in a row. Get it? Writing "consecutive" makes "in a row" redundant.

Superlatives do not admit of degree. It is redundant for a merchant to describe an object as "uniquely one of a kind," because if it is unique, then by definition it is one of a kind. An infatuated boy, noting that the prettiest girl he ever saw was sipping cider through a straw, would not push his luck by describing her as the "most prettiest girl he ever saw." The rule becomes blurred when using the superlative *perfect*. The preamble to the U.S. Constitution begins, "We the People of the United States, in order to form a more perfect Union . . . " In addition, "very unique" has become commonly used, but it is still grating for us to hear.

Other terms, through accepted usage, violate the redundancy proscription with impunity. One of the more egregious of these is the part of the brain called the prefrontal area. How can an area be *pre* (meaning "in front of") the front? Another term, used widely in advertising, is *free gift*. If it is a gift, then it is free; if it is free, then it is given away. Beware, also, of redundancies when languages are combined. Students taking winter break at *the El San Juan Hotel* in Puerto Rico probably enjoyed a *merry feliz Navidad*. Other redundant terms are found in this construction: number + "different" + varieties, kinds, or types. If a client received three kinds of language assessments, then it is redundant to write that they were "different" kinds. Hegde (2003, p. 72) has compiled a list of redundant phrases. Which word (or part) in the following phrases, appearing in our students' reports, should be deleted as redundant?

successfully completed	repeat again
precondition	hospital facilities
facilitate better comprehension	explicitly instructed
objective judges	as of yet
actual facts	in-depth analysis

The redundant word or part of word is indicated in parentheses

(successfully) completed	repeat (again)
(pre)condition	hospital (facilities)
facilitate (better) comprehension	(explicitly) instructed

(objective) judges — as (of) yet

(actual) facts — (in-depth) analysis

Find the redundancies.

1. Three weeks following the experiment, the participants with brain damage repeated the same experiment a second time, undergoing an identical procedure.

   Answer: The word "repeated" means that the participants undertook the experiment a second time. Repeating "the same experiment" means they were undergoing an identical procedure.
2. The story was presented to the participant, who was then instructed to retell the story (back) to the experimenter.
3. As aphasia severity increased, the patients were more impaired. Degree of language impairment increases with severity level in aphasia.

Modifying prepositional phrases

A prepositional phrase may be defined as a modifying phrase consisting of a preposition and its object. These phrases can modify nouns, verbs, phrases, or complete clauses. They are not complete sentences. Prepositional phrases may appear at the end of a sentence (called right-branching, e.g., Students must submit paperwork on time *to pass the course.*), at the beginning of a sentence (called left branching, e.g., *To pass the course*, students must submit paperwork on time.), or in the middle of a sentence (e.g., Students, *to pass the course*, must submit paperwork on time.).

Hyperbole: "I've told you a million times, don't exaggerate."

The term *hyperbole* refers to poetic exaggeration. Most instances of hyperbole result from the clinician's inexperience. One's first client is bound to be the most fascinating, interesting, challenging, rewarding, and so on—not that we have become jaded after more than a combined half-century of academic and clinical practice. To the contrary, we continue to be surprised by how much our students and clients teach us, and we are genuinely delighted when we can make a positive impact. It is in our writing that we are less effusive.

We frequently read reports which are flowery, overwritten, and overwrought. You may note that some of the following examples contain both hyperbole and redundancy:

EXAMPLES:

1. Language and communication are two such closely interweaving elements as to oftentimes be virtually indistinguishable.
2. As language and communication are far from synonymous, research does well to conjecture that perhaps the collective level of communication exceeds expectations as far as the language impairment would dictate.
3. Evaluating the patients were eleven objective judges.
4. This particular study involved in-depth analysis, utilizing countless hours of videotapes, patient observations, interviews, and videotape review.
5. Throughout the exhaustive analysis of these two patients, clinicians were targeting the use of compensatory strategies employed by the patients to combat their disability.

Parallelism

Parallel Lines Meet at the ASHA Convention

Imagine if Hamlet said, "To be or not being." Components of a construction must be matched. George Bernard Shaw's play *Pygmalion* (1916, Act II) featured the phonetician Henry Higgins (based on the English phonetics professor Henry Sweet), who was impressed by Eliza Doolittle's low-class father's use of parallelism.

> DOOLITTLE ["*most musical, most melancholy*"]: I'll tell you, Governor, if you'll only let me get a word in. I'm willing to tell you. I'm wanting to tell you. I'm waiting to tell you.
>
> HIGGINS: Pickering: this chap has a certain natural gift of rhetoric. Observe the rhythm of his native woodnotes wild. "I'm willing to tell you: I'm wanting to tell

you: I'm waiting to tell you." Sentimental rhetoric!

Elegance of sentence construction is not a major goal of professional writing. After all, content is more important than style. We cite lack of parallelism in syntax as a more minor concern, but one that separates adequate writing from the professional construction expected in a journal article or a diagnostic report.

Lack of balance in pairs and series feels like the lurch of the standard transmission car you drove in college; parallelism rides like a well-tuned Porsche.

EXAMPLES:

Unbalanced: Distractibility contributed to John's poor compliance and was a reason why his test scores were not reliable.

Parallel (balanced): Distractibility contributed to John's poor compliance and poor test score reliability.

Be especially cognizant of correlative conjunctions, such as *either . . . or*, *neither . . . nor*, *both . . . and*, and *not only* when balancing coordinate elements.

Unbalanced: Recommended follow-up is either in-person contact at the clinic or calling him at home.

Parallel: Recommended follow-up is either in-person contact at the clinic or telephone contact at home.

Driscoll (2017) indicates two easy ways to think about parallelism in sentences. Given a sentence such as, "Mary likes to screen, to score, and do audiological testing," there are two easy fixes. Using the *ing* form (the gerund form in this case, because the verb becomes a noun with *ing*), the sentence becomes, "Mary likes audiological testing, screening, and scoring." The other easy fix is to use infinitive phrases (such as we just did with "to use"), as in, "Mary likes to test, to screen, and to score in audiology." For more information on parallelism, see Cook's chapter entitled, "Ill-Matched Partners" (Cook, 1985, pp. 54–74).

Target Skills: Definite, Specific, Concrete Language

"The Facts, Ma'am, Just the Facts"

One of the earliest police dramas on television was *Dragnet*, in which the detective, Sgt. Joe Friday, dealt with hysterical and evasive testimony by requesting "*the facts, ma'am, just the facts.*" Sgt. Friday would have had difficulty with this first sentence of an assignment to include evidence-based practice in a progress report:

EXAMPLE:

Extensive research studies have been conducted to determine the exact nature and extent of the complexity and complications involved with the impairment.

Here is another sentence that needs to go on a diet.

The first study focuses on the fact that when a word that has a stronger meaning inherent in the word or representation, the word will have a stronger impression on the memory of the patient with aphasia.

Delete the first sentence, and rephrase the second. The report now begins as follows:

Author (year) provided evidence that meaningful words improve memory in aphasia.

Answering the Question

Following is an actual trial transcription involving the lawyer (Q), the expert witness (A), and the trial judge (The Court):

Q: Looking at Exhibits H and RR, having reviewed those documents, in your opinion was PH misdiagnosed in any way?

A: Let me first refer to Exhibit H, which is the speech-language evaluation report. There are three purposes for an initial speech-language evaluation. The first purpose is to —

> The Court: No, no, please. I am in a position where if I have to try to absorb what turns out to be useless information, after a while I discard it. I am not going to be helped with a long dissertation. I would appreciate it if you would respond to the question. He asked the question as to whether or not, in your opinion, using these two documents, AB had been misdiagnosed. I would like you to answer that question first and tell me then why. Then you can expound on that in any way you wish.

The witness was evasive, because he was uncomfortable saying a colleague misdiagnosed a patient and was appropriately chastised by the judge for not answering the lawyer's question. Later in the transcript, a chastened witness responded to a query by the plaintiff's attorney.

> Q: I think you testified that you think BA is wrong at least to some very important elements of that evaluation, that is, her comprehension.
>
> A: She misdiagnosed conduction aphasia and misdiagnosed paragrammatism.

Target Skills: Our Students Never Stop Teaching Us What They Need

Spaced Out

We were taught to press the space bar once between words and twice after periods at the ends of sentences. The reason was to improve clarity of documents written with a typewriter. However, most publications now recommend that you use only one space after a period. These rules necessarily change if you opt to right-justify your margins; that is, words in sentences line up flush on the left and on the right, as in this textbook. We also note spacing for an elision in another section. Spaces between three periods, called an ellipsis are required to signify that some words have been omitted.

We have also noted a recent tendency for students to use spacing to separate parts of a single word, especially *a part* and *in tact,* as in, "Why did you take one session plan a part and leave the other one in tact?" There are times when use of a part and apart are both correct, as in, "It is *a part* of a clinical supervisor's job to take students' session plans *apart*." However, it is never correct to write *in tact* instead of *intact* (even when referring to B.F. Skinner's coinage of the terms *mands* and *tacts*). We have also noted the absence of spacing, as in the following example from a student's paper: "Dyslexia is a disorder that is based on a disrupted phonological processing component of language and is frequently unexpected compared to other cognitive abilities that *maybe* (emphasis added) relatively stronger."

Off Base

> We are also confounded by the usage of "based off of" instead of *based on* to describe the foundation of, say, a clinical hypothesis. Behrens and Mercer (2007) proposed in a theory of prepositional change that "based off of" is analogous to "jump off of." They are both metaphorical, rather than literal, prepositions and are prone to change. In baseball, you are out if you are tagged while off base, and you are safe when you are on base. So base your reasoning on (not off of) evidence, and you will be safe. Did you find where the student author's writing was off base? Did you notice that the year, but not the author's name, should have appeared in parentheses?

See if you can rewrite the following sentence (we added a citation error, because it has also begun to creep into professional writing):

> My rationale for the treatment of John's stuttering was based off of the recent work of (Smith, 2018), who used the speech science laboratory to support her theories.

Has-Beens

In Chapter 1, we write about out-of-control sentences that result in grammatical errors. See if you can figure out which one of the following sentences correctly includes* a *has been* and which should be changed to *have been.*

*Note that includes (not include) is correct, because "Which of the following sentences . . . " specifies *which one.*

1. In the last decade, the neural basis of speech and language and the fiber pathway connectivity relating to word retrieval difficulty (has/have) been questioned.
2. ASHA is pleased to announce that Abercrombie & Fitch (has/have) been selected to make new T-shirts for the association.

The correct answer in the first sentence is *have been*, because the author questions two possible causes of word retrieval difficulty. It is still a sentence that the student should rewrite for clarity.

The second sentence refers to one store (even though the store has two names), so *has been* is correct (although our colleagues in the United Kingdom might prefer *have been* here; to conform to British custom, pay attention to the two names, not the one store).

EXERCISES

Exercise 2–1. Is a Comma Missing? Should the Comma Be Deleted?

1. Before you do a hearing screening make sure your audiometer is calibrated.

 ____

2. Take a case history, give the *PPVT*, and, observe attending behaviors.

 ____

3. This 68-year-old man presented with aphasia, and apraxia of speech.

 ____

4. We will use stickers and playtime as reinforcers.

 ____

5. Articulation errors consisted of substitutions, omissions and distortions of fricatives.

 ____

6. Confirmation of the existence of the Higgs boson was based on the work of over 10000 scientists from more than 100 countries, including nearly 2000 from the U.S.

 ____

7. Although, subjects are required to be on a consistent pharmacological regimen for 3 months prior to inclusion, it would be expected that by the time of the 3 to 6 month postoperative evaluation the medications would have been adjusted (from an actual IRB proposal review).

 ____

8. The evaluation revealed an air-bone gap, and a conductive hearing loss.

 ____

9. However, hungry you get you can't eat between meals.

____

10. According to the "open punctuation" model there is no need for a comma before the last item in a series of three or more.

Exercise 2–2. Is the Hyphen Needed?

1. semi-colon

____

2. after-noon

____

3. post-treatment

____

4. inter-related

____

5. under-wear

____

6. pseudo-bulbar palsy

____

7. anti-biotic

____

8. re-peat

____

9. extra-curricular

____

10. un-American

____

Exercise 2–3. Insert a Colon or Semicolon (or No Punctuation)

1. Here is what I need ___ parsley, sage, rosemary, and thyme.

   ____

2. The winners are ___ Flo, Fran, and Reem.

   ____

3. Following are the winners ___ Flo, Fran, and Reem.

   ____

4. Take the bus ___ the train is delayed.

   ____

5. Get to bed by 11 ___ 30).

   ____

6. I grew up in Wheeling, West Virginia ___ and went to school in Lafayette, Indiana.

   ____

7. The odds of winning the raffle are 1,000 ___ 1.

   ____

8. Get me to the church on time ___ I'm getting married.

   ____

9. The long article runs on pp. 1 ___ 6–9.

   ____

10. Please go by yourself ___ I'm too tired.

Exercise 2–4. Change the Stilted Word

1. Thusly→ ______________________________
2. Hence→ ______________________________
3. Utilize→ ______________________________
4. Whilst→ ______________________________
5. Amongst→ ______________________________

Exercise 2–5. Correct the Apostrophe Errors

1. Their's still time left to turn in your report.

 ____

2. The toys are in the children's' playroom.

 ____

3. How many time's do I have to remind you?

 ____

4. They're keeping up with the Jones'.

 ____

5. Here is a list of do's and don't's.

 ____

6. Once we got married, half of everything was her's.

 ____

7. The brides veil was different from any other wedding gown's we saw.

 ____

8. He always has to put his two cent's in.

 ____

9. Worker's of the world, unite; you have nothing to lose but your chain's (from the *Communist Manifesto*).

 ____

10. Egghead's of the world, unite; you have nothing to lose but your yolk's (Correct version is attributed to Adlai Stevenson.).

 ____

Exercise 2–6. Identify the Apostrophe in the Contractions as Correct, or Correct the Errors

1. The responsibility is our's.

 ____

2. Give the Devil it's due.

 ____

3. It's time to go home.

 ____

4. It's time is up.

 ____

5. The therapy plan is her's.

 ____

6. Their testing for bone conduction today.

 ____

7. Its time your registered for clinic.

 ____

8. The student's are all in their rooms.

 ____

9. I'm happy if your happy.

 ____

10. See if its the right test to give.

 ____

Exercise 2–7. Correct the Capital Letter Errors (Use of Upper or Lowercase), or Identify the Sentence as Correct

1. Mr. Trump was out of town. The President was attending a european conference.

    ____

2. The President of the bailed-out bank testified before congress.

    ____

3. I didn't know that king George vi stuttered.

    ____

4. Give me anything but jello for dessert.

    ____

5. Her performance of Rachmaninoff's Piano Concerto, No. 2 indicated superb command of the Piano.

    ____

6. Learn some new tests, not just the Peabody Picture Vocabulary test.

    ____

7. Dr. Serpanos is an ASHA-Certified Audiologist.

    ____

8. We are graduate students in the department of Communication Sciences and Disorders.

    ____

9. Do we call the people who come for therapy Clients, Patients, or Consumers?

    ____

10. Dr. Goldfarb has been a professor for many years.

    ____

Exercise 2–8. Correct Errors in Agreement

1. Air conduction testing, used in most hearing screenings, and bone conduction testing ***gives*** us valuable information.

   ____

2. We went to the student cafeteria, which ***has*** nothing we wanted.

   ____

3. Only one of the five courses I'm taking ***require*** a term paper.

   ____

4. Any person who fails the Praxis II exam ***take*** it again without penalty.

   ____

5. So I ***says*** to my friend, "Don't take Singh for phonetics."

   ____

6. She ***says***, "I had Singh, and he was great."

   ____

7. He ***says*** the same thing every time I ask him.

   ____

8. Everybody in the college ***want*** to graduate on time.

   ____

9. All ***want*** to graduate on time.

   ____

10. John ***don't*** want to graduate on time, because he has another year of eligibility for football.

    ____

Exercise 2–9. Determine the Correct Use of Imply/Infer

In the following examples using Jack and Jill, determine who implies and who infers.

1. Jill told Jack that the lawn was getting overgrown.
   a. Jill (implied/inferred) that Jack should mow the lawn.

   ____

   b. Jack (implied/inferred) that he should get out the lawn mower.

   ____

2. Jack and Jill were planning Thanksgiving dinner for 20 people
   a. From their discussion Jill (implied/inferred) that they would need a very large turkey.

   ____

   b. Jack (implied/inferred) that the turkey could be smaller, because half the guests were vegetarians.

   ____

3. Jill congratulated a beaming Jack on his new job.
   a. We can (imply/infer) that Jack had gone on a job interview.

   ____

   b. Jill (implied/inferred) that she was happy for Jack.

   ____

4. Jack, who called himself "king of the gutter ball," went bowling with Jill.
   a. Jack (implied/inferred) that he would earn a low score.

   ____

   b. We can (imply/infer) that Jill was a good sport for going bowling with Jack.

   ____

Exercise 2–10. Practice Correct Usage

1. Change *an apraxic* to . . .

2. Change *deaf mute* to . . .

3. Change *retarded child* to . . .

4. Change *Mongoloid* to . . .

5. Change *dumb* to . . .

6. Change *aphasic child* to . . .

7. Change *speech therapist* to . . .

8. Change *lisper* to . . .

9. Change *dysarthric adult* to . . .

10. Change *stammerer* to . . .

Exercise 2–11. Correct or Incorrect Use of However?

In the spaces below, change the punctuation of incorrect sentences.

1. I love chocolate cake. However I'm on a diet.

____

____

2. Please call your parents. However, much they annoy you, they're still your parents.

____

____

3. I want to go however, I don't have the money.

____

____

4. Everyone says not to rush on tests. However they are timed.

____

____

5. I know about citing authors in a term paper, however, I am confused about citing page numbers.

____

____

6. Tomorrow's class will be held at 8:00 am. However, you decide to get yourself up, make sure you are on time.

____

____

7. Feel free to celebrate; however; don't bother the neighbors.

____

____

8. Practice giving the BDAE on a neurotypical adult first however you eventually will have to give it to someone who has aphasia.

____

____

9. Not everyone needs a complete audiologic evaluation, however. For some, a screening will be sufficient.

____

____

10. Pure-tone thresholds do not, however tell us everything we need to know.

____

____

Exercise 2–12. Correct the Errors in Participles

1. Dubarry done gone again. (This was the title of a folk song written by Chad Mitchell and Tom Paxton.)

2. If you would have went earlier, the outcome might have been different.

3. I didn't just do it, I been did it last week.

4. She was overjoy with the results.

5. We will have ate dinner by the time you come.

6. They haven't saw the movie that everyone's talking about.

7. The play had last three hours, which was too long for me.

8. Why couldn't you have tell him sooner that you were afraid of commitment?

____

____

9. Test for dysphagia using a modify barium swallow.

____

____

10. Shouldn't we have use all the materials we brought to therapy?

____

____

Exercise 2–13. Correct the Errors in Numbers or Numerals

1. 13 is lucky for some, unlucky for others.

   ____

2. We will meet at half past Two.

   ____

3. Our college's sports teams play in division 2.

   ____

4. My great-grandfather fought in world war II.

   ____

5. Go 2 the store for some bread.

   ____

6. I like Paul Simon's song, "Fifty Ways to Leave Your Lover."

   ____

7. One of the authors is Robert Goldfarb I.

   ____

8. Dr. Seuss writes about thing 1 and thing 2 in "The Cat in the Hat."

   ____

9. I'll meet you at III o'clock.

   ____

10. I asked 4 a hospital placement.

    ____

Exercise 2–14. Amount Versus Number

Correct or incorrect? Try to find which half of the following examples is incorrect, and change the incorrect examples in the spaces that follow them.

1. The number of pages I have to read is crazy.

____

____

2. The amount of reading I have is crazy.

____

____

3. I am increasing the number I can read before I get bored.

____

____

4. Professor Jones used to assign three books, but now it's twice that amount.

____

____

5. The number of dollars I write on my college tuition check keeps getting larger.

____

____

6. The number of money college costs is staggering.

____

____

7. The amount of tuition is rising by 5% next year.

____

____

8. The amount of required courses keeps going up.

____

____

9. The patient's speech consists of a large amount of articulation errors.

____

____

10. Only a small number of words were missed on the speech recognition score task.

____

____

Exercise 2–15. Less Versus Fewer. Correct or Incorrect?

Try to find which half of the following examples is incorrect, and change the incorrect examples in the spaces below.

1. She lost fewer pounds than I did.

2. I weigh less pounds than I did last semester.

3. I weigh fewer than she does.

4. She lost less weight than I did.

5. She ate less than I did.

6. Lite beer has less calories than regular beer.

7. She lost weight by eating fewer calories.

8. If you want to be a designated driver, drink fewer.

9. My instructor assigns fewer homework than yours.

10. She scored fewer points on the exam than I did.

Exercise 2–16. Forms of Address

Discuss the following:

1. Guillermo has left his native Spain to study in the graduate program at Yankee University. Prof. Sheets told Guillermo that because the student was now in an American city, it was time to change his name to Bill.

2. Howard, studying opera at Trinity College, decided to Anglicize the composer's name (Giuseppe Verdi) to "Joe Green" in his report on *Rigoletto*.

3. At her cocktail party, Helen Fuddyduddy introduced her guests, Ms. Smith and Mrs. Jones.

4. The office administrator introduced Donald Saunders, PhD to the client waiting for a complete audiological evaluation, saying, "The doctor will see you now."

5. When Barry entered politics, he decided it was time for people to start calling him by his formal given name of Barack.

6. The singer Prince asked journalists to write his name as a symbol he invented, and to refer to him as "The Artist Formerly Known as Prince." Many journalists refused.

7. Early in his career, the television personality Geraldo Rivera called himself Gerald Rivers.

____

____

8. Yula Cherpelis Serpanos uses her maiden name as her middle name to honor her paternal family ancestry.

____

____

9. Big band singers, such as Frank Sinatra, would often ask the band leader to "Play it in E-flat, Professor."

____

____

10. Robert Goldfarb called one set of grandparents "Grandma and Grandpa" and the other set "Bubbie and Zaydie."

____

____

Exercise 2–17. Agreement and Gender Neutrality

Rewrite the sentences below to maintain agreement and gender neutrality.

1. The parents indicated that the report could be sent either to him or her.

2. The student handed in their assignment late.

3. A clinician can improve one's skills with continued practice.

4. The patients are told that they must sign in at the front desk before their session.

5. Before a student can complete practicum, s/he must obtain clearance from their adviser.

6. Everyone in the class said they would be willing to sign up for the research study.

7. Neither of the student's clients showed up for their appointments.

____

____

8. Mrs. Smith accompanied Connor to the session. She indicated that his language is delayed and that he receives therapy three times a week.

____

____

9. Anyone attending his or her graduation ceremony in the spring must fill out an application.

____

____

10. If a student does not pass the comprehensive exam, s/he may retake it in the following semester.

____

____

Exercise 2–18. Superlatives. Correct or Incorrect?

Try to find which of the following examples are incorrect, and change them in the spaces that follow.

1. We the people of the United States, in order to form a more perfect union . . .

 ____

 ____

2. Democracy is the last, best hope of Earth.

 ____

 ____

3. In *Playhouse 90*, Shirley Booth played the hostess with the mostess.

 ____

 ____

4. It was the most unique course I've ever had.

 ____

 ____

5. She is worst than I am in grammar.

 ____

 ____

6. Marie is the eldest in her family.

 ____

 ____

7. It was a less ultimate experience than you think.

____

____

8. I'm going to have a very deluxe wedding.

____

____

9. Brutus was the nobelest Roman of them all.

____

____

10. She went the forest possible in therapy.

____

____

Exercise 2–19. Abbreviations

A. Write 10 sentences with each containing two professional abbreviations from the list provided in the chapter.

1. ______________________________

____

2. ______________________________

____

3. ______________________________

____

4. ______________________________

____

5. ______________________________

____

6. ______________________________

____

7. ______________________________

____

8. ______________________________

____

9. ______________________________

____

10. ______________________________

____

B. Explain what the abbreviations mean.

1. ______________________________

____

2. ______________________________

____

3. ______________________________

____

4. ______________________________

____

5. ______________________________

____

6. ______________________________

____

7. ______________________________

____

8. ______________________________

____

9. ______________________________

____

10. ______________________________

____

Exercise 2–20. Latin Abbreviations

Insert *i.e.*, *e.g.*, *et al.*, or *etc.*, as required in the blank spaces.

1. She needed to ace her last two exams, _______ phonetics and hearing science, to receive departmental honors.

2. The selection of courses required for the major, _______ phonetics and hearing science, was confusing.

3. The applicant was very strong in basic courses _______ phonetics and hearing science.

4. The article I need was written by Smith _______.

5. Put everything away, such as books, scrap paper, _______ before you start the exam.

Exercise 2–21. Expand the Clinical Statements

1. HS is currently receiving ABA 5x week for treatment of his autism.

2. TH was prescribed with BTE hearing aids for his sensorineural hearing loss.

Exercise 2–22. Edit the Redundancy

Here are some composite examples, taken from many student papers to prevent embarrassing a single author. Try to rewrite the sentence in a way that would avoid censure by The Squad Squad.

1. Andrews et al. (1983) cite the World Health Organization's (WHO) definition of stuttering which defines stuttering as involuntary repetition, prolongation, or cessation of sound.

2. An individual with first-degree relatives who are disfluent has a risk of stuttering three times that of the general population of being disfluent.

3. Video and audio-recording can be used to record a speech sample of the child.

4. The clinician repeated the exam again.

5. The audiologist gave the exact same test to another client.

6. He notes a decline in his ears and his understanding and comprehension have decreased.

7. Acoustic immittance revealed type A patterns for both ears bilaterally.

____

____

8. The client is fitted with binaural amplification, but does not ever wear his hearing aids at all.

____

____

9. Mr. Smith reports a constant tinnitus in his ears that does not go away.

____

____

10. The speech recognition score was 45 dB HL for the right ear and the speech recognition score was 45 dB HL for the left ear.

____

____

Exercise 2–23. Modifying Prepositional Phrases.

Some of the images conjured by the sentences below can be funny. We resist the urge to laugh, and, instead, ask that you change them to represent the meaning that the author probably intended. In the spaces below, rewrite the sentences so as to correct the dangling prepositional phrases.

1. Guitar (2006) recommends a 5-minute speech sample, measuring only while the child is speaking with an accurate stopwatch.

   ____

   ____

2. Play with the child to get an accurate language sample on the floor.

   ____

   ____

3. The best way to give the PICA is by spreading across the table in order the 10 stimulus objects.

   ____

   ____

4. Red is right on the ears when placing headphones.

   ____

   ____

5. Look for signs exhibited by the child who is self-stimulating with autism.

   ____

   ____

6. How do you test a child on the TOLD with a hearing impairment?

   ____

   ____

7. Check for gurgling sounds after the client swallows in her voice.

___

___

8. Count the number of errors as soon as you finish so you don't forget on the speech recognition task.

___

___

9. Remember to sterilize the immittance probe tips from the client's ears after they are removed.

___

___

10. Inspect the ear canals carefully for cerumen prior to obtaining an earmold impression with an Otoscope.

___

___

Exercise 2–24. Parallelism

In the spaces below, rewrite the sentences below to improve parallelism.

1. Reading to a large audience and the unfamiliarity of a word will increase the likelihood of stuttering.

2. The clinician can see if the child is aware of stuttering, secondary behaviors, and whether or not the child seems to be ashamed of stuttering.

3. The clinician makes sure that the child's hearing has been checked, and assess the child's physical and cognitive development.

4. The errors either were in the first syllable of the spondee word or the second syllable.

5. Mr. Smith was instructed to listen carefully to the words, repeat them back, and that he should take a guess if he was not sure.

6. The casing of the left hearing aid not only was scratched, but was cracked.

7. Neither the output level of the first audiometer or the second had been calibrated.

____

____

8. The child's test reliability was poor as he was both tired as well as hungry.

____

____

9. Frequencies were tested between 250 Hz to 4000 Hz.

____

____

10. Outcomes revealed that high-frequency thresholds increased and speech recognition scores decreased over the past 5 years.

____

____

Exercise 2–25. General Errors in Writing

Find and correct the errors, or recast the sentence.

1. The book's are Joans, not her's.

2. John was phonically challenged after his partial laryngectomy.

3. As a member of the deaf community, Bill hoped his new baby would be born Deaf.

4. The complete package includes hearing aid, case and batteries.

5. The diagnosis was Asperger's syndrome, a mild form of Autism.

6. If s/he wants a 2:00 appointment, try to give it to him/her.

7. You may extract a biscuit from the tin if you name the correct colour.

8. A child has a right to express their own opinion.

9. At the beginning of therapy, Mary presented with a voice quality that sounds breathy.

10. Goals were met, because he answered correctly three times in a row, consecutively.

11. He made fantastic progress in therapy.

____

12. She improved in reading, writing, and ability to produce gestures.

____

13. Jim was treated for speech problems related to CP.

____

14. Linda can produce some consonant clusters, but not others.

____

15. John was tested on Form a of the *Peabody Picture Vocabulary Test*, IInd edition.

____

16. Mike has expressive aphasia.

____

17. 15 students were registered for clinic on the same day.

____

18. The child asked if he could extract a biscuit from the tin as a reward.

____

19. The hearing aid should be placed *a.d.*, right ear.

____

20. We gave *PPVT's* at the beginning and end of therapy.

____

Exercise 2–26. General Errors in Writing

Correct the sentences, writing corrections in the spaces below.

1. It is important to complete the portion of the assessment in which the child is directly involved and the nature of the disorder, and only then offer recommendations.

____

____

2. This allows for the clinician can observe firsthand the nature of the disorder.

____

____

3. The goal of the protocol is to assess the frequency, severity, and duration the adult stutters.

____

____

4. Mrs. Smith's medical history includes issues with her optic nerves and spinal pressure.

____

____

5. The mother reported that her son has kidney problems, Hydronephrosis.

____

____

6. Mr. Frank is Single-Sided Deafness (SSD) for the right ear due to an acoustic neuroma in August, 1983.

____

____

7. Following a high fever experienced a week ago, the client reported his right ear had no hearing.

____

____

8. The child reportedly received speech therapy once a week every Tuesdays.

____

____

9. The patient was counseled of the nature and degree of his hearing loss and is a candidate for monaural amplification.

____

____

10. A speech recognition score was not obtained in the right ear and a speech recognition score obtained at 55 dB HL was 92% in the left ear.

____

____

Exercise 2–27. General Errors in Writing

Correct the eight errors in the paragraph below on the worksheet that follows.

The ages of birth to three years[1] are the critical period of language learning for children, so these parents are rightfully concerned that there[2] child of 1.1[3] has not yet spoken clear 1st[4] words. Regardless of the fact that this child has passed the newborn hearing screening,[5] in accordance with the JCIH 2007 Position Statement, Sarah should continue to receive ongoing surveillance of her communicative development. A through[6] audiologic assessment should be done[7] which is[8] case history, Otoscopy, pure-tone air and bone conduction testing, speech audiometry, and immittance.

In the spaces below, identify and correct the errors in the paragraph above.

1. ______________________________

____

2. ______________________________

____

3. ______________________________

____

4. ______________________________

____

5. ______________________________

____

6. ______________________________

____

7. ______________________________

____

8. ______________________________

____

Exercise 2–28. General Errors in Writing

Correct the eight errors in the paragraph below on the worksheet that follows.

Populations that can benefit from classroom amplification include children with fluctuating CHL[1], unilateral hearing loss, slight permanent hearing loss, and (a) language, (b) learning, (c) attention, (d) auditory processing problems[2], and even those with normal hearing. 5[3] physical factors that can influence speech intelligibility are: intensity level of speech; distance of listener from the sound source; background noise,[4] signal to noise ratio[5] (SRN)[6]; and room reverberation (sound's[7] reflections). According to ASHA 2005, an ideal classroom SNR should be at least +15[8] at the child's ears.

In the spaces below, identify and correct the errors in the paragraph above.

1. ______________________________

2. ______________________________

3. ______________________________

4. ______________________________

5. ______________________________

6. ______________________________

7. ______________________________

8. ______________________________

Exercise 2–29. General Errors in Writing

Correct the eight errors in the paragraph below on the worksheet that follows.

OME[1] may cause conductive hearing loss. A child with OME may have auditory and speech language effects.[2] Their[3] speech/language[4] may be delayed if they have chronic OME because they can't hear very good.[5] During birth to 3 yrs[6], this[7] is the prime time when kids are learning language and acquiring the rules.[8] It is therefore very important for children to have routine hearing screenings.

In the spaces below, identify and correct the errors in the paragraph above.

1. ______________________________

____

2. ______________________________

____

3. ______________________________

____

4. ______________________________

____

5. ______________________________

____

6. ______________________________

____

7. ______________________________

____

8. ______________________________

____

Exercise 2–30. General Errors in Writing

Correct the eight errors in the paragraph below on the worksheet that follows.

It is difficult to evaluate behavioral hearing in infants <[1] 6 months of age. Behavioral observation audiometry is an unconditioned test that can be used in this population—[2] the audiologist watches for a change in the child's behavior in response to a sound. BOA[3] may be used in conjunction with electrophysiologic testing such as the auditory brainstem response (ABR) or otoacoustic emissions (OAE) to assess their[4] hearing because it's[5] difficult to evaluate behavioral hearing in infants less than 6 months of age. ABR's[6] provide information about the auditory system up to the level of the brainstem,[7] OAE testing evaluates the function of the cochlear outer hair cells.[8]

In the spaces below, identify and correct the errors in the paragraph above.

1. ______________________________

2. ______________________________

3. ______________________________

4. ______________________________

5. ______________________________

6. ______________________________

7. ______________________________

8. ______________________________

Exercise 2–31. General Errors in Writing

Find the errors in form in the paragraph below.

AB has progress throughout the semester in the area of expressive language, social-cognitive skills, and pragmatic/gesteral skills. He is engaged in most of the speechgroup activitie's. He has shown increase expressive abilities in the area of labelling, and verbal requesting. In the area of social-cognitive skills, AB has improvement in the use of two toys in a multi scheme context. Pragmatically AB occasionally sings the hello, and "goodbye" songs. he interacts with his age peers in several ways (i.e., playing ball).

In the spaces below, indicate whether there are any of the following:

1. Proofreading errors, such as errors in capitalization or spacing?

____

____

2. Spelling errors?

____

____

3. Punctuation errors?

____

____

4. Omissions or substitutions of grammatical morphemes?

____

____

5. Incorrect use of abbreviations?

____

____

6. Anything else?

____

____

Exercise 2–32. General Errors in Writing

Find the errors in content and composition in the paragraphs below.

Now that you have checked your writing for errors in form, we can turn to content and composition. See Chapter 1 for a discussion of run-on sentences and sentence fragments. Also focus on agreement and gender neutrality. Be aware of some other errors, including spacing and use of phonetic symbols. Find the errors in the paragraph below:

The clinician will engage the client in conversational speech conversation. The clinician will facilitate responses by ask the client questions regarding their interests, and what did you like about prior therapy sessions. The client will be instruction to read a newspaper magazine out loud. The clinician will record phonological errors (ex., substitution of "f" for the consonant blend "th" in the final position). The client will be asked if they noticed any speech, language, or hearing errors. Then be asked to read the exact same paragraph again two times in a row, consecutively.

In the spaces below, indicate whether there are any of the following:

1. Sentence fragment or run-on sentence?

____

____

2. Redundancies?

____

____

3. Lack of noun-pronoun agreement?

____

____

4. Errors in grammatical morphemes?

____

____

5. Incorrect use of abbreviations?

____

____

6. Anything else?

____

____

Exercise 2–33. Choose the correct answer in parentheses.

1. Alex Sharp had (a part/apart) in *The Curious Incident of the Dog in the Night-Time*, a play about autism.
2. It is not easy to take (a part/apart) a hearing aid.
3. An (in tact/intact) tympanic membrane does not rule out conductive hearing loss.
4. In mild non-fluent aphasia, some language production skills are impaired, but some language comprehension skills may be (in tact/intact).
5. A popular song is "Call Me (Maybe/May Be)."
6. One branch of the vagus nerve (maybe/may be) damaged in unilateral adductor vocal fold paralysis.
7. The body-cover model is based (off of/on) the five layers of the vocal folds.
8. A finding of conductive hearing loss is based (off of/on) an air-bone gap.
9. "Individuals with autism spectrum disorders," rather than "autistics" (has/have) been the preferred way of classifying such people for the past 10 years.
10. Genetic characteristics (has/have) been identified in individuals who stutter.

Final Note

Here is a bit of doggerel. Consider your reaction.

With your figure asymmetrical,
Tho' you drink a case o' Metrecal,
You're a fatter man than I am,
Double Chin.

Did you notice that *tho'* really should have been written as *although* and that there really was no need to abbreviate *of* as *o*?

Or did you notice the play on Rudyard Kipling's rhythm, a tortured rhyme owing a debt to W. S. Gilbert (of Gilbert and Sullivan), and a tag line that rhymes with *Gunga Din*?

If you answered affirmatively to part (or all) of the first question, you'll probably make a good copyeditor, but aren't having fun with language. If you said "Yes" to part (or all) of the second question, then language is becoming your toy.

References

American Academy of Audiology. (2018). *Academy information*. Retrieved from http://www.audiology.org/about/information/Pages/default.aspx

American Psychological Association. (2010). *Publication manual of the American Psychological Association* (6th ed.). Washington, DC: Author.

Battistella, E. (1990). Language, gender, and professional writing: Theoretical approaches and guidelines for nonsexist use. *Language, 66*, 190–191.

Behrens, S. J. (2010). *Grammar: A pocket guide*. New York, NY: Routledge.

Behrens, S. J., & Mercer, C. (2007). The style of which this is written: Neutralization of prepositions in English. *NADE Digest, 3*, 45–56.

Bess, F. H., & Humes, L. E. (2003). *Audiology: The fundamentals*. Baltimore, MD: Lippincott Williams & Wilkins.

Cook, C. K. (1985). *Line by line: How to edit your own writing*. Boston, MA: Houghton Mifflin.

Debonis, D. A., & Donohue, C. L. (2004). *Survey of audiology: Fundamentals for audiologists and health professionals*. Boston, MA: Allyn & Bacon.

Driscoll, D. L. (2017). Parallel structure. *OWL Purdue online writing lab*. Retrieved from https://owl.english.purdue.edu/owl/resource/623/01/

Fuchs, E. (1981). *Comprehension of explicit and implicit information in adult aphasia* (Unpublished PhD dissertation). Columbia University, New York, NY.

Goldberg, E., & Goldfarb, R. (2005). Grammatical category ambiguity in aphasia. *Brain and Language, 95*, 293–303.

Goldfarb, R. (1985). Speech disorders/communication problems. In T. Husen & T. N. Postlethwaite (Eds.), *The international encyclopedia of education* (pp. 4760–4766). Oxford, UK: Pergamon.

Goldfarb, R. (1996). Transposition of words as indicators of semantic state in aphasia. *Perceptual and Motor Skills, 82*, 112–114.

Graff, G. (2003). *Clueless in academe: How schooling obscures the life of the mind*. New Haven, CT: Yale University Press.

Hegde, M. N. (2010). *A coursebook on scientific and professional writing for speech-language pathology* (4th ed.). Clifton Park, NY: Thomson Delmar Learning.

Jones, J., Obler, L. K., Gitterman, M., & Goldfarb, R. (2002). The interface of phonology and morphology in agrammatism: Negation in African American vernacular English. *Brain and Language, 83*, 164–166.

Katz, J. (2002). Clinical audiology. In J. Katz (Ed.), *Handbook of clinical audiology*, (5th ed., pp. 3–8). Baltimore, MD: Lippincott Williams & Wilkins.

LaPointe, L. L. (2006). Profanity. *Journal of Medical Speech-Language Pathology, 14*, vii–ix.

Lebrun, Y. (1997). Subcortical structures and non-volitional verbal behaviour. *Journal of Neurolinguistics, 10*, 313–323.

Lees, A. J., Robertson, M., Trimble, M. R., & Murray, N. M. (1984). A clinical study of Gilles de la Tourette syndrome in the United Kingdom. *Journal of Neurology, Neurosurgery, and Psychiatry, 47*, 1–8.

Martin, F. N., & Clark, J. G. (2006). *Introduction to audiology* (9th ed.). Boston, MA: Allyn & Bacon.

Morris, H. R., Thacker, A. J., Newman, P. K., & Lees, A. J. (2000). Sign language tics in a prelingually deaf man. *Movement Disorders: Official Journal of the Movement Disorder Society, 15*, 318–320.

NCTE. (2002). Guidelines for gender–fair use of language. *National council of teachers of English*, revised by N. Prosenjak, et al., National Council of Teachers of English, revised ed. Retrieved from http://www.ncte.org/positions/statements/genderfairuseoflang

Paden, E. P. (1975). ASHA in retrospect: Fiftieth anniversary reflections. *ASHA*, *17*(9), 571–572.

Pena-Casanova, J., Bertran-Serra, I., Serra, A., & Bori, I. (2002). Uncommonly long sequences of speech automatisms in a young woman with traumatic brain injury. *Journal of Neurolinguistics*, *15*, 109–128.

Rolnick, M., & Hoops, M. (1969). Aphasia as seen by the aphasic. *Journal of Speech and Hearing Disorders*, *34*, 48–53.

Santo Pietro, M. J., & Goldfarb, R. (1995). *Techniques for aphasia rehabilitation generating effective treatment (TARGET)*. Vero Beach, FL: The Speech Bin.

Shipley, K. G. (Ed.). (1982). *A style guide for writers in communicative disorders*. Tucson, AZ: Communication Skill Builders.

Stern, E., Silbersweig, D. A., Chee, K. Y., Holmes, A., Robertson, M. M., Trimble, M., . . . Dolan, R. J. (2000). A functional neuroanatomy of tics in Tourette syndrome. *Archives of General Psychiatry*, *57*, 741–748.

Van Lancker Sidtis, D. (2004). When novel sentences spoken or heard for the first time in the history of the universe are not enough: Toward a dual-process model of language. *International Journal of Language and Communication Disorders/Royal College of Speech and Language Therapists*, *39*, 1–44.

Evidence-Based Writing

This chapter reviews concepts in writing a professional paper in the form of a journal article.

You will be required to:

1. Evaluate and critique the title, abstract, introduction, and methods sections of a research study
2. Write components of a results and conclusions section of a research study
3. Design a methods section in a proposed research study.

Writing a Professional Paper/Journal Article

This chapter reviews concepts in writing a professional paper in the form of a journal article. In this section, we refer to the triangle and the spiral. Keeping these shapes in mind may help when writing a professional paper in the form of a journal article. We will also refer to a PowerPoint™ presentation From Adelphi University: Syntax Training (FAUST) available on the website that describes a simulated experiment and guides the student in writing a related experiment. The format of FAUST follows the structure of a typical journal article.

The author of a journal article tends to spend a great deal of time in following the format that we describe below, but the work continues in rewriting the article after critical review. Many journals have a lead editor who will provide immediate feedback when a manuscript is submitted. At this stage, the manuscript may be deemed inappropriate for the content or mission of the journal, and it will be rejected. Alternatively, with the lead editor's approval, the manuscript may be considered for publication and will be sent to an associate editor with expertise in the research area addressed by the authors. The associate editor will contact *ad hoc* peer reviewers who volunteer their services to provide an in-depth critique of the manuscript.

The outcome of the critique may be for acceptance of the manuscript without revisions (a very rare occurrence), acceptance with minor or major revisions, or rejection. The authors have the opportunity to respond to the comments from peer reviewers by adding requested information or literature support (even running additional experiments if necessary), correcting errors in the manuscript, or explaining why they disagree with the peer reviewers on particular points.

The authors of the present book have both been *ad hoc* peer reviewers for many journals over many years. It is our way of providing service to our professional committee and assuring adherence to standards of excellence in the publication of journal articles. In addition, service (to the department, school or college, and university, as well as professional service) is one of the three areas (along with scholarship and teaching) in which professors are evaluated for reappointment, promotion, and tenure.

For more information about the peer-review process in refereed journals, see Chapter 5.

A. Title

Inform the reader of both the classification variables under study and the target population. Try also to attract the reader's interest, and, where possible, to limit the title to 10 or fewer words. Here are some examples of our own articles, with comments.

> Goldfarb, R., & Bekker, N. (2009). Noun-verb ambiguity in chronic undifferentiated schizophrenia. *Journal of Communication Disorders, 42*, 74–88.

Comment: This is an example of seven words used effectively to fulfill the requirements of a title cited above.

> Serpanos, Y. C., & Jarmel, F. (2007). Quantitative and qualitative follow-up outcomes from a preschool audiologic screening program: Perspectives over a decade. *American Journal of Audiology, 16*, 4–12.

Comment: This title does go on a bit, but the authors could not select a word or area for deletion without sacrificing an essential element.

> Goldfarb, R., & Bader, E. (1979). Espousing melodic intonation therapy in aphasia rehabilitation: A case study. *International Journal of Rehabilitation Research, 2*, 333–342.

Comment: This title is a little too cute. The focus was on training the wife of the patient in the study, and the pun indicating that the authors were both advocating the therapy and using the spouse as a partner in therapy was probably lost on the reader.

B. Abstract

Most peer-reviewed journals in communication sciences and disorders follow the APA style manual (APA, 2010) and recommend that the abstract should be no longer than 250 words. The abstract should include the following information:

1. Purpose, or problem under investigation (in one sentence)
2. Pertinent characteristics of participants (e.g., number, type, age, and sex); journals that publish research on animals include information on genus and species in the abstract
3. Experimental method including apparatus, data-gathering procedures, and complete test
4. Names and complete generic names and dosage and routes of administration of any drugs (particularly if the drugs are novel or important to the study)
5. Results: findings, including statistical significance levels
6. Conclusions: the implications or applications of the findings

The spiral begins with the abstract, where the terms used in the title are clarified, elaborated, and defined. The abstract includes purposes of the study, a brief outline of the important results, and implications of the research. Some journals include key words and learning outcomes in the abstract.

C. Introduction

Think of the literature review (or introduction in a peer-reviewed article) as a triangle with the tip pointing down, and the widest part on top ▼. The first part of the introduction will have a wide view, such as a statement about language disorders in autism, and, as the review progresses, the focus will be narrowed to the current field of study and end with the hypotheses. This section aims to review the literature relevant to your study, and to motivate your hypotheses. Your literature review should not be completely uncritical; that is, you should not merely report what others have done, but provide the following:

> an original synthesis of a large body of information;
>
> a theoretical basis for the research you are doing;
>
> alternative theories on the specific or related subject;

an indication of what is valuable in these studies; and

an indication of what is weak or erroneous in these studies.

The information in the introduction widens the spiral by referring to previous statements and providing much more detail. Begin with a general statement of the problem, and make this the focus of the introduction. Clearly specify, at greater length than in the abstract, the purposes of the study.

Operational Definitions

All terms in a descriptive statement must be carefully defined in terms of the operations involved in manipulating or observing their referents. As an illustration, treatment for aphasia varies according to type and severity of the disorder. A strategy of delay will help the patient with mild aphasia more than the one with severe aphasia, and a cue of the initial phoneme will be more effective at triggering the target word for a patient with nonfluent aphasia than one with fluent aphasia. The following example needs the term *benefit* to be defined operationally:

Patients who benefit most from group treatment have been diagnosed with

(___) mild aphasia (___) moderate aphasia (___) severe aphasia.

If *benefit* is defined as improved word retrieval, then the answer would be mild aphasia, but if *benefit* is defined as improved quality of life, then the answer might be severe aphasia.

You should write operational definitions for any terms used in the title or description that may be interpreted in more than one way. For example, you may think the word "infant" applies to a human being under the age of 12 months. In fact, an "infant of the court" is an individual younger than 21 years of age. Present your information from many points of view, using a combination of mostly recent, but some classical references, where appropriate. The best references are primary sources, such as journal articles, rather than secondary sources, such as books (even this one). The problem with secondary sources is one of depending on someone else's interpretation, rather than your own. For example, if you read a summary of Smith's article as cited in Jones' book, you are depending on Jones to report Smith's work accurately. You are much more likely to be accurate if you go back to the original Smith article.

Finally, all roads in the introduction lead to hypotheses. You may present your hypotheses as statements or questions, but they must be motivated by the preceding review of the literature, and they must be falsifiable. Theories, therapies, and hypotheses may never be proven to be universally correct, but they can be shown to be incorrect. The simple reason is that we can never test everyone in the population that interests us, so we use what we hope is a representative sample of the population. There may be a child in Burkina Faso with autism spectrum behavioral disorders (ASD) that no one has seen before, and these behaviors never appear on a scale to evaluate ASD. Similarly, an adult in Siberia with post-stroke aphasia may recover language in a pattern never described in the literature.

Some disciplines, for example, descriptive linguistics, do not depend on falsifiable hypotheses in order to develop models for further study. Saying that TPWSGWTAU (the place where sentences go when they are understood) exists somewhere in the brain is not a falsifiable hypothesis. However, it permits the development of models of language processing, even if it is unlikely that the specific existence of TPWSGWTAU will be discovered.

For the purpose of practice, list at least one principle hypothesis and at least one secondary hypothesis. It is also good practice to list null hypotheses. The following examples are taken from FAUST.

Principle hypothesis: Successful training of forms of *to be* as a verbal auxiliary will generalize to untrained copula in 4-year-old children with specific language impairment.

Secondary hypothesis: Generalization from verbal auxiliary to copula will be better for contractible than for noncontractible pronouns.

Null hypotheses: Add the word "not" in the appropriate place. For example, "Successful training of forms of *to be* as a verbal auxiliary will NOT generalize to untrained copula in 4-year-old children with specific language impairment," and, "Generalization will NOT be better for contractible than for noncontractible pronouns."

In general, the null hypothesis indicates that there was no effect of the experimental or clinical treatment or that there were no differences between experimental and control groups. It is possible to make two kinds of errors involving the null hypothesis. In a Type I (note that Roman numerals are used here) error, the null hypothesis is rejected when it should have been the accepted alternative. In a Type II error, the null hypothesis is accepted when it should have been the rejected alternative.

D. Methods

Subjects (or more properly, Participants): The spiral here refers back to the individuals or groups cited in the title and abstract, and described in the introduction. Clearly identify the proposed population(s), as well as the bases for participant selection. If a control group is or is not being used, explain why or why not. What variables are you controlling with regard to participants? Why have you selected these and omitted others? Will the sample size be adequate to permit statistical analysis and generalization? If the population includes participants with communication disorders, how will these disorders be assessed? Who will perform the diagnostic evaluation? How will severity and type of impairment be controlled? Remember that certain uncontrolled variables, such as age, gender, education, and socioeconomic status can confound your results.

Information about drugs in communication sciences and disorders (CSD) research tends to appear, if at all, in participant characteristics when the study involves a medically-based disorder. For example, in research on the language of schizophrenia, duration and level of typical or atypical antipsychotic medications should be included.

Inclusionary and exclusionary criteria refer to what must be present and what must not be present as participant characteristics. For example, some inclusionary criteria in addition to the variables listed above might be handedness, race or ethnicity, and employment history. Studies of medical etiologies in speech-language pathology and audiology might list specific type of disorder and time since onset as inclusionary criteria. For example, the tested population might include only adults with nonfluent aphasia secondary to a stroke that occurred no longer than 6 months before testing. Presence of communication disorder is crucial in our research and might need clarification. For example, a study on conductive hearing loss should not include individuals with sensorineural hearing loss, and a study on nonfluent aphasia should not include individuals with fluent aphasia. Some exclusionary criteria, unless they are the substance of the study, might be uncorrected loss in hearing or vision, bilingual or polyglot status, and presence of medical conditions other than the one being studied. Ideally, a control group will also be included in the experiment, and the control group should be matched with the experimental group on all participant characteristics except for presence of communication disorder.

Materials: Will they be standardized? If not, why not? If equipment is to be used, how will correct calibration be ensured? Who is qualified to use this equipment?

Procedures: How are you conducting your research? Describe in sufficient detail to permit the study to be repeated, every step of the way. How will the materials be presented? Why? Who will present these materials? Why? How will your participants respond? Why? Who will score the responses? How and why? Also note how the following will be controlled:

order of presentation;

randomization of stimuli;

practice effect (learning to learn);

recording of responses; and

reliability of, and correlation between, and among, scorers.

Baseline data and baseline recovery data are essential in intervention studies. Writing this information ensures that claims of change have a basis in evidence. Baseline data can include the "hard" data of standardized testing as well as "soft" data, such as reports of observations of children at play. Following is an example of baseline data to assess a child's use of forms of *to be* as a verbal auxiliary or copula (see FAUST):

All 30 children will be tested

1. Informally in free play; review of video to analyze first 10 obliged uses of *to be*.
2. Formally with random presentation of 10 pronoun (PN) + V (for verbal auxiliary) and 10 PN + Adj (for copula) pictures (that will not be used in training). S^D: "Tell me about this one."

Measures will be repeated with different stimuli for formal testing in baseline recovery.

If the research is clinical, describe the program of intervention in detail, including number of trials, number of consecutive sessions, and criterion levels for mastery.

E. Results

The results section continues the spiral. In the results section, key findings of the study are reported, but not interpreted. A summary of the data is presented in table or figure format, following APA style. Visual displays of data often appear in a line graph, bar graph, or histogram. The text should explain the main outcomes in sequence to address the research questions and/or hypotheses and refer to information presented in tables and figures. All findings should be reported, even those that do not support the hypotheses. A description of the statistical analysis of the data and outcomes should be indicated; complex analyses may be presented in visual display.

F. Discussion and Conclusion

For the last time, spiral back to earlier sections of your paper. The Discussion section provides a thorough interpretation of the study results. Begin by comparing a summary of your findings to some of the research you reported in your introduction section. Explain any similarities or differences. Are your hypotheses supported (they are never "proven") or falsified? What do your results have to do with the theories that supported your hypotheses? Have you considered alternative theories or explanations? The importance of an underlying theory should be woven throughout your paper. What are the implications for clinical intervention, diagnosis and appraisal, and future research? The Conclusion section ends the research article. Here, the main research findings are presented briefly in a few sentences.

G. References

References should be presented alphabetically in APA style, unless you are submitting your article to a medical journal. Avoid using abstracts and Internet sites (although peer-reviewed online journals are fine; see Chapter 6). Unpublished observations and personal communications may not be used as references. Manuscripts accepted but not yet published may be cited, followed by a notation of "in press" where the year of publication typically would be indicated. All references cited in the body of the paper must be included, and articles not cited in the body of the paper must not be included in the reference section.

EXERCISES

Exercise 3–1. Chapter Review

1. References in a professional paper or journal article are typically in ________ format.
   a. MLA
   b. Chicago
   c. APA
   d. Vancouver
   e. Harvard

2. Participant characteristics in a study are specified in the _____________ section of a journal article.
   a. Introduction
   b. Methods
   c. Procedures
   d. Materials

3. The abstract of a professional journal article:
   a. appears immediately following the title.
   b. should include references.
   c. follows the Conclusions section.
   d. typically has no word limit.

4. In a professional paper, key findings from a research study are interpreted in the ____________ section.
   a. Methods
   b. Results
   c. Discussion
   d. Conclusion

5. The following statement about the Introduction section of a journal article is true:
   a. It begins with a narrow focus in the field of study.
   b. The section ends with research questions or hypotheses.
   c. The literature review only includes references that support the research hypothesis.
   d. Only the most recent literature should be included.

6. In an introduction,
   a. the literature review motivates the hypothesis.
   b. the hypothesis motivates the literature review.
   c. the literature review and the hypothesis are independent of each other.
   d. all references in the literature review must be from publications within the last 10 years.
   e. cite as many books as you can, because the author has already synthesized the literature.

7. If we think of the literature review (or introduction in a peer-reviewed article) as a triangle with the tip pointing down, and the widest part on top ▼, then
   a. the wide part of the triangle is devoted to the research and null hypotheses.
   b. the wide part of the triangle is devoted to uncritical review, and the tip addresses the literature critically.
   c. there may be only one hypothesis at the tip, because it is so small.
   d. the literature review is an original synthesis of a large body of information relevant to your study.
   e. applicable theories are not raised in this section .

8. Visual displays of data in the results section may be
   a. tables but not figures.
   b. figures but not tables.
   c. tables or figures.
   d. polygraphs.
   e. graphemes.

9. The null hypothesis may indicate that
   a. there is a statistically significant difference between experimental and control groups.
   b. there is no difference between experimental and control groups.
   c. speech and language therapy has been successful.
   d. the experiment was poorly designed.
   e. the experiment was well designed.

10. Which of the following is an operational definition?
    a. Uncorrected hearing loss from birth can affect speech and language development.
    b. A mild hearing loss indicates a threshold level of between 26-40 dB in the better ear.
    c. Stuttering is everything you do to stop stuttering.
    d. Non-fluent aphasia indicates stuttering in addition to a language disorder.

Exercise 3–2. Evaluation of Student's Evidence-Based Writing in Speech-Language Pathology

The following is edited from an actual report. In the spaces below, correct the examples of incorrect usage. Each item is followed by a number in parentheses.

Clinical hypothesis.
A phonological approach will improve production of postvocalic /t/ and /p/ more than a traditional approach in a preschool male.

Client profile. Z.Z. is a three year, four month old (1) male who presents with a speech delay. Observations indicate that he omits the final /p/ and /t/ sounds in words. His mother expressed concern that he did not finish the endings of his words. His mother also added that his immediate family understands him, but other adults often display difficulty understanding his speech.

Pretreatment baseline data. The following data was (2) collected prior to initiation of his treatment program: The client was producing the final /t/ sound in words with 40% accuracy. The client was producing the final /p/ sound in words with 50% accuracy. (3)

Treatment technique. The clinician used an alternating treatment approach for a single subject. (4) The two treatments used during therapy included a phonological approach and a traditional approach. The clinician used minimal pairs during phonological therapy to emphasize the consonants at the end of words. The client refused to participate in this task. Whether due to lack of interest, (5) or the unability (6) to comprehend this goal, this approach was discarded. (7) The remaining therapy sessions focused on the traditional approach. The techniques used during traditional articulation therapy included modeling, direct imitation, and motor exercises. These techniques, as well as visual prompts, elicited the final /t/ and /p/ sounds at the word, phrase, and sentence levels.

Treatment efficacy evidence. Klein (1996) observed that a study indicated that children who received traditional therapy did not perform as well as children who received phonological therapy. The children in the phonological group were all released from therapy, whereas only two of the children (8) in the traditional therapy group reached age-appropriate speech.

Data following 10 weeks of treatment. The client produced the final /p/ in words with 90% accuracy and the final /t/ in words with 85% accuracy. (9)

Conclusion. Results suggest that traditional therapy is improving Z.Z.'s intelligibility by emphasizing the final /T/ and /P/ (10) in words, with carryover observed at the phrase and sentence levels.

Reference
Klein, E. S. (1996). Phonological/traditional approaches to articulation therapy: A retrospective group comparison. *Language, Speech, and Hearing Services in Schools*, *27*, 314–323.

1. ____

____

2. ____

____

3. ____

____

4. ____

____

5. ____

____

6. ____

____

7. ____

____

8. ____

____

9. ____

____

10. ____

____

Exercise 3–3. Evaluate the Abstracts

Here are two incomplete abstracts, one in speech-language pathology and one in audiology. Based on the information provided, indicate the parts of the abstract that are missing.

A. Abstract in Speech-Language Pathology:

Purpose: The present study was designed to determine if there is any systematic effect of use on swallow function, specifically an increase in oral and/or pharyngeal swallowing time in adults with acute stroke when an effort is made to "fatigue" the swallowing mechanism, and to consider underlying causes other than peripheral neuromuscular fatigue (i.e. neurophysiological, neurochemical, and/or central fatigue).

Methods: In 13 patients aged 52 to 80 years (mean, 65 years) with acute stroke and clinically suspected oropharyngeal dysphagia, the temporal sequences of six, 1-mL liquid oropharyngeal swallowing events were measured pre- and post-videofluoroscopic swallowing evaluation.

(Reference: Baylow, H., Goldfarb, R., & Steinberg, R. (2014). Swallowing effect and suspected neuromuscular fatigue in adults with acute stroke: A videofluorographic analysis. *Journal of Medical Speech-Language Pathology*, *21*, 333-342.)

List the information missing from Abstract A above:

____

____

____

____

____

____

____

____

B. Abstract in Audiology:

Purpose: This study was conducted to investigate the efficacy of routine screening for high-frequency hearing loss (HFHL) including 3000, 6000, and 8000 Hz frequencies with conventional test frequencies (1000, 2000, and 4000 Hz). Method: Screening outcomes were examined in 2 cohorts. Results: Average total test time significantly increased ($p < .0001$) and nearly doubled with inclusion of 3000-, 6000-, and 8000-Hz frequencies, adding approximately 1 min. Rescreen referral rates decreased by approximately 2%–16% at 1000–8000 Hz (approximately 13%–16% at 6000 and 8000 Hz) using the modified protocol, supporting false-positive responses using supra-aural headphones.

Conclusion: Screening for HFHL should include insert earphones in order to prevent potential errors, particularly at 6000 and 8000 Hz.

(Reference: Serpanos, Y.C., Senzer, D., Renne, B., Langer, R., & Hoffman, R. (2015). The efficacy of routine screening for high frequency hearing loss (HFHL) in adults and children. *American Journal of Audiology, 24,* 377–383. doi:10.1044/2015_AJA-15-0014)

List the information missing from Abstract B above:

____

____

____

____

____

____

____

____

Exercises 3–4 to 3–12. Evaluate a Clinical Research Project

Several of the exercises below refer to the FAUST (From Adelphi University: Syntax Training) PowerPoint™ from your textbook website. The purpose of FAUST is to demonstrate a way to plan and conduct a clinical research project. In the present instance, the project involves a plan of therapy to train regular forms of the verb "to be" when used as a verbal auxiliary (e.g., he IS eating), and to measure generalization to untrained forms of "to be" when used as a copula (e.g., she IS tall). The student is then required to write a parallel clinical hypothesis and design a treatment study to examine generalization of trained regular plural allomorphs (e.g., [z] in two home RUNS) to untrained forms of first person singular (e.g., [z] in he RUNS home).

Exercise 3–4. Critique the Title

Refer to the FAUST PowerPoint™. Note the proposed title is, "Effect of Verbal Auxiliary Training on Untrained Copula in SLI." Now write another title, using no more than 10 words.

____

____

Exercise 3–5. Review Concepts of an Abstract Section

Write a list of the components of an abstract that are needed for a scientific paper.

____

____

____

____

Exercise 3–6. Critique the Abstract

The following is an abstract from a recent journal article (Goldfarb & Bekker, 2009; see complete reference above). Answer the questions on the worksheet that follows.

This study investigated noun–verb retrieval patterns of 30 adults with chronic undifferentiated schizophrenia and 67 typical adults, to determine if schizophrenia affected nouns (associated with temporal lobe function) differently from verbs (associated with frontal lobe function). Stimuli were homophonic homographic homonyms, balanced according to frequency of occurrence, where N > V, N < V, or N~V. Systematicity effects, in which systematic noun and verb meanings are transparently related (e.g., "drain"), and unsystematic noun and verb meanings appear to be unrelated (e.g., "seal"), were also examined. Adults with schizophrenia overselected nouns, in both phrase and sentence tasks. Typical participants strongly preferred verbs in the phrase task, but nouns in the sentence task. Frequency of occurrence yielded statistically significant effects in control, but not in experimental groups. Effects of systematicity were statistically significant in some, but not all, tasks and conditions. Age of typical participants was not significant.

Learning outcomes: Readers will be introduced to: (a) evidence of noun–verb organization in the brain; (b) evidence of ambiguous noun–verb preference to differentiate the language of schizophrenia from the language of typical adults; and (c) evidence of ambiguous noun–verb preference to differentiate the language of schizophrenia from fluent aphasia.

1. What do you like about this abstract?

___

___

___

___

2. What do you think could be better?

___

___

___

___

3. Do the learning outcomes make you want to read the paper? Why or why not?

____

____

____

____

Exercise 3–7. Identify and Correct the Errors in the Abstract of a Research Paper

Following is a sample of an abstract section of a research paper based on FAUST. We have taken our students' excellent written work and created errors to be identified according to the categories listed below. Please upload the FAUST PowerPoint file on the website provided with this book for reference as you identify the errors in the sample abstract using the classification below. Then, correct the errors on the worksheet below.

Identify the errors using the following classification:

G1, G2, G3 . . . errors in grammar

P1, P2, P3 . . . errors in punctuation

R1, R2, R3 . . . errors in referencing

S1, S2, S3 . . . errors in spelling

U1, U2, U3 . . . errors in usage

V1, V2, V3 . . . errors in vocabulary

Generalization of Regular Plural to Present Simple in SLI

ABSTRACT

Children with Specific Language Impairment have a very unique difficulty learning morphological aspects of language. This study examined weather training in use of the regular plural form /s/ to use of /s/ in the present simple tense in four-year-old children with specific language impairment. 30 children diagnosed as having specific language impairment, ranging in age from 4.2 to 4.8 years of age; were studied. One group of fifteen children were provided with explicit instruction in "regular" forms of plural [s], [z], and [iz], whereas the control group of fifteen children receive typical KIDTalk language therapy, they were than tested on their ability to generalize these forms to use of the present simple. The results that instruction in correct usage of plural forms did not generalize to use of the present simple tense.

____

____

____

____

____

Exercise 3–8. Review Concepts of an Introduction Section

1. Write an explanation of the concept of the upside-down triangle.

____

____

____

____

2. Refer to the FAUST PowerPoint™ on the website. Write a research hypothesis and a null hypothesis for the presented study.

____

____

____

____

Exercise 3–9. Identify and Correct the Errors in the Introduction Section of a Research Paper

Identify the errors in the sample introduction section, using the classification below. Then, correct the errors on the worksheet below.

Identify the errors using the following classification:

G1, G2, G3 . . . errors in grammar
P1, P2, P3 . . . errors in punctuation
R1, R2, R3 . . . errors in referencing
S1, S2, S3 . . . errors in spelling
U1, U2, U3 . . . errors in usage
V1, V2, V3 . . . errors in vocabulary

Generalization of Regular Plural to Present Simple in SLI

INTRODUCTION

Specific language impairment is characteristic by difficulty acquiring appropriate developmental language skills, despite otherwise typical development of nonlanguage skills. Children with specific language impairment have particular difficulty acquiring appropriate developmental language skills, such as inflectional morphology, when compared to typically developing children (Leonard, Bortolini, Caselli, McGregor, & Sabbadini, 1992, as cited by Swisher and Snow, 1994). This difficulty is preponderant even when children are in a linguistic environment, that supports normal language development.

____

____

____

____

____

Exercise 3–10. Review Concepts of a Methods Section

Refer to the FAUST PowerPoint from the website.

1. Participants: Write a list, with explanations, of characteristics of the population that need to be controlled.

 ____

 ____

 ____

 ____

2. Procedures: Write a list, with explanations, of the aspects of the treatment that need to be clear enough for the experiment to be replicated.

 ____

 ____

 ____

 ____

Exercise 3–11. Practice Writing Components of a Results Section

Refer to the FAUST PowerPoint from the website.

Pretend that you actually ran the study. Spiral back to earlier sections of the paper to suggest what you should anticipate happening. Although it is optional, it would be pleasant and impressive to know what statistical treatment you would use and why you would choose these statistical measures. How would you summarize your results? Show how you can best display your results, in figures and tables (such as F tables; figures of histograms or frequency polygons).

1. Write a summary of the findings indicated in the histograms in Figures 1 and 2 in the PowerPoint.

____

____

____

____

2. Reconfigure the data in the form of two frequency polygons.

Figure 3–1. Comparison of SLI pre- and post-VA training measures.

Figure 3–2. Comparison of SLI children with and without VA treatment.

3. Explain if training of the verbal auxiliary generalized to improvement in untrained copula.

___

___

___

Exercise 3–12. Practice Writing a Concluding Paragraph

Refer to the FAUST PowerPoint from the website.

1. Did the study support the research hypothesis or the null hypothesis? Why?

   ____

   ____

   ____

2. Write one clinical implication of the study.

   ____

   ____

   ____

Exercise 3–13. Design a Methods Section in Original Research

The methods section of a study includes description of participants, materials, and procedures. Using the sentence stimuli provided below (in section 2 of this exercise), create an experiment. Assume that the introduction, including literature review and statement of hypotheses, has already been written.

1. Write the **Participants** portion of a Methods section.

   Design a study, using the stimuli to see how older children or adults respond to 36 sentences that contain ambiguous words (that is, the word may be interpreted as a noun or a verb), 36 sentences that contain unambiguous words (18 nouns and 18 verbs), and 36 sentences that contain nonwords. Your participants may be neurotypical or representative of a population with disorders (e.g., teens with autistic spectrum disorders; college-age students with auditory processing disorders; elderly individuals with aphasia). Identify both inclusionary and exclusionary criteria (see examples).

   Examples of inclusionary criteria:

   Age range of participants
   Gender
   Educational level
   Socioeconomic status
   Type of disorder
   Severity of disorder
   Type and dosage of medications
   Other

   Examples of exclusionary criteria:

   No uncorrected auditory or visual acuity impairment
   Only monolingual speakers of English
   Exclude most or least severe impairments
   Limit time post-onset of disorder
   Other

   Participants

   ____

   ____

   ____

   ____

2. Write the **Materials** portion of a Methods section.

   Use the sentence stimuli below. Describe instrumentation, which may range from paper-and-pencil representation of the sentences to computerized reaction time programs to event-related brain potentials. How are stimuli controlled (e.g., randomization) and instrumentation calibrated?

Stimuli:

Ambiguous Sentences

1. I saw her film.
2. I saw her farm.
3. I saw her garden.
4. I saw her head.
5. I saw her order.
6. I saw her phone.
7. I saw her signal.
8. I saw her call.
9. I saw her knock.
10. I saw her laugh.
11. I saw her shout.
12. I saw her talk.
13. I saw her wash.
14. I saw her cry.
15. I saw her dress.
16. I saw her glance.
17. I saw her glow.
18. I saw her gulp.
19. I saw her work.
20. I saw her band.
21. I saw her board.
22. I saw her box.
23. I saw her flag.
24. I saw her trip.
25. I saw her iron.
26. I saw her hide.
27. I saw her mount.
28. I saw her nod.
29. I saw her stoop.
30. I saw her watch.
31. I saw her lie.
32. I saw her crash.
33. I saw her prop.
34. I saw her battle.
35. I saw her tape.
36. I saw her slip.

Nonambiguous Sentences:

18 Verbs

1. I saw her enter.
2. I saw her write.
3. I saw her cling.
4. I saw her speak.
5. I saw her listen.
6. I saw her learn.
7. I saw her grow.
8. I saw her sell.
9. I saw her sit.
10. I saw her compete.
11. I saw her teach.
12. I saw her bake.
13. I saw her fail.
14. I saw her erase.
15. I saw her choose.
16. I saw her twirl.
17. I saw her read.
18. I saw her eat.

18 Nouns

19. I saw her apple.
20. I saw her leg.
21. I saw her sofa.
22. I saw her cat.
23. I saw her hat.
24. I saw her glass.
25. I saw her street.
26. I saw her lamp.
27. I saw her home.
28. I saw her magazine.
29. I saw her laundry.
30. I saw her daughter.
31. I saw her passport.
32. I saw her piano.
33. I saw her doll.
34. I saw her computer.
35. I saw her meal.
36. I saw her uniform.

Nonwords

1. I saw her zat.
2. I saw her ped.
3. I saw her dav.
4. I saw her mog.

5. I saw her vun.
6. I saw her foit.
7. I saw her moof.
8. I saw her porth.
9. I saw her foy.
10. I saw her jern.
11. I saw her stot.
12. I saw her sheg
13. I saw her cliss.
14. I saw her chab.
15. I saw her foap.
16. I saw her sote.
17. I saw her sny
18. I saw her heest.
19. I saw her bruck.
20. I saw her shain.
21. I saw her hep.
22. I saw her rud.
23. I saw her lurst.
24. I saw her stook.
25. I saw her fim.
26. I saw her phum.
27. I saw her weam.
28. I saw her boj
29. I saw her waz
30. I saw her rin.
31. I saw her bap.
32. I saw her zel.
33. I saw her fub.
34. I saw her nos.
35. I saw her mup.
36. I saw her vib.

Materials

____

____

____

____

3. Write the **Procedures** portion of a Methods section.

   Describe the procedure in sufficient detail that an independent laboratory can replicate the experiment. How are threats to internal and external validity controlled? How is inter-rater reliability controlled?

Procedures

____

____

____

____

References

Albert, M., Sparks, R., & Helm, N. (1973). Melodic intonation therapy for aphasia. *Archives of Neurology, 29*, 130–131.

American Psychological Association (2010). *Publication manual of the American Psychological Association* (6th ed.). Washington, DC: Author.

American Speech-Language-Hearing Association. (2005). *Evidence-based practice in communication disorders* [Position statement]. Retrieved from http://www.asha.org/docs/html/PS2005-00221.html

Anderson, B. F. (1971). *The psychology experiment*. Belmont, CA: Brooks/Cole.

Finn, P., Bothe, A. K., & Bramlett, R. E. (2005). Science and pseudoscience in communication disorders: Criteria and applications. *American Journal of Speech-Language Pathology, 14*, 172–186.

Santo Pietro, M. J., & Goldfarb, R. (1995). *Techniques for aphasia rehabilitation generating effective treatment (TARGET)*. Vero Beach, FL: The Speech Bin.

Schuell, H., Jenkins, J., & Jimenez-Pabon, E. (1964). *Aphasia in adults: Diagnosis, prognosis, and treatment*. New York, NY: Hoeber Medical Division, Harper.

Ethics of Professional Writing

In Chapter 6 on writing using Internet resources, we identify several areas of ethical concern in research. The focus of the present chapter is on ethical considerations in professional and clinical writing.

By *ethics* we mean moral decision-making. A too-common example of an ethical lapse is the discussion of patients by medical personnel that we overhear when riding in the hospital elevator. Imagine the pain of a visitor who hears an intern casually indicate to a colleague that the visitor's relative "isn't going to make it."

In this chapter several writing exercises will be completed on ethical principles. You will:

1. Review and comment on a set of ethical dilemmas
2. Refer to a PowerPoint™ presentation on your website entitled, "Sample of a Short Course"
3. Read the Belmont Report and view the 9-minute video of participants of the National Commission for the Protection of Human Subjects of Biomedical and Behavioral Research
4. Take the computer-based NIH training course on the protection of human research participants
5. Read the ASHA Code of Ethics (2016)
6. Visit one of the sites from the list of annotated Web links.

We begin this chapter with an annotated Code of Ethics, continue with a discussion of relevant legal guidelines regarding ethical practice, and conclude with a sample form for compliance with ethical standards.

Robert William West (1892–1968) was the first president of what we now call the American Speech-Language-Hearing Association (ASHA). He thought our professions should have an ethical philosophy similar to that of physicians, and proposed the following as our version of the Hippocratic Oath:

> The speech of the children of man is our interest; and the communion of man is our concern. We seek out those who are halting in speech; and we offer help to those whose ears have been confused by disease. Life without speech is empty; and life devoid of communication is scarcely better than death. Therefore, the duty we owe is sacred; and our calling is gravely important.

Ethics of professional writing require that authors cite references appropriately and gain written permission to use the work of others. For example, in the present volume, the authors have submitted the following written approvals to Plural Publishing, Inc.: permission to use photographs of individuals fitted with electroencephalographic nets from Electrical Geodesics, Inc.; to copy the information for authors and the peer review policy from the *Journal of Speech-Language Pathology and Applied Behavior Analysis*; and to use examples of ethical writing from the *American Journal of Speech-Language Pathology*.

The ASHA Code of Ethics

The American Speech-Language-Hearing Association (ASHA) began a decade-long process of revising its *Code of Ethics* in August 2000, focusing on ethics in research and professional practice. The first revised *Code of Ethics* took effect on January 1, 2003, with the most recent revision in 2016 (reprinted by permission from ASHA). The Code of Ethics may be considered our discipline's compass (Rao, 2011).

The Preamble begins as follows:

> The preservation of the highest standards of integrity and ethical principles is vital to the responsible discharge of obligations by audiologists, speech-language pathologists, and speech, language, and hearing scientists who serve as clinicians, educators, mentors, researchers, supervisors, and administrators. This Code of Ethics sets forth the fundamental principles and rules considered essential to this purpose.

In annotating parts of the *Code of Ethics*, the authors are attempting to highlight only those portions that refer to clinical and professional practice, and to omit those portions that refer to research or treatment of animals. We have used elisions (three periods separated by spaces) to indicate portions omitted, and brackets to add a word for grammatical purposes when elisions affected sentence structure. The editorial opinions of the authors will be preceded by *Comment.*

Principle of Ethics I

Individuals shall honor their responsibility to hold paramount the welfare of persons they serve professionally.

Comment: The revisions in Principle of Ethics I add humane treatment of animals to the section on welfare of research participants and also address issues of nondiscrimination, informed consent, confidentiality, and security of research data.

Rules of Ethics

A. Individuals shall provide all clinical services and scientific activities competently.

Comment: ASHA members who hold the certificate of clinical competence (CCC) have, by virtue of completing an advanced degree from an accredited college or university, passing the national examination in speech language pathology or audiology, and completing the supervised clinical fellowship, demonstrated the ability to provide competent services. Should ASHA members with the CCC be considered competent in all areas of clinical practice? Many newly licensed and certified speech-language pathologists have never earned practicum hours with clients who have fluency or voice disorders; are they equipped to treat stuttering or spasmodic dysphonia? Few students in audiology are ever provided with clinical training in intraoperative monitoring; are they qualified to perform and interpret auditory evoked measures during surgical procedures?

B. Individuals shall use every resource, including referral and/or interprofessional collaboration when appropriate, to ensure that quality service is provided.

Comment: Rule B answers the comment raised in A, and requires that individuals without proper education, training, or experience in a particular area of communication disorders refer clients with such disorders to a practitioner with proper education, training, and experience. Offering credentials in specialization areas will facilitate appropriate referrals.

C. Individuals shall not discriminate in the delivery of professional services or in the conduct of research and scholarly activities on the basis of race, ethnicity, sex, gender identity/gender expression, sexual orientation, age, religion, national origin, disability, culture, language, or dialect.

Comment: None.

D. Individuals shall not misrepresent the credentials of aides, assistants, technicians, support personnel, students, research interns, Clinical Fellows, or any others under their supervision, and they shall inform those they serve professionally of the name, role, and professional credentials of persons providing services.

Comment: Student clinicians should sign their names above the title "Clinical Intern," or a similar designation approved by the institution, on all diagnostic evaluations, daily log notes, progress reports, and clinical summaries. The clinical supervisor who holds full credentials should also sign these documents.

E. Individuals who hold the Certificate of Clinical Competence may delegate tasks related to the provision of clinical services to aides, assistants, technicians, support personnel, or any other persons only if those persons are adequately prepared and are appropriately supervised. The responsibility for the welfare of those being served remains with the certified individual.

Comment: See F below

F. Individuals who hold the Certificate of Clinical Competence shall not delegate tasks that require the unique skills, knowledge, judgment, or credentials that are within the scope of their profession to aides, assistants, technicians, support personnel, or any nonprofessionals over whom they have supervisory responsibility.

Comment: These comments relate to E and F above, as well as G below. Council of Academic Accreditation (CAA) standards have changed regarding direct supervision of student clinicians, who formerly were required to be directly supervised by an individual holding the CCC for 25% of therapy time and 50% of diagnostic time. By signing a student's hourly log and affixing the ASHA account number, the supervisor guaranteed that these requirements had been met or exceeded.

The current CAA position for clinical supervision in audiology and speech-language pathology is (reprinted with permission):

Clinical supervision is commensurate with the clinical knowledge and skills of each student, and clinical procedures ensure that the welfare of each person served by students is protected, in accord with recognized standards of ethical practice and relevant federal and state regulations.

The program must have written policies that describe how the manner and amount of supervision are determined and adjusted to reflect the competence of each student and the specific needs of the clients/patients served. The written policies must describe the extent to which students are supervised and receive supervisor or preceptor consultation when providing services to client/patients. Procedures for client/patient safety, confidentiality, and security of client/patient records must also be clearly described in the program's written policies, in accordance with relevant federal and state regulations. Ethical standards must be clearly documented in the program's published materials.]

The complete list of CAA standards is available at http://caa.asha.org/wp-content/uploads/Accreditation-Standards-for-Graduate-Programs.pdf. A side-by-side comparison of CAA standards before and after changes that took effect on August 1, 2017 is available at http://caa.asha.org/wp-content/uploads/Accreditation-Standards-Revisions-Summary.pdf

G. Individuals who hold the Certificate of Clinical Competence may delegate to students tasks related to the provision of clinical services that require the unique skills, knowledge, and judgment that are within the scope of practice of their profession only if those students are adequately prepared and are appropriately supervised. The responsibility for the welfare of those being served remains with the certified individual.

Comment: See F above

H. Individuals shall obtain informed consent from the persons they serve about the nature and possible risks and effects of services provided, technology employed, and products dispensed. This obligation also includes informing persons served about possible effects of not engaging in treatment or not following clinical recommendations . . .

Comment: We recommend that individuals disclose to persons served (or their advocates) any financial or nonfinancial interest in technology or products dispensed.

I. Individuals shall enroll and include persons as participants in research or teaching demonstrations only if participation is voluntary, without coercion, and with informed consent.

Comment: Student clinicians should obtain release forms for video and audio recording before beginning therapy. These forms should indicate that recordings and other information will be used for teaching purposes only.

J. Individuals shall accurately represent the intended purpose of a service, product, or research endeavor and shall abide by established guidelines for clinical practice and the responsible conduct of research.

Comment: See K below

K. Individuals who hold the Certificate of Clinical Competence shall evaluate the effectiveness of services provided, technology employed, and products dispensed, and they shall provide services or dispense products only when benefit can reasonably be expected.

Comment: Relating to Rules J and K, understanding the differences between science and pseudoscience in communication disorders will facilitate critical evaluation of controversial practices and products, as Finn, Bothe, and Bramlett (2005) do with facilitated communication and Fast ForWord, as well as with the SpeechEasy device.

L. Individuals may make a reasonable statement of prognosis, but they shall not guarantee—directly or by implication—the results of any treatment or procedure.

Comment: In fitting a hearing aid, an audiologist may anticipate that the patient's amplified hearing may approach typical levels, but may not state that the device will restore normal hearing.

M. Individuals who hold the Certificate of Clinical Competence shall use independent and evidence-based clinical judgment, keeping paramount the best interests of those being served.

Comment: The ASHA 2005 Position Statement *Evidence-Based Practice in Communication Disorders* emphasizes the importance of an evidence-based approach in clinical practice by audiologists and speech-language pathologists. The document can be accessed at http://www.asha.org/policy/PS2005-00221.htm

N. Individuals who hold the Certificate of Clinical Competence shall not provide clinical services solely by correspondence, but may provide services via telepractice consistent with professional standards and state and federal regulations.

Comment: Although individual practitioners typically hold the CCC, a national accreditation, they are required in most cases to be licensed by the state in which they practice. State laws supersede rules of ethics regarding Rule N.

O. Individuals shall protect the confidentiality and security of records of professional services provided, research and scholarly activities conducted, and products dispensed. Access to these records shall be allowed only when doing so is necessary to protect the welfare of the person or of the community, is legally authorized, or is otherwise required by law.

Comment: See P below

P. Individuals shall protect the confidentiality of any professional or personal information about persons served professionally or participants involved in research and scholarly activities and may disclose confidential information only when doing so is necessary to protect the welfare of the person or of the community, is legally authorized, or is otherwise required by law.

Comment: For Rules O and P, see the section on the Health Insurance Portability and Accountability act of 1996 (HIPAA) as well as the Belmont Report for elaboration.

Q. Individuals shall maintain timely records and accurately record and bill for services provided and products dispensed and shall not misrepresent services provided, products dispensed, or research and scholarly activities conducted.

Comment: Per HIPAA regulations, any documents with identifying information of persons being treated must be kept securely in a locked cabinet.

R. Individuals whose professional practice is adversely affected by substance abuse, addiction, or other health-related conditions are impaired practitioners and shall seek professional assistance and, where appropriate, withdraw from the affected areas of practice.

Comment: Student clinicians with the above conditions should notify the clinical supervisor and the clinic director. In some cases, affected student clinicians might also contact the university office of mental health or disability services. When the health-related condition is a pregnancy, the student clinician should advise the persons in charge of internship and externship placements if delivery is expected midsemester.

S. Individuals who have knowledge that a colleague is unable to provide professional services with reasonable skill and safety shall report this information to the appropriate authority, internally if a mechanism exists and, otherwise, externally.

Comment: Most institutions have a Human Resources department. We suggest you contact that department first.

T. Individuals shall provide reasonable notice and information about alternatives for obtaining care in the event that they can no longer provide professional services.

Comment: One reason we are called *speech-language pathologists* and *audiologists*, as opposed to speech and hearing therapists, is that we do not need medical authorization to do our own discharge planning. With that privilege comes the responsibility to conduct discharge planning ethically.

Principle of Ethics II

Individuals shall honor their responsibility to achieve and maintain the highest level of professional competence and performance.

Comment: Principle of ethics II refers to professional competency. The philosophy articulated by ASHA parallels that of hospitals, where physicians may have general, specialized, or research privileges (Goldfarb, 1989). Research and specialized privileges include all general privileges and responsibilities. Specialized privileges, such as evaluating a client's suitability for a cochlear implant or an alternative augmentative communication device, are earned through additional credentialing, coursework, or continuing education.

Rules of Ethics

A. Individuals who hold the Certificate of Clinical Competence shall engage in only those aspects of the professions that are within the scope of their professional practice and competence, considering their certification status, education, training, and experience.

Comment: The United States Bureau of Labor Statistics has listed the professions of speech-language pathology and audiology among the leading growth professions for the coming decade (and has done so for many years). The shortage of fully credentialed practitioners has led some employers, particularly school districts, to appeal for and be granted exemption from the *highest quality provider* requirement of the state. Nevertheless, ASHA is exercising moral decision making by stipulating the CCC as a minimum requirement for best practice.

B. Members who do not hold the Certificate of Clinical Competence may not engage in the provision of clinical services; however, individuals who are in the certification application process may engage in the provision of clinical services consistent with current local and state laws and regulations and with ASHA certification requirements.

Comment: This rule is similar to, and was addressed in, comments to rules IA and IB.

C. Individuals who engage in research shall comply with all institutional, state, and federal regulations that address any aspects of research, including those that involve human participants and animals.

Comment: See sections below on *The Institutional Review Board*, and *The Belmont Report.*

D. Individuals shall enhance and refine their professional competence and expertise through engagement in lifelong learning applicable to their professional activities and skills.

Comment: The professions of speech-language pathology and audiology require lifelong learning for maintaining and developing new knowledge and skills. Although ASHA and most states require completion of 30 hours of continuing education every 3 years, many ASHA members, including the present authors, have earned ASHA's award for continuing education (ACE), which requires completion of 70 hours of continuing education in 3 years.

E. Individuals in administrative or supervisory roles shall not require or permit their professional staff to provide services or conduct research activities that exceed the staff member's certification status, competence, education, training, and experience.

Comment: See II F below.

F. Individuals in administrative or supervisory roles shall not require or permit their professional staff to provide services or conduct clinical activities that compromise the staff member's independent and objective professional judgment.

Comment: One of the more sensitive issues of ethics is coercion, as applicable to Rules II E and II F. The possibility of staff members who are unsure of their job security being tyrannized by a coercive director is, of course, of ethical concern. Of equal concern is the staff member who considers the individual in charge to be a mentor. Whenever there is a power differential, the individual in the position of power must be especially sensitive to the possibility of perhaps unintended coercion. See Schmidt, Galletta, and Obler (2006) for more information on coercion and power differentials.

G. Individuals shall make use of technology and instrumentation consistent with accepted professional guidelines in their areas of practice. When such technology is not available, an appropriate referral may be made.

Comment: See II H below.

H. Individuals shall ensure that all technology and instrumentation used to provide services or to conduct research and scholarly activities are in proper working order and are properly calibrated.

Comment: Related to Rules II G and II H, the effectiveness of clinical services is dependent upon on the accurate performance of any equipment used to perform them. Clinicians who rely on the use of equipment in service delivery must systematically assess the equipment function according to manufacturer specifications, and at minimum, ASHA guidelines. In audiology, where there is a heavy reliance on equipment for most services, biologic (listening), quarterly, and annual calibrations are routinely performed in order to ascertain proper equipment function (Wilber & Burkard, 2009).

Principle of Ethics III

Individuals shall honor their responsibility to the public when advocating for the unmet communication and swallowing needs of the public and shall provide accurate information involving any aspect of the professions.

Comment: Principle of Ethics III relates to accurate and honest information about an individual's contributions to scholarly and research activities.

Rules of Ethics

A. Individuals shall not misrepresent their credentials, competence, education, training, experience, and scholarly contributions.

Comment: We knew of an individual who described himself as a neuroaudiologist, a title that does not exist. ASHA will need to be clear about which new titles will be permissible with specialized credentialing (e.g., Will "board-certified aphasiologist" be acceptable?).

B. Individuals shall avoid engaging in conflicts of interest whereby personal, financial, or other considerations have the potential to influence or compromise professional judgment and objectivity.

Comment: As with coercion, conflict of interest is a subtle and thorny issue. When the first author directed a PhD program, the faculty engaged in some stimulating discussions. In one case, we resolved that it would be a conflict of interest for a doctoral student to engage in dissertation research at a paid employment site, unless the employment was a research fellowship. In another case, we permitted a student who had not yet earned CCC to undertake a clinical externship with a supervisor who did not have a PhD. We were concerned that the supervisor might be considering pursuing a doctoral degree at our program, and that placing one of our students in an externship might be coercive. It also might be a conflict of interest if the individual decided to apply for admission to the doctoral program while serving as a supervisor.

C. Individuals shall not misrepresent research and scholarly activities, diagnostic information, services provided, results of services provided, products dispensed, or the effects of products dispensed.

Comment: (See Chapter 8 for information about writing the diagnostic report.) Digital signal processing is considered a technological advancement over analog hearing aid circuits. In the 1990s when digital hearing aid processing became clinically available, there was a considerable price differentiation between the existing (analog) and very expensive new technology. Clinical studies at that time, however, did not support significantly better performance outcomes for patients fitted with digital as compared to analog hearing aids. It would therefore have been unethical to recommend a digital device to a client on the basis that it is "better" in terms of hearing improvement over a comparable analog device.

D. Individuals shall not defraud through intent, ignorance, or negligence or engage in any scheme to defraud in connection with obtaining payment, reimbursement, or grants and contracts for services provided, research conducted, or products dispensed.

Comment: In many instances, these are also criminal offenses.

E. Individuals' statements to the public shall provide accurate and complete information about the nature and management of communication disorders, about the professions, about professional services, about products for sale, and about research and scholarly activities.

Comment: Any written or oral statements made by student clinicians, in the form of a press release, advertisement, or interview, should be vetted by the clinic director, as well as approved through the chain of command, which might include the program director, department chair, divisional dean, and university offices of information services or institutional advancement. This should takc placc even if the written or oral statement refers to an externship facility.

F. Individuals' statements to the public shall adhere to prevailing professional norms and shall not contain misrepresentations when advertising, announcing, and promoting their professional services and products and when reporting research results.

   Comment: Approvals through the chain of command indicated for rule III E apply to III F as well.

G. Individuals shall not knowingly make false financial or nonfinancial statements and shall complete all materials honestly and without omission.

   Comment: As indicated for rule III D, falsifying financial information may be a criminal offense.

Principle of Ethics IV

Individuals shall uphold the dignity and autonomy of the professions, maintain collaborative and harmonious interprofessional and intraprofessional relationships, and accept the professions' self-imposed standards.

Comment: The rule of law prevails, but rules of ethics may hold a higher standard. The ethical rules that follow, presented without comment, include proscriptions previously discussed, which include deceit, coercion, conflict of interest, and abuse of power.

Rules of Ethics

A. Individuals shall work collaboratively, when appropriate, with members of one's own profession and/or members of other professions to deliver the highest quality of care.

B. Individuals shall exercise independent professional judgment in recommending and providing professional services when an administrative mandate, referral source, or prescription prevents keeping the welfare of persons served paramount.

C. Individuals' statements to colleagues about professional services, research results, and products shall adhere to prevailing professional standards and shall contain no misrepresentations.

D. Individuals shall not engage in any form of conduct that adversely reflects on the professions or on the individual's fitness to serve persons professionally.

E. Individuals shall not engage in dishonesty, negligence, fraud, deceit, or misrepresentation.

F. Applicants for certification or membership, and individuals making disclosures, shall not knowingly make false statements and shall complete all application and disclosure materials honestly and without omission.

G. Individuals shall not engage in any form of harassment, power abuse, or sexual harassment.

H. Individuals shall not engage in sexual activities with individuals (other than a spouse or other individual with whom a prior consensual relationship exists) over whom they exercise professional authority or power, including persons receiving services, assistants, students, or research participants.

I. Individuals shall not knowingly allow anyone under their supervision to engage in any practice that violates the Code of Ethics.

J. Individuals shall assign credit only to those who have contributed to a publication, presentation, process, or product. Credit shall be assigned in proportion to the contribution and only with the contributor's consent.

K. Individuals shall reference the source when using other persons' ideas, research, presentations, results, or products in written, oral, or any other media presentation or summary. To do otherwise constitutes plagiarism.

L. Individuals shall not discriminate in their relationships with colleagues, assistants, students, support personnel, and members of other professions and disciplines on the basis of race, ethnicity, sex, gender identity/

gender expression, sexual orientation, age, religion, national origin, disability, culture, language, dialect, or socioeconomic status.

M. Individuals with evidence that the Code of Ethics may have been violated have the responsibility to work collaboratively to resolve the situation where possible or to inform the Board of Ethics through its established procedures.

N. Individuals shall report members of other professions who they know have violated standards of care to the appropriate professional licensing authority or board, other professional regulatory body, or professional association when such violation compromises the welfare of persons served and/or research participants.

O. Individuals shall not file or encourage others to file complaints that disregard or ignore facts that would disprove the allegation; the Code of Ethics shall not be used for personal reprisal, as a means of addressing personal animosity, or as a vehicle for retaliation.

P. Individuals making and responding to complaints shall comply fully with the policies of the Board of Ethics in its consideration, adjudication, and resolution of complaints of alleged violations of the Code of Ethics.

Q. Individuals involved in ethics complaints shall not knowingly make false statements of fact or withhold relevant facts necessary to fairly adjudicate the complaints.

R. Individuals shall comply with local, state, and federal laws and regulations applicable to professional practice, research ethics, and the responsible conduct of research.

S. Individuals who have been convicted; been found guilty; or entered a plea of guilty or nolo contendere to (1) any misdemeanor involving dishonesty, physical harm—or the threat of physical harm—to the person or property of another, or (2) any felony, shall self-report by notifying ASHA Standards and Ethics . . .

T. Individuals who have been publicly sanctioned or denied a license or a professional credential by any professional association, professional licensing authority or board, or other professional regulatory body shall self-report by notifying ASHA Standards and Ethics . . .

Final Comment: the *ASHA Leader* will occasionally report members who have violated one or more rules in the *Code of Ethics*. The principles and rules violated will be cited, as well as the punishment for the violation.

Health Insurance Portability and Accountability Act of 1996 (HIPAA)

Consider the following scenario: Your mother (or father, sibling, or spouse) has just come out of surgery. You call the hospital for an update and are told that you are not authorized to receive any information about the patient. You should:

1. scream indignantly, "But it's my mother (father, sibling, spouse)!"
2. threaten to sue,
3. sob hysterically, or
4. be grateful that your loved one's medical confidentiality is being protected.

HIPAA was established by the 104th Congress on August 21, 1996, as Public Law 104-191, which amended the Internal Revenue Code of 1986. The purpose of the new law was to combat waste, fraud, and abuse in health-care delivery. The function of HIPAA was to establish standards and requirements for electronic transmission of health information and to encourage the development of a health information system.

Many aspects of HIPAA are relevant to students and practitioners in communication sciences and disorders. The term *health information* refers to oral or recorded forms, created by a health care provider (including a speech-language pathologist or audiologist), school, or university, which address the physical or mental health of an individual in the present, past, or future.

Confidentiality protection under HIPAA refers to individually identifiable health information. Any demographic or other physical or mental health information that can reasonably be believed to identify a person is included. The 16-page document addresses security standards and safeguards, such as keeping confidential records in locked file cabinets in locked rooms away from waiting areas.

There are monetary and incarceration penalties for failure to comply with HIPAA requirements and standards. In addition, the site visit team from ASHA's Council on Academic Accreditation will determine if confidentiality protections are enforced by a college or university speech and hearing center before awarding accreditation to that program. Finally, some third-party payers will refuse payment to a speech and hearing center that does not provide adequate documentation and protection of health information.

The Institutional Review Board

There is a laudable trend in graduate and even some undergraduate programs in communication sciences and disorders (CSD) to require students to present documentation of their evidence-based (research-based) clinical practice (see Chapter 3). Some programs set aside an evening for student presentations as a poster session, with invitations sent throughout the university and even the neighboring community. Students stay next to their posters and answer questions, as visitors circulate among the many impressive presentations. This project serves many functions:

1. It serves to reinforce the clinician-researcher connection.
2. It advertises the excellent work of the speech and hearing center.
3. It highlights the achievements of CSD students to members of the department, school, and university.

The project also raises some ethical questions:

1. How will confidentiality of participants be ensured?
2. How have ethical standards of treatment for human participants been assured?
   a. Safety and appropriateness of research methodology
   b. Informed consent
3. How has the potential for coercion in the supervisor–student or mentor–student relationship been avoided?

Some of the ethical questions have already been addressed in this chapter. For example, HIPAA is concerned with issues of confidentiality, and the ASHA Code of Ethics sets limits on the types of interactions, even friendships, permitted in supervisor-student and mentor-student relationships. Another level of ethical protection is provided by the Institutional Review Board (IRB). Clinicians and students engaging in clinical research that will be submitted for presentation at a poster session must write a proposal for approval by the IRB.

The Hammurabi code of "First, do no harm" is usually cited as the beginning of patient welfare concern (Schwartz, 2006). Compare this code to the "experiments" conducted by physicians in Nazi Germany, which led to the Nuremberg Code. At the end of World War II, the Nuremberg Military Tribunal established standards for research and conduct with human participants. These standards must also be applied in the clinical intervention conducted in our speech and hearing centers. They include:

1. Voluntary consent. The participant must also have the capacity to consent, the consent has to be given without direct or indirect coercion, and the participant must understand the risks and benefits of the treatment. The participant's age or degree of impairment may require an advocate to approve the treatment. For example, a participant or advocate must understand that there may be discomfort (i.e., elicited dizziness) associated with portions of vestibular electronystagmography (ENG) testing, or that there may be a risk of aspiration associated with the treatment of dysphagia.

2. Risk-to-benefit ratio. The ratio must be favorable to the participant, with risks minimized, and the participant is permitted to withdraw from treatment at any time.

The Belmont Report

In 1979, the *Belmont Report* set out three core ethical principles for human participants in research. We have extended them to include participants in clinical intervention. The Belmont Report Historical Archive is available (subject to change) at https://www.hhs.gov/ohrp/regulations-and-policy/belmont-report/index.html and includes interviews with participants of the National Commission for the Protection of Human Subjects of Biomedical and Behavioral Research (1974–1978). There is also a 9-minute video, featuring participants of the commission.

1. Respect for persons. Individuals have the right to decide whether or not they want to participate in treatment or research. These decisions should be based on full information and free from coercion.
2. Beneficence. The researcher or clinician has an obligation to minimize possible harm and to maximize potential benefits.
3. Justice. Benefits and risks of research and treatment should be fairly distributed across the population, as well as be fairly applied to individuals. For example, a drug currently in clinical trials (pagoclone, a GABA-receptor modulator) may be effective in controlling stuttering. If efficacy is adequately demonstrated, the drug must be distributed according to the ethical principles identified in the *Belmont Report*.

National Institutes of Health (NIH) Training Course

Clinical writing may lead to professional and research writing. Any individual submitting a grant proposal to the National Institutes of Health (NIH; effective 2000) has been required to complete a computer-based training course on the protection of human research participants. The online course is free and may be accessed (subject to change) at https://phrp.nihtraining.com/users/login.php. The course takes about 2 to 3 hours and permits the printing of a certificate of completion. It is an excellent overview of research ethics and should be completed by anyone providing clinical intervention to human participants.

Conclusion

Before beginning any clinical research project involving human beings, the investigator (even if the investigator is a student taking a clinical practicum course) must obtain approval from the Institutional Review Board. Forms are reasonably standard across institutions (see Appendix 4A, sample IRB form, adapted from Adelphi University), and require a brief description of the project's purposes, methodology, and design; dates for initiation and completion of the project; number and characteristics of participants; method of recruitment; and any potential risks, stresses, or discomforts and the precautions taken to minimize them. Investigators must include an informed consent form and a representative sample of materials. There may also be a required debriefing form, as well as a sign-up sheet or advertisement.

Exercises

Exercise 4–1. Chapter Review

1. Before beginning any clinical research project involving human beings, the investigator must obtain approval from the:
   a. ASHA
   b. state licensing office
   c. Council on Academic Accreditation (CAA)
   d. Institutional review board (IRB) office
   e. all of the above

2. In the *Belmont Report*, the three core ethical principles for human participants in research are: respect for persons, ____________, and justice.
   a. fairness
   b. beneficence
   c. privacy
   d. protection
   e. honesty

3. The federal law that provides data privacy and confidentiality protection for health information is the:
   a. Health Insurance Portability and Accountability Act (HIPAA)
   b. ASHA Code of Ethics
   c. IRB
   d. Hammurabi Code
   e. Belmont Report

4. As professionals in the communication sciences, we abide by ethical principles stated by the:
   a. ASHA Code of Ethics
   b. state licensing office
   c. IRB office
   d. HIPAA
   e. all of the above

5. True or False: State regulations supersede ASHA Scope of Practice guidelines.

Exercise 4–2. Ethical Dilemmas

1. In the spaces below, correct the writing and the ethical errors in the following letter to a former professor:

    Hey Dr. G, January 1, 2018

    I'm going on a job interview next week and I need your help. If you could write me a letter of recommendation. The supervisor of speech wants to go for a doctorate at Adelphi, and you would certainly have some leverage as the program director, if you say she should hire me, she probably would, because she wants to make a favorable impression on you. Thanks.

    Sincerely,
    Will di Sappoint

    ____

    ____

    ____

    ____

2. Scandinavicon, a new manufacturer of digital hearing aids, is offering free trips to its flagship store in Copenhagen. United States-based audiologists who have active practices including prescribing hearing aids are invited to apply to participate in a weekend conference in Denmark on Scandinavicon aids, with all expenses paid. Should you apply? What should you write in your letter?

    ____

    ____

    ____

    ____

3. How do you write a letter to a physician or psychologist, asking for a financial benefit (or offering a financial benefit) for recommending clients? After all, attorneys specializing in accident and malpractice claims give a portion of their contingency fees to lawyers who refer clients.

____

____

____

____

4. I want to offer free hearing screenings to the elderly in my community. It will serve the purposes of addressing an unmet need of this population and drawing attention to my audiology practice. Is this ethical? If it is, how do I do it?

____

____

____

____

5. I can't afford the high registration fees and transportation costs of attending the ASHA or AAA conventions, but I need to get 30 hours of continuing education every 3 years to keep my CCC and my state license. What should I write to ASHA about this?

____

____

____

____

Exercise 4–3. Writing on Ethics

Download the PowerPoint on the website, entitled, "Sample of a Short Course," and refer to Goldfarb (2006) to see the fallout of errors in ethical judgment.

A. Identify three ethical failures of the Tudor study.

1. ______________________________

____

____

2. ______________________________

____

____

3. ______________________________

____

____

B. How could a revised Tudor study conform to today's ethical standards?

____

____

____

____

Exercise 4–4. The Belmont Report

Read the Belmont Report and view the 9-minute video of participants of the National Commission for the Protection of Human Subjects of Biomedical and Behavioral Research at http://www.hhs.gov/ohrp/humansubjects/guidance/belmont.html

A. Write an explanation of the concepts of respect for persons, beneficence, and justice.

____

____

B. Write an essay explaining one of the three sections.

The distinction between clinical practice and research

The set of core ethical principles for the conduct of research

The definitions of ethical practice in research

____

____

____

____

____

Exercise 4–5. Protection of Human Research Subjects Training Course

Take the computer-based NIH training course on the protection of human research subjects at http://cme.cancer.gov/c01

a. Earn a passing grade on the tutorial.

b. Show the Certificate of Completion to the course instructor.

Exercise 4–6. ASHA Code of Ethics (2016)

Read the ASHA Code of Ethics (2016) with a focus on ethics in research and professional practice at http://www.asha.org/uploadedFiles/ET2016-00342.pdf

A. Write an essay about the Principle of Ethics I that addresses issues of nondiscrimination, informed consent, confidentiality, and security of research data.

____

____

____

B. Write an essay about the Principle of Ethics II that refers to professional competency.

____

____

____

Exercise 4–7. Web Links

Visit one of the sites from the list of annotated Web links below (excluding those accessed above).

Note: Please be advised that all links are subject to change.

APA Style Manual
The Publication Manual of the American Psychological Association, currently in its 6th edition (2010), is generally available for online purchase in hardcover or paperback form, and often at discounted prices, from Internet sites such as http://www/amazon.com.

It also may be available in a Kindle version. The department of English at Purdue University has been generous enough to post an APA Formatting and Style Guide, free of charge, on the Internet at http://owl.english.purdue.edu/owl/resource/560/01/

ASHA Code of Ethics
According to the 2016 revision, every person who is an ASHA member, a nonmember who holds the CCC, an applicant for membership, or a clinical fellow is required to abide by the code of ethics, which may be accessed at http://www.asha.org/uploadedFiles/ET2016-00342.pdf

Belmont Report Historical Archive
The Belmont Report is divided into three sections that distinguish between clinical practice and research, identify a set of core ethical principles for conducting research, and define ethical practices in research. The core ethical principles are respect for persons, beneficence, and justice. It is available online at htttps://www.hhs.gov/ohrp/regulations-and-policy/belmont-report/index.html and includes interviews with participants of the National Commission for the Protection of Human Subjects of Biomedical and Behavioral Research. There also is a 9-minute video featuring participants of the commission.

Centers for Disease Control and Prevention
Information on human subject research is available from http://www.cdc.gov. Scroll along the alphabetical listings for a wealth of information.

Declaration of Helsinki
The World Medical Association developed the Declaration of Helsinki ethical principles for medical research involving human subjects described in the NIH training course (see below). The document can be accessed at https://www.wma.net/policies-post/wma-declaration-of-helsinki-ethical-principles-for-medical-research-involving-human-subjects/

Department of Energy
The Department of Energy's advisory committee on Human Radiation Experiments Report, entitled, "DOE Oneness: Human Radiation Experiments" is available at https://ehss.energy.gov/ohre/roadmap/roadmap/index.html

Department of Health and Human Services
Educational material for researchers from the office for Human Research Protections is available at https://www.hhs.gov/ohrp/

The report of the Office of Inspector General on protecting human research subjects may be found at http://www.oig.hhs.gov/oei/reports/oei 01 97 00197.pdf

National Security Archive
The Advisory Committee on Human Radiation Experiments Report, Part I, Chapter 3 is available on the site of the National Security Archive at http://nsarchive.gwu.edu/radiation/

National Library of Medicine
Bibliographies in medicine pertaining to ethical issues in research involving human participants are available from https://www.nlm.nih.gov/archive/20040829/pubs/cbm/hum_exp.html

Nuremberg Trials
Trials of war criminals before the Nuremberg military tribunals, resulting in the Nuremberg Code, may be found at https://history.nih.gov/research/downloads/nuremberg.pdf

United Nations
The Universal Declaration of Human Rights is the most translated document in the world. It is available at http://www.un.org/en/universal-declaration-human-rights/ It is also instructive to go to "Issues on UN Agenda" for an alphabetical list.

World Health Organization
Go to the site and click on "Health Topics" to learn about ethics and health at http://www.who.int/en/

Read and follow the links on one of the websites above. Write an essay describing the site.

___

___

___

___

___

___

___

___

___

___

___

___

References

American Speech-Language-Hearing Association. (2010). *Code of ethics* [Ethics]. Available from http://www.asha .org/policy. doi:10.1044/policy.ET2010-00309

Dillon, H. (2001). *Hearing aids*. New York, NY: Thieme.

Finn, P., Bothe, A. K., & Bramlett, R. E. (2005). Science and pseudoscience in communication disorders: Criteria and applications. *American Journal of Speech- Language Pathology, 14*, 172–186.

Goldfarb, R. (Ed.). (2006). *Ethics: A case study from fluency*. San Diego, CA: Plural.

Goldfarb, R. (1989). Organization of speech, language, and hearing programmes in United States hospitals. *College of Speech Therapists Bulletin, 452*, 2–7.

Health Insurance Portability and Accountability Act (HIPAA) of 1996. Public Law 104–191, 104th Congress.

New York State Department of State Division of Licensing Services. Registration of Hearing Aid Dispensers 2001. General Business Law, Article 37-A.

Office for Protection from Research Risks, Protection of Human Subjects. National Commission for the Protection of Human Subjects of Biomedical and Behavioral Research. (1979). *The Belmont Report: Ethical principles and guidelines for the protections of human subjects of research* (GPO Office 887–890). Washington, DC: Government Printing Office.

Rao, P. R. (2011, August 02). From the President: ASHA's compass: The revised code of ethics. *ASHA Leader*.

Schmidt, B., Galleta, E., & Obler, L. K. (2006). Teaching research ethics in communication disorders programs. In R. Goldfarb (Ed.), *Ethics: A case study from fluency* (pp. 63–82). San Diego, CA: Plural.

Schwartz, R. G. (2006). Would today's IRB approve the Tudor study? Ethical considerations in conducting research involving children with communication disorders. In R. Goldfarb (Ed.), *Ethics: A case study from fluency* (pp. 83–96). San Diego, CA: Plural.

Wilber, L. A. & Burkhard, R. (2009). Calibration: Puretone, speech, and noise signals. In J. Katz (Ed.), *Handbook of clinical audiology* (pp. 7–29). Baltimore, MD: Lippincott Williams & Wilkins.

APPENDIX 4–A
Sample Institutional Review Board Research Review Form

Date submitted:

TITLE OF PROJECT:

PRINCIPAL INVESTIGATOR/CO-INVESTIGATOR:

Address:

Phone:

Email:

You must complete a training program in the protection of human research participants before you can begin your research. Please indicate the date the training was completed and include a copy of the certification with this application.

If you have not completed a training program, follow the links to http://cme.cancer.gov/c01 or http://my.research.umich.edu/peerrs/ or http://www.nyu.edu/ucaihs/tutorial/

I. Brief description of the project's purposes:

II. Planned dates for initiation and completion of the project:

III. Number of subjects:

IV. Characteristics of subjects (e.g., age range, special populations, etc.):

V. Method of subject recruitment:

VI. Brief description of project's methods and research design:

VII. Sequence of activities required of the subject:

VIII. Estimated time commitment required of the subjects:

IX. Any potential risks, discomforts, or stresses and the precautions taken to minimize them:

Signatures and date of all researchers who will be working in direct contact with study participants. These signatures indicate that all the researchers have familiarized themselves with policies regarding the legal and ethical treatment of human subjects in research, and are certified in human subjects protections training.

Name: ______________________________

Date: ______________________________

Signature: ______________________________

Affiliation: ______________________________
(institution/organization)

ATTACHMENTS CHECKLIST:

1. Informed Consent Form
2. Debriefing Form (if applicable)
3. Representative sample of materials/test/questionnaire items
4. Sign-up sheet, solicitation script, or advertisement (whichever is applicable)
5. Other attachments

Referencing Resources

It's hard to imagine a time when printed information couldn't be retrieved by sitting in front of a computer and clicking a button, yet certainly tangible collections of print works have existed (and still do) in storage areas well known as libraries, which date far back over 5000 years to ancient Mesopotamia. Because much printed information typically housed in libraries can also be accessed electronically via the Internet, the reader is referred to Chapter 6, "Internet Resources." This chapter, however, will focus mainly on the information and physical services available to the student of communication sciences and disorders in university libraries.

In this chapter, you will be required to:

1. Review APA style referencing.
2. Practice writing reference lists and in-text citations in correct APA style.
3. Access library services and conduct a tour of the university library.

History of the Library

Private "libraries" or collections of written works originated in the Near East and have existed for thousands of years. The practice prospered with the ancient Greeks through their enlightened curiosity in intellectual life and literacy. The concept of a public library surfaced by the 4th century BC (Krasner-Khait, 2001). The first public library in the United States appeared in 1833 in New Hampshire, with hundreds more opened throughout the country following the surge of immigration and the idea of a free public education for all children.

Catering primarily to the needs of the educated—scholars, scientists, teachers—and later to the larger masses, libraries would clearly play a major role in higher education. The first American university library was established in 1638 at Harvard, the oldest American institution of higher learning, with a donation of over 300 books by the Massachusetts clergyman, John Harvard (Shores, 1972). Today there are approximately 120,000 libraries of all types in the United States including academic, armed forces, corporate, government, law, medical, public, religious, and school libraries (American Library Association, 2015). Although the type of information housed in libraries has changed drastically over the years, from scrolls to cyberspace bytes, the search for knowledge, and a place to store it, will continue throughout the ages, or as long as there are individuals who seek it.

The student in communication sciences and disorders has access to a wealth of information stored in the university's library. Initially a repository for books, the modern university library additionally includes collections of information such as journals, video and audio recordings, microforms, government documents, and electronic resources. Many also have quiet seating areas to which students can retreat for moments of silent reading or study time during breaks from a busy day of classes or clinical work.

Collections

Books

The Library of Congress (LC) classification system is used by most academic libraries in the country to organize and ease search for books. In this system, a distinctive call number is assigned to each book, which allows organization by subject matter with a combination of letters and numbers (Library of Congress, n.d.). The books are arranged in alphanumerical order using the call number, which appears (in order from top to bottom) on the book binding:

RC

423

.V45

2006

1. The first letter of the call number represents the subject.
2. The second letter represents a subdivision of that subject.
3. The first set of numbers refers to an area of study within that subdivision.
4. The second set of numbers is a code that represents the author's name, book title, and subject. It should be read as a decimal, for example, .45.
5. The last number represents the year of publication.

In the example above, *R* represents *Medicine*, and *C* is *Internal Medicine, Practice of Medicine.*

Although the electronic age has dramatically decreased the need for printed materials in general, for practical reasons the printed book is still preferred by some readers, and libraries still maintain large print collections for their patrons.

Scholarly Journals

A typical form of publication in the medical, scientific, and technological disciplines, and certainly in the communication sciences, is that of the journal-style article. This type of short work, typically of original research, is written in a discrete subject area and became a common form of disseminating scientific information by the end of the 18th century. The journal is a serial publication, usually published by an academic or professional association or press. If a journal is *refereed* or *peer-reviewed*, that indicates that the articles were evaluated by a team of scholars assembled by the editor with expertise in that particular subject matter. The peer reviewers assess the quality of the work, such as the content, mechanics of the writing (grammar, spelling, sentence structure, etc.), and accuracy of the citations, and provide their comments to the author and editor. It is the editor who ultimately decides whether the manuscript is rejected or accepted with or without recommended revisions (Budd, 2005).

The first American professional journal in our discipline, *The Voice*, was published from 1879 to 1892 by the clinician Edgar Werner and focused on the topic of speech disorders, specifically on stuttering. Interestingly, it was the National Society for the Study and Correction of Speech Disorders (NSSCSD), an organization preceding the American Speech-Language-Hearing Association (ASHA), that published the first journal by a professional organization of the communication sciences in July 1918, entitled the *American Journal of Speech Disorders and Correction*. ASHA first published the *Journal of Speech Disorders* in March 1936 (Malone, 1999; Paden, 1975).

Today there are hundreds of journals devoted to various issues and topics in our discipline. Most print journals also allow users electronic access to their articles, and many journals now appear in online-only formats. Journal collections vary by institution as cost and space are considerations for maintaining them, and therefore not all journals in a specific field may be carried by an academic library. Because libraries must pay journal subscription fees and at the same time adhere to budget restrictions, journal collections are carefully evaluated and periodically reassessed. Print journals are usually arranged on stacked shelving in alphabetical order by title. These take up physical space that may also restrict the holdings, although the wide availability of electronic formats has made space less of an issue.

Audiovisual Materials

In addition to print media, many informational and instructional materials are available in audiovisual format, including audio cassette or compact disc (CD) recordings; video films, tapes, or digital video discs (DVDs); and electronic software. Instructors may put such items, often limited in number, on reserve to supplement lecture topics. Depending on the specific library policy, the student may have limited access to these materials on-site or with borrowing privileges.

Microforms

Before the wide availability of computers and electronic versions of print documents, librarians found other ways to contend with the growing problem of space. Printed materials, typically books and newspapers, were transferred onto minutely small nonprint media in the form of film, collectively known as microforms. Common types found in libraries include *microfilm*, which refers to 35 mm film wound onto open reels or inserted into cassettes, and *microfiche*, which is a flat piece of film typically stored in filing envelopes. As microforms are reproduced into smaller photographic film images, they then require special magnifying machines for viewing, which can be cumbersome and time consuming to the user. Print copies of the images can be made, but they are often of inferior quality. Because they are analog media, an additional problem with microforms is that they are susceptible to deterioration (Veaner, 2002). Hooray for the digital era!

Services

The Organization of Information: Catalogs and Databases

In order to search effectively for information on a given subject, there must be a systematic method for organization, storage, and retrieval of that information. *Catalogs*, or lists of a library's holdings, were in early centuries simple handwritten registers, usually alphabetized, of the books contained within. Indeed, the library catalog can be considered "the oldest type of booklist known" (Vickery, 1970, p. 20). Such lists were simple to prepare and maintain as long as the collection itself, and interest in it, were minimal. Catalogs were prepared by individuals at separate libraries without a universal system, and therefore varied greatly in organization and quality up until the 19th century. One can only imagine the hours of intensive labor put into handwriting or manually typing such lists (and periodically updating them) prior to the advent of computers. Over the years, various classification schemes emerged in an effort to simplify the task of book searches and retrieval. Contemporary American librarianship began in 1876 with the formation of a professional organization, the American Library Association (ALA), and attempts toward a more systematic approach to cataloging. During the 20th century, the LC advanced the practice of shared cataloging among libraries. The ALA is currently the largest and oldest library organization in the world, providing library and information services, standards for the profession and professional services, and publications to members and the public (ALA, n.d.). A division of the ALA, the Association of College and Research Libraries (ACRL), is concerned with aspects of the academic library (ALA, 2018).

With the electronic age came the ability to organize and store vast amounts of cataloged information digitally into *databases* that allowed for easier sharing of this information among libraries and organizations, and for online search and retrieval of materials (Blake, 2002; Shoffner, 2002). The use of electronic catalogs was nearly universal in academic libraries by the year 2000 (U.S. Department of Education, 2005). Databases may be isolated to book or journal listings within a single institution or may be so expansive as to include all types of materials in libraries throughout the world, such as WorldCat, a catalog supported by the Online Computer Library Center (OCLC) and serving over 57,000 libraries in over 100 countries and territories (OCLC, 2018). University library catalogs are available to students on site or via remote access (from outside the university). In addition, the library may provide access to a variety of other electronic catalogs or databases such as those of neighboring public or other university libraries as well as state, organizational, or international systems, through the academic library. Although the library is required to pay a site license fee for the use of most databases, in general access to library databases is free of charge to students as part of their library privileges at their academic institution.

A valuable database for students and professionals in the communication sciences is PubMed, a free service developed by the National Center for Biotechnology Information (NCBI) and provided by the U.S. National Library of Medicine and the National Institutes of Health. PubMed encompasses over 22 million citations from the biomedical and life science literature (dentistry, medicine, nursing, veterinary medicine, the health care system, and the preclinical sciences) published worldwide, and includes MEDLINE, its largest database component (NCBI, n.d.). There are even databases dedicated solely to reference sources within our field. One such database, ComDisDome (published by ProQuest), focuses on information sources from the hundreds of books, refereed journals, dissertations, grants, and other related published documents exclusive to the communication sciences and disorders (ComDisDome, n.d.). An advantage of a discipline-specific database may be that searches often yield more precise and relevant citations to the search topic than when conducted with cross-disciplinary systems such as PubMed. On the other hand, such searches may be limited to the narrower source base of the discipline-specific database. The student must, of course, consider these issues when conducting a search. These text-based databases provide citations and may permit access, with or without charge, to abstracts and full-text articles at journal websites or through the library holdings (depending on journal subscription and library site license status) and other related Web resources.

Conducting a Search

Search and you shall find. Today, electronic databases are used to search and access the information in a library's holdings (and beyond) literally in seconds. Most library catalog searches are initiated by typing in a specific piece of information such as a keyword, subject heading, title, author, or catalog number. The databases may also be searched using other numbers including non-LC call numbers, Government Document numbers, ISBN (International Standard Book Number), or ISSN (International Standard Serial Number). Figure 5–1 is a sample library catalogue database search.

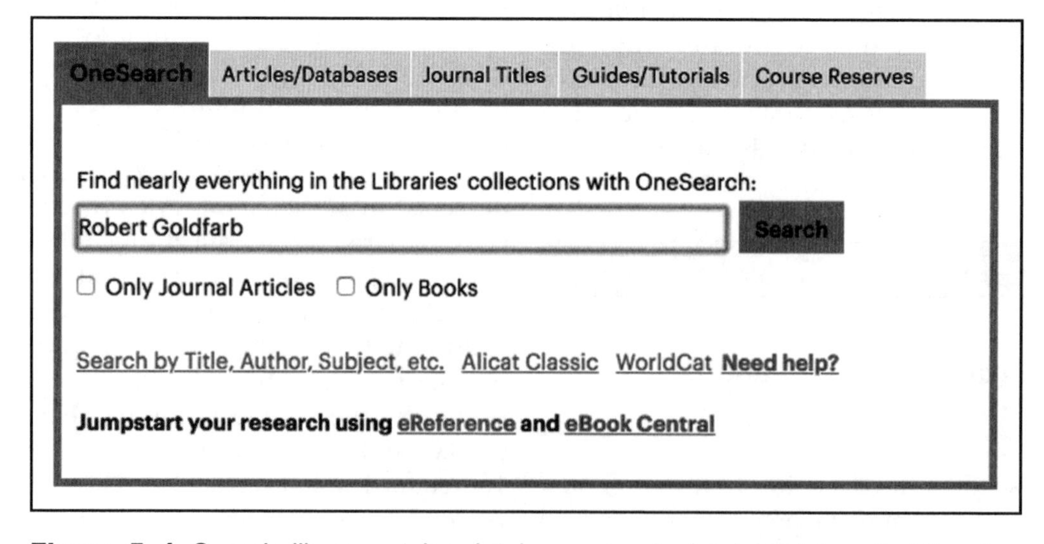

Figure 5–1. Sample library catalog database search, Adelphi University Libraries. Retrieved from https://libraries.adelphi.edu/

Once processed, the result screen will display whether the item is available for circulation or accessible electronically. Books will be identified by call number and a location for retrieval will be provided (see example in Figure 5–2). An option may also be given to place a hold on the item. Journal listings will include the specific volumes owned by the library and whether they are in print or electronic form.

Figure 5–3 is an example of a cross-disciplinary database search by topic (citations excluded). In the example, 3163 articles were found for the topic of sudden deafness using a cross-disciplinary database. A similar search on a disciplinary-specific database system produced 601 results, a smaller number, but still an inordinate amount to sift through. It is therefore wise to narrow the search as much as possible by typing in as many key

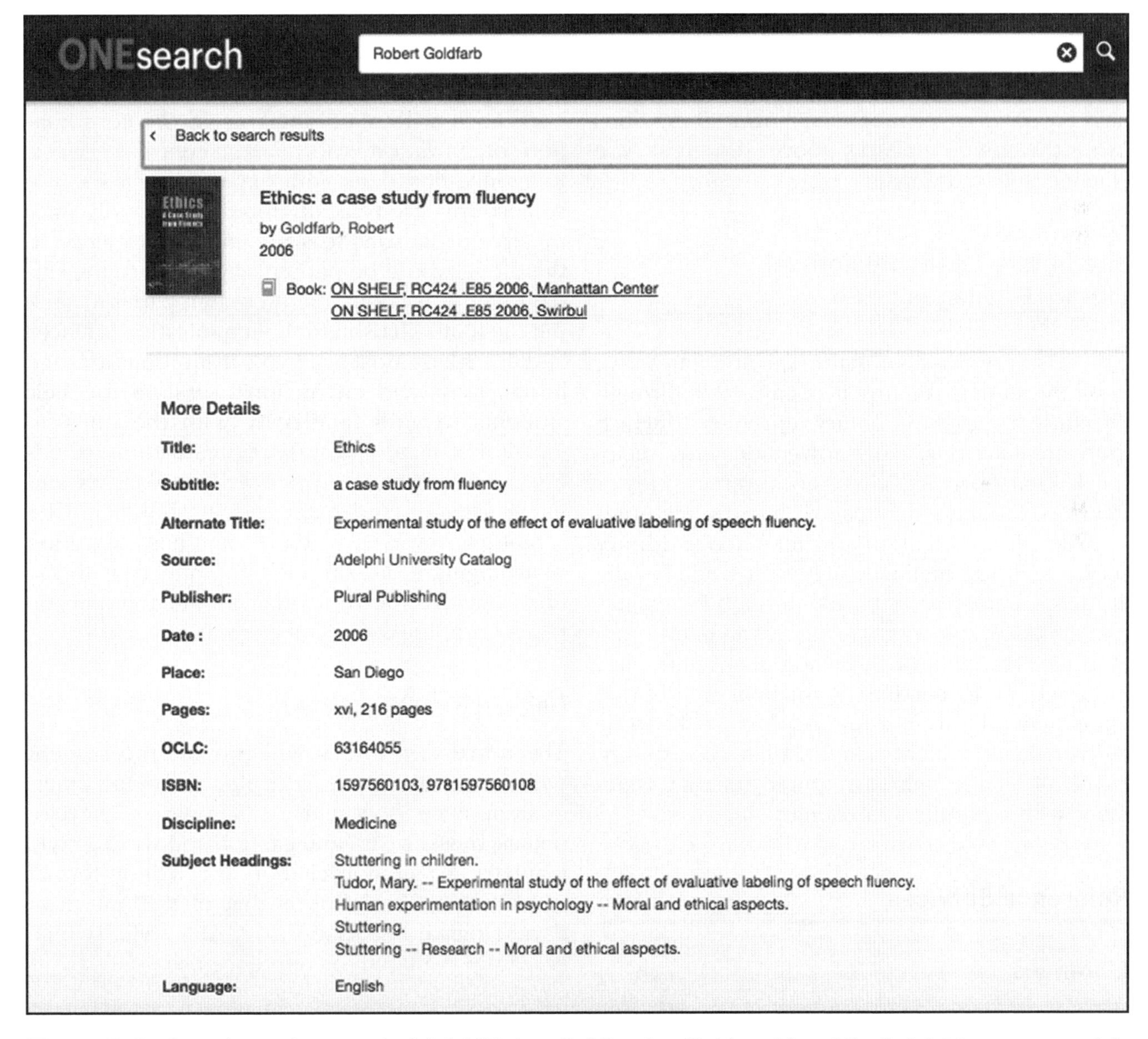

Figure 5–2. Sample catalog search, Adelphi University Libraries. Retrieved from http://adelphi.summon.serialssolutions.com/?fvf=ContentType%2CBook+Review%2Ct&q=Robert+Goldfarb&fvf=ContentType%2CBook+%2F+eBook#!/search/document?ho=t&fvf=ContentType,Book%20Review,t%7CContentType,Book%20%2F%20eBook,f&l=en&q=Robert%20Goldfarb&id=FETCHMERGED-adelphi_catalog_b1499138x2

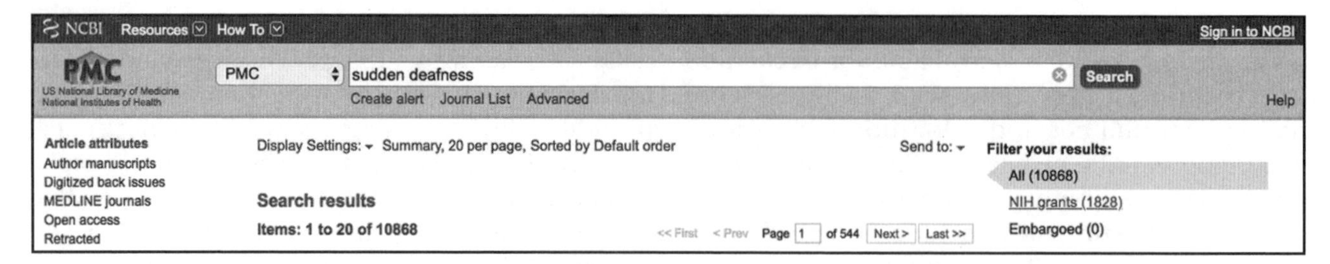

Figure 5–3. Sample cross-disciplinary database search by topic (citations excluded). Retrieved from https://www-ncbi-nlm-nih-gov.libproxy.adelphi.edu:2443/pmc/?term=sudden+deafness

words that are relative to the topic as possible. For example, limiting the topic to sudden deafness *in children* produced 473 and 90 citations using the same databases above, respectively, a considerably more manageable outcome.

Interlibrary Loans/Reciprocal Library Privileges

It is very possible that a specific journal or book the student requires is not available through the student's academic library, a problem to which there are solutions. Many universities have reciprocal library privileges with local universities or libraries. Students may use or borrow materials available for circulation and may access library services. When materials are not owned by the academic library or accessible through its reciprocal databases, students may request an interlibrary loan electronically or in person at the reference or help desk. Depending on the item, interlibrary loans may take from a few days to weeks to be delivered, so students should plan accordingly, especially if the item is required for an assignment with a rapidly approaching due date.

Reference Services

Librarians

With the digital age and anonymity of computer use, one may forget that the library does offer opportunities to connect (either electronically or in person) with an expert who is specially trained to work with individuals on researching a particular topic or locating material. In fact, most large academic libraries employ numerous staff members, each with a unique role in the coordination, organization, and management of services. Reference librarians with expertise in a specific subject area are typically hired by the university to serve as liaisons to academic departments. It, therefore, would be particularly useful to the student who is working on a research paper to seek out the library liaison for communication sciences and disorders. Most academic institutions arrange library tours and instructional sessions for their students to gain familiarity with the physical location of materials and services within, including demonstrations on performing searches and using catalogs and databases. It should not be forgotten, however, that a student has the option of arranging a one-on-one appointment with the librarian, an opportunity that should definitely be taken (Brophy, 2005; Guerrero, 2006).

Reference Tools

The university library will provide the student with on-site or remote electronic access to numerous reference tools such as dictionaries, encyclopedias, thesauruses, and citation and writing style manuals. A common citation and writing format used by our discipline is that of the American Psychological Association, or "APA style," which is readily available for reference use.

Research Guides

Printed or downloadable versions of guides for writing and research have been prepared by academic libraries for student use. Such "how-to" guides are extremely useful for the independent student who needs some help with preparing a research paper, with information ranging from searching and evaluating sources to properly documenting them. Some topics may include information and tips for:

Using library databases and catalogs

Remote access to library databases

Identifying scholarly versus popular journals

Research and writing

Plagiarism

Documenting scientific writing

Web evaluation

Reserve Items

The library permits faculty to put items that are recommended or required for courses such as books, journal articles, or audiovisual materials aside or *on reserve* for student use. Electronic reserve items are known as *e-reserves*. This service ensures that materials that may be difficult to acquire (such as those limited in number or not typically available in the library collection) are readily available to students. Access to physical reserve items requires a visit to the library service desk and is often time-restricted, usually limiting the user to a few hours or days. More conveniently, e-reserves can be electronically downloaded by the students, as long as there is access to a computer with Internet connection. Students may consider asking the instructor to make use of the reserve service when recommended or required course materials are difficult to obtain.

Course Packs

Many instructors recommend or require reading assignments from sources other than the designated textbook for the course (e.g., journal articles and individual book chapters from other texts). Following copyright approval, photocopies of these reading materials are collected and bound in book form known as a *course pack* and are prepared as a matter of convenience for students. Typically, the instructor provides titles or photocopies of the materials to the university library, printing office, or other service area, which, in turn, prepares the course pack. Course packs are particularly handy when there are numerous readings or when items are difficult to locate (e.g., out of print, not available in the university library). They may be provided to students for free as handouts, or sold for a fee through the university bookstore or by the instructor.

Copyright Material

The term *copyright* refers to the legal rights and protection given to authors of their published or unpublished literary or artistic work as provided by the U.S. Constitution and federal law (*Title 17*, U.S. Code). Copyright protection is automatic once the work is created and does not need to be officially registered, though many authors choose to do so in order to obtain a public record or certificate of the registration and eligibility for additional legal and monetary rights (U.S. Copyright Office, 2017). The student should assume, unless it is made known otherwise, that all materials housed in the library that are electronically accessed, and that occur in any other forms or obtained elsewhere, are copyrighted. This generally means that reproductions of such materials can be made only with the permission of the copyright holder; however, there are exceptions.

The 1976 Copyright Act delineated the "fair use" modification to copyright violation (or infringement) by allowing limited copies to be made for noncommercial purposes such as for personal study, research, scholarship, or teaching. Therefore, an individual may legally reproduce material under this premise, but could be found liable for copyright violation if at a later time the material is used for purposes beyond fair use. Academic libraries are also, under specific conditions, granted the authority to reproduce materials within the institution itself or for others, but may deny a copy order if it is deemed potentially a copyright infringement. Consider the following distinction. A student is permitted to photocopy a journal article for the purpose of a reading assignment for class. If that student decides, however, to make multiple copies of that article for the purpose of sale to classmates, that would be considered in excess of fair use and that student would be in violation of the copyright law.

Copyright issues have arisen in academic libraries over recent years with the availability of such services as e-reserves and course packs (discussed above) that may infringe on copyright laws, depending on the number and type of items used without author permission. Academic libraries now have guidelines for instructors who use those services in an effort to ensure compliance with the free-use criteria.

Plagiarism

The term *plagiarism* refers to the act of using another's work (ideational, written, or spoken) and intentionally or unintentionally misrepresenting it as one's own. This is essentially considered a form of academic dishonesty or "cheating" by most universities, for which there may be significant repercussions in the academic standing of a student. University students must be especially aware of what constitutes plagiarism, because writing is a major part of academic study. The issue of plagiarism has become more pervasive among institutions over the past years as a result of the widespread use of the Internet by individuals and specifically in academe. Virtually any piece of information on any topic can be found electronically and downloaded rapidly. The ability to access a completed research paper online or to find information on a web page without an obvious author may make it very enticing for one to "borrow" the information. Just as easily, however, instructors have access to search engines specifically geared to finding possible instances of plagiarism, making the offense quickly identifiable.

Certainly, copying another's writing exactly without quotations and reference to the author is an obvious form of plagiarism. However, there are other forms that are not as apparent, leading the student to plagiarize inadvertently. Rewording or paraphrasing the words of someone else without credit to the author is another type of plagiarism. Furthermore, writing ideas that are not one's own without reference to the originator of those ideas is also plagiarism. A simple rule of thumb would be always to provide a reference for the source of information used. The best defense against plagiarism is for the student to be well informed on the subject, and there are numerous sources from which to obtain this information. Most universities have prepared guidelines on plagiarism that are easily available to students through the university library, through a writing center, or electronically. Publication manuals such as the *American Psychological Association Publication Manual* (2010) provide examples of properly referencing and writing citations and are important resources for the student.

Finally, we counsel sensitivity in dealing with cultures whose custom of honoring ancestors extends to copying what they wrote.

Citing References From Print Books and Journals

In APA format, the references used for the content of a publication are cited in the body of the text by author(s) and date, and also appear in an alphabetical listing in the references section toward the end of the work. The writer must ensure that there is agreement between the references cited in the text and those listed in the references section.

Writing References in APA Style: Review of Selected APA-Style (2010) Reference List and In-Text Citation Formats

Following are most common uses of APA (2010) style for referencing books and journal articles. The list is not exhaustive, and therefore the reader is referred to the APA style manual for further examples.

General Note: For references obtained electronically or online, include the digital object identifier (DOI) if one has been assigned. The DOI follows the period after the page number of the reference as follows: doi:xxxxxxx

If content has been retrieved online and no DOI is assigned, indicate the home page URL of the book, journal, and so forth.

Journal Article (One Author)

Reference:

Serpanos, Y. C. (2004). ABR and DPOAE indices of normal loudness in children and adults. *Journal of the American Academy of Audiology*, *15*(8), 555–565.

Note:

1. The title of the journal article is in sentence case; the journal title is in title case.
2. Journal title and issue are italicized.
3. The journal issue number is added in parentheses only if the journal is paginated by issue.

In-Text:

xxxxx xxxxx (Serpanos, 2004).

Serpanos (2004) xxxxx xxxxx

Journal Article (Two Authors)

Reference:

Serpanos, Y. C., & Jarmel, F. (2007). Quantitative and qualitative follow-up outcomes from a preschool audiologic screening program: Perspectives over a decade. *American Journal of Audiology*, *16*, 4–12. doi:10.1044/1059-0889(2007/002)

Note: The first word following the colon in the title of a journal article is also capitalized.

In-Text:

xxxxx xxxxx (Serpanos & Jarmel, 2007).

Serpanos and Jarmel (2007) xxxxx xxxxx

Journal Article (Three to Five Authors)

Reference:

Halpern, H., Goldfarb, R. M., Brandon, J. M., & McCartin-Clark, M. (1985). Word-association responses to time-altered stimuli by schizophrenic adults. *Perceptual and Motor Skills*, *61*, 239–253.

In-Text:

xxxxx xxxxx (Halpern, Goldfarb, Brandon, & McCartin-Clark, 1985).

Halpern, Goldfarb, Brandon, and McCartin-Clark (1985) xxxx xxxx

Note: In works with three to five authors, all author names should be cited the first time the reference is used in the text.

In-Text (subsequent references):

xxxxx xxxxx (Halpern et al., 1985).

Halpern et al. (1985) xxxxx xxxxx

Note: In subsequent references the surname of the first author is followed by the term **et al.**

Journal Article (Six or Seven Authors)

Reference:

Thompson, D. C., McPhillips, H., Davis, R. L., Lieu, T. A., Homer, C. J., & Helfand, M. (2001). Universal newborn hearing screening summary of evidence. *Journal of the American Medical Association, 286*(16), 2000–2010. doi:10.1001/jama.286.16.2000

Note: In journal articles with up to seven authors, provide the surnames and initials of all authors in the reference list.

In-Text:

xxxxx xxxxx (Thompson et al., 2001).

Thompson et al. (2001) xxxxx xxxxx

Note: Only the surname of the first author is used followed by **et al.** the first and subsequent times the reference is cited in the text.

Journal Article (Eight or More Authors)

Reference:

Gravel, J., Berg, A., Bradley, M., Cacace, A., Campbell, D., Dalzell, L., . . . Prieve, B. A. (2000). New York State universal newborn hearing screening demonstration project: Effects of screening protocol on inpatient outcome measures. *Ear and Hearing, 1*(2), 131–140.

Note: In journal articles with eight or more authors, provide the surnames and initials of the first six authors followed by three ellipsis points (periods) and add the last author name in the reference list.

In-Text:

xxxxx xxxxx (Gravel et al., 2000).
Gravel et al. (2000) xxxxx xxxxx

Note: Only the surname of the first author is used followed by **et al.** the first and subsequent times the reference is cited in the text.

Entire Book

Reference:

Raphael, L. J., Borden, G. J., & Harris, K. S. (2007). *Speech science primer: Physiology, acoustics, and perception of speech* (5th ed.). Baltimore, MD: Lippincott Williams & Wilkins.

Note:

1. The book title is in sentence case and italicized.
2. A book edition is denoted by the edition number followed by **ed.** in parentheses after the book title.
3. The city and state are listed for publishers in the U.S. and the city and country are listed for those outside the U.S.

In-Text:

xxxxx xxxxx (Raphael, Borden, & Harris, 2007).

Raphael, Borden, and Harris (2007) xxxxx xxxxx

Note: Follow rules for citing multiple authors in book references as described in the journal article citation section.

Edited Book

Reference:

Goldfarb, R. (Ed.). (2006). *Ethics: A case study from fluency.* San Diego, CA: Plural.

Note: Use (Eds.) if there is more than one editor.

In-Text:

xxxxx xxxxx (Goldfarb, 2006).

Goldfarb (2006) xxxxx xxxxx]

Chapter in an Edited Book

Reference:

Goldfarb, R., & Halpern, H. (1980). A syntactic analysis of word association responses of aphasic and non-aphasic subjects. In D. Oborne, M. Gruenberg, & J. Eiser (Eds.), *Research in psychology and medicine* (pp. 354–359). London, UK: Academic.

Note:

1. Both the chapter and book title are in sentence case; the book title is italicized.
2. A frequent error of citation occurs when the editor of a book is listed as the author, but the relevant chapter was written by someone other than the editor.
3. The reference in text would be Goldfarb and Halpern not Oborne, Gruenberg, and Eiser.

In-Text:

xxxxx xxxxx (Goldfarb & Halpern, 1980).

Goldfarb and Halpern (1980) xxxxx xxxxx

Internet Document/Report

Reference:

American Academy of Audiology. (2018). *Academy information*. Retrieved from https://www.audiology.org/about-us/academy-information

Note:

1. Author is indicated.
2. If there is no date provided for the document use (n.d.) to indicate no date.
3. Title of publication is in sentence case and italicized.
4. Internet address is provided

In-Text:

xxxxx xxxxx (American Academy of Audiology [AAA], 2018).

Subsequent reference: AAA (2018) xxxxx xxxxx

Poster Session Presented at a Professional Meeting

Reference:

Schoepflin, J., & Serpanos, Y. (2007, April). *Frequent music listeners: Listening levels and hearing*. Poster session presented at the annual meeting of the American Academy of Audiology, Denver, CO.

Note:

1. Provide year and month of the presentation.
2. The title of the presentation is in sentence case.
3. Provide the name of the meeting and location.

In-Text:

xxxxx xxxxx (Schoepflin & Serpanos, 2007)

Schoepflin and Serpanos (2007) xxxxx xxxx

In-Text Citation of Two or More Publications

xxxxx xxxxx (Goldfarb, 2006, 2008; Raphael et al., 2007).

Note:

1. List two or more publications cited in text within the same parentheses in alphabetical order by the first author's surname.
2. Separate works by different authors with a semicolon.
3. List multiple works by the same author in date order, separated by commas.

Quoted Material

Reference:

Follow the examples above for referencing journal articles, books, and portions of books.

In-text:

"xxxxx xxxxx" (Goldfarb & Halpern, 1989, p. 35)

Goldfarb and Halpern (1989) xxxxx "xxxxx xxxxx" (p. 35)

Note: When material is being directly quoted from another source, the word-for-word section is enclosed within double quotation marks in the body of the text with the author's name, year of publication, and page number of the specific section quoted.

Unpublished Paper Presented at a Professional Meeting

Reference:

Goldfarb, R., & Bekker, N. (2006, April). *Grammatical category ambiguity in aging, aphasia, and schizophrenia.* Paper presented at the annual meeting of the New York State Speech, Language, and Hearing Association, Saratoga, NY.

Notes:

1. The month of the date of the presentation follows the year by a comma in parentheses.
2. The title of the presentation is in italicized sentence case.
3. Indicate if the professional meeting is annual.
4. Follow the title of the meeting with a comma, then with the city and state abbreviation.

In-text:

xxxxx xxxxx (Goldfarb & Bekker, 2006)

Goldfarb and Bekker (2006) xxxxx xxxxx

EXERCISES

Exercise 5–1. Chapter Review

1. In the following alphanumeric display of the Library of Congress classification system, which is NOT true?

RC
423
.V45
2006

   a. The first letter of the call number represents the subject.
   b. The second letter represents the object.
   c. The first set of numbers refers to an area of study within that subdivision.
   d. The second set of numbers is a code that represents the author's name, book title, and subject. It should be read as a decimal, for example, .45.
   e. The last number represents the year of publication.

2. If journals are *refereed* or *peer-reviewed*, that indicates that:
   a. The articles were evaluated by a team of scholars, assembled by the editor, with expertise in that particular subject matter.
   b. Peer reviewers assessed the content of the work, but not the mechanics of the writing (grammar, spelling, sentence structure, etc.).
   c. The citations were in APA style.
   d. Peer reviewers ultimately decide whether the manuscript is rejected or accepted with or without recommended revisions.
   e. The journal is published quarterly (four times a year).

3. The largest and oldest library organization in the world is the:
   a. Library of Congress
   b. Association of College and Research Libraries (ACRL)
   c. British Museum
   d. American Library Association (ALA)
   e. Google

4. A database dedicated solely to reference sources within our field is:
   a. PubMed
   b. Science Direct
   c. MEDLINE
   d. NIH
   e. ComDisDome

5. On-site or remote electronic access to numerous reference tools such as dictionaries, encyclopedias, thesauruses, and citation and writing style manuals can also be called:
   a. reference librarians
   b. course packs
   c. reference tools
   d. research guides
   e. reserve items

Exercise 5–2. Practice Writing Reference List and In-Text Citations Correctly Using APA-Style

(Use the APA style format above as a guide).

#	Information
1.	**Title:** *Connexin 26 mutations in hereditary non-syndromic sensorineural deafness* **Journal / Volume / Pages / Year / DOI:** Nature / 387 / 80 – 83 / 1997 doi:10.1038/387080a0 **Authors:** D. P. KELSELL, J. DUNLOP, H. P. STEVENS, N. J. LENCH, J. N. LIANG, G. PARRY, R. F. MUELLER & I. M. LEIGH **Write the reference correctly:** ____________________ ____________________ **Cite in text, beginning of sentence:** ____________________ ____________________ **Cite in text, end of sentence:** ____________________ ____________________

2. **Title:**
THE DEAF POPULATION OF THE UNITED STATES

Book Publisher / Location / Year:
National Association of the Deaf / 814 Thayer Avenue, Silver Spring, Maryland 20910 / 1974

Authors:
Schein, Jerome D.; Delk, Marcus T., Jr.

Write the reference correctly:

____

____

Cite in text, beginning of sentence:

____

____

Cite in text, end of sentence:

____

____

3. **Title:**
Sign Language Structure: An Outline of the Visual Communication Systems of the American Deaf

Journal / Volume / Pages / Year:
Journal of Deaf Studies and Deaf Education / 10, Issue 1 / 3-37 / 2005

Author:
William C. Stokoe Jr.

Write the reference correctly:

____

____

Cite in text, beginning of sentence:

____

____

Cite in text, end of sentence:

____

____

4. **Title:**
Beginning to teach the end: the importance of including discharge from aphasia therapy in the curriculum.

Authors:
Hersh, Deborah; Cruice, Madeline

Journal / Volume / Pages / Year / DOI:
International journal of language & communication disorders / 45(3)/ 263-274 / 2010
doi:10.3109/13682820902994200

Write the reference correctly:

____

____

Cite in text, beginning of sentence:

____

____

Cite in text, end of sentence:

____

____

5. **Title:**
It's a Noisy Planet

Author:
National Institute on Deafness and Communication Disorders (NIDCD)

URL Address:
http://www.noisyplanet.nidcd.nih.gov

Write the reference correctly:

____

____

Cite in text, beginning of sentence:

____

____

Cite in text, end of sentence:

____

____

6. **Title:**
   A PET study of word finding

   Authors:
   C.D. Frith, K.J. Friston, P.F. Liddle and R.S.J. Frackowia

   Journal / Volume / Pages / Year:
   Neuropsychologia / 29(12) / 1137-1148 / 1991

   Write the reference correctly:

   ____

   ____

   Cite in text, beginning of sentence:

   ____

   ____

   Cite in text, end of sentence:

   ____

   ____

7. **Title:**
Speech fluency in neurofibromatosis type 1

Authors:
Cosyns, Marjan; Mortier, Geert; Janssens, Sandra; Saharan, Nidhi; Stevens, Eileen; Van Borsel, John

Journal / Volume / Pages / Year / DOI:
Journal of fluency disorders / 35(1) / 59-69 / 2010
doi:10.1016/j.jfludis.2010.01.002

Write the reference correctly:

___

___

Cite in text, beginning of sentence:

___

___

Cite in text, end of sentence:

___

___

8. Chapter Title:
Auditory brainstem response in audiometric threshold prediction

Author:
Sininger YS, Hyde, ML.

Book Title / Edition / Publisher / Location / Year / Pages:
Handbook of Clinical Audiology / 5th ed. / Lippincott Williams & Wilkins / Baltimore, MD / 2009 / 293-321

Book Editor:
Katz J

Write the reference correctly:

____

____

Cite in text, beginning of sentence:

____

____

Cite in text, end of sentence:

____

____

9. **Title:**
Status of state early hearing detection and intervention (EHDI) laws.

Author:
American Speech-Language-Hearing Association

URL Address:
http://www.asha.org/advocacy/federal/ehdi/

Write the reference correctly:

____

____

Cite in text, beginning of sentence:

____

____

Cite in text, end of sentence:

____

____

10. Title:
Aphasia: A Clinical Approach

Authors:
Rosenbek John C.; LaPointe Leonard Lyell; Wertz Robert Terrence

Book Publisher / Location / Year:
Pro-Ed / Austin, Texas / 1991

Write the reference correctly:

____

____

Cite in text, beginning of sentence:

____

____

Cite in text, end of sentence:

____

____

Exercise 5–3. Write the References in Appropriate APA Style, Alphabetized Correctly in a Reference List

Use the reference information below to write the references in appropriate APA style, alphabetized correctly in a reference list.

#	Information
1.	**Title:** Identification of Hearing Loss & Middle-Ear Dysfunction in Preschool & School-Age Children. **Author/Year:** American Academy of Audiology, 2007 **URL Address:** http://www.audiology.org/resources/documentlibrary/Pages/HearingLossChildren.aspx
2.	**Chapter Title:** "The Quantitative Measurement of the Effect of Certain Situations on Stuttering," **Author:** Van Riper, C. & Hull, C. J **Book Title / Publisher / Location / Year / Pages:** *Stuttering in Children and Adults* / Minneapolis, University of Minnesota Press, 1955. 199–206 **Book Editors:** Johnson, W. & Leutenegger, R. R.
3.	**Title:** Prevalence And Risk Factors Of Hearing Impairment Among Primary-School Children In Shebin El-Kom District, Egypt. **Authors:** Taha, Azza A; Pratt, Sheila R; Farahat, Taghreed M; Abdel-Rasoul, Gaafar M; Albtanony, Manal A; Elrashiedy, Abdel-Latif E; Alwakeel, Hany R; Zein, Ahmed **Journal / Volume / Pages / Year / DOI:** American journal of audiology / 19(1) / 46-60 / 2010 doi:10.1044/1059-0889(2010/09-0030)

4. **Title:**
   Surgical Solutions for Conductive Hearing Loss

   Author:
   Mirko, Tos

   Book Publisher / Location / Year:
   Thieme Medical Publishers / New York, New York / 2000

5. **Title:**
   National survey of pediatricians' opinions about and practices for acute otitis media and xylitol use.

   Authors:
   Danhauer JL, Johnson CE, Rotan SN, Snelson TA, Stockwell JS.

   Journal / Volume / Pages / Year:
   J Am Acad Audiol / 21(5) / 329-46 / 2010

6. **Title:**
   The role of motor learning in *stuttering* adaptation: repeated versus novel utterances in a practice-retention paradigm.

   Authors:
   Max, Ludo; Baldwin, Caitlin J

   Journal / Volume / Pages / Year / DOI:
   Journal of fluency disorders, 35(1):33-43 / 2010
   doi:10.1016/j.jfludis.2009.12.003

7. **Title:**
   Hearing loss

   Author/Year:
   Vorvick, LJ (2010)

   URL Address:
   http://www.nlm.nih.gov/medlineplus/ency/article/003044.htm

8. **Chapter Title:**
   Neuromotor processes underlying *stuttering*

   Author:
   Caruso, A. J.

   Book Title / Publisher / Location / Year / Pages:
   Speech Motor Control And Stuttering / Excerpta Medica / Amsterdam / 1991 / 101–116

   Book Editors:
   Peters, H. F. M., Hulstijn, W. & Starkweather, C. W.

9. **Title:**
   Localization Of Cognitive Operations In The Human Brain

   Authors:
   Posner MI, Petersen SE, Fox PT, Raichle ME

   Journal / Volume / Pages / Year:
   Science / 240 / 1627-31 / 1988

10. **Book Title / Edition / Publisher / Location / Year:**
    The Nature and Treatment of Stuttering: New Directions / 2nd edition / Allyn & Bacon / Boston / 1997

    Book Editor:
    Richard F. Curlee, Gerald M. Siegel

#	Write A Reference List
1.	
2.	
3.	

4.

5.

6.

7.

8.

9.

10

____

____

____

____

____

____

Exercise 5–4. In-Text Citations

Using the reference information provided on multiple works below, write appropriately the in-text citation of two or more publications. (Use the APA style format above as a guide).

#	Information	Write a Multiple Publication Citation
1.	WILLIAM C. STOKOE JR., 2005 D. P. Kelsell, J. Dunlop, H. P. Stevens, N. J. Lench, J. N. Liang, G. Parry, R. F. Mueller & I. M. Leigh, 1997 Schein, Jerome D.; Delk, Marcus T., Jr.,1974	(__________ __________ __________ __________ __________ __________ __________)
2.	Sininger YS, Hyde, ML, 2009 American Speech-Language-Hearing Association (ASHA), 2010 National Institute On Deafness And Communication Disorders (NIDCD), 2010	(__________ __________ __________ __________ __________ __________ __________)

3. Hersh, Deborah; Cruice, Madeline, 2010 C.D. Frith, K.J. Friston, P.F. Liddle and R.S.J. Frackowia, 1991 Cosyns, Marjan; Mortier, Geert; Janssens, Sandra; Saharan, Nidhi; Stevens, Elien; Van Borsel, John, 2010	(______________________ ______________________ ______________________ ______________________ ______________________ ______________________ ______________________)
4. Taha,Azza A; Pratt, Sheila R; Farahat, Taghreed M; Abdel-Rasoul, Gaafar M; Albtanony, Manal A; Elrashiedy, Abdel-Latif E; Alwakeel, Hany R; Zein,Ahmed, 2010 Mirko,Tos, 2000 Danhauer JL, Johnson CE, Rotan SN, Snelson TA, Stockwell JS, 2010 National Institutes of Health (NIH), 2010	(______________________ ______________________ ______________________ ______________________ ______________________ ______________________ ______________________)
5. Richard F. Curlee, Gerald M. Siegel,_1997 Posner M. I., Petersen S. E., Fox P. T., Raichle M. E., 1988 Caruso, A. J., 1991 Max, Ludo; Baldwin, Caitlin, 2010 Van Riper, C. & Hull, C. J, 1955	(______________________ ______________________ ______________________ ______________________ ______________________ ______________________ ______________________)

6. Serpanos,Y. & Gravel, J, 2000 Serpanos,Y. & Gravel, J, 2002 Serpanos,Y. & Gravel, J, 2004 Serpanos,Y. & Jarmel, F, 2007	(__________ __________ __________ __________ __________ __________ __________)
7. Bellis,Teri James; Billiet, Cassie; Ross, Jody (2008) Shinn, JB; Chermak, GD; Musiek, FE (2009) Bellis,TJ (2003) Smith, Corinne and Strick, Lisa (1997)	(__________ __________ __________ __________ __________ __________ __________)
8. Goldfarb & Halpern, 1981 Goldfarb & Halpern, 1989 Goldfarb and Halpern, 1980 Goldfarb and Halpern, 1979 Goldfarb & Halpern, 1984	(__________ __________ __________ __________ __________ __________ __________)

9. Forguer, BD (1979) Fielding & Rawool (2002) Flottorp, Djupesland,Winther (1971) Fria, LeBlanc, Dristensen, Alberti (1975) Ferguson, Smith, Lutman, Mason, Coles, Gibbin (1996)	(____________________ ____________________ ____________________ ____________________ ____________________ ____________________ ____________________ ____________________)
10. American Academy of Audiology, (2010) National Center for Hearing Assessment & Management (2007) American Speech-Language-Hearing Association (1997) New York State Speech-Language-Hearing Association, 2010	(____________________ ____________________ ____________________ ____________________ ____________________ ____________________ ____________________ ____________________ ____________________)

Exercise 5–5. Demonstrate Access to University Library Services

In the following exercises, demonstrate access to university library services by conducting a search and documenting the outcomes in the worksheet below. Choose a topic of interest and conduct the following:

1. Search book catalog databases; provide a list of three sources.
2. Search article/journal databases (print and e-journals); provide a list of three sources.
3. Search video and other audiovisual material databases; provide a list of three sources.
4. Request an interlibrary loan service; choose one item that is not available in your university library from the searches conducted above and request an interlibrary loan.

Topic of Interest: ______________________________

Book Catalog Database Search

1. ______________________________
2. ______________________________
3. ______________________________

Article/Journal Database Search

1. ______________________________
2. ______________________________
3. ______________________________

Audiovisual Material Database Search

1. ______________________________
2. ______________________________
3. ______________________________

Interlibrary Loan Service

Item Requested: ______________________________

Library Source: ______________________________

Anticipated Date of Receipt: ______________________________

Exercise 5–6. Participate in a Library Field Trip

Participate in a library field trip with a guided tour through your university's library. Write three outcomes below based on this experience. Use performance-oriented verbs (e.g., search, compare, synthesize), rather than more passive verbs (e.g., think, understand, consider), and begin your sentence with, "I can" or "I will."

Provide three responses to the following:

After conducting a tour of my university library, I can:

1. ______________________________

____

2. ______________________________

____

3. ______________________________

____

REFERENCES

American Library Association. (2018). *Standards for libraries in higher education*. Retrieved from http://www.ala.org/acrl/standards/standardslibraries

American Library Association. (2015). *Number of libraries in the United States*. Retrieved from http://www.ala.org/tools/libfactsheets/alalibraryfactsheet01

American Library Association. (n.d.). *What is ALA?* Retrieved from http://www.ala.org/aboutala/

American Psychological Association (APA). (2010). *Publication manual of the American Psychological Association* (6th ed.). Washington, DC: Author.

Blake, V. L. P. (2002). Forging the Anglo-American Cataloging Alliance: Descriptive cataloging, 1830–1908. In M. D. Joachim (Ed.), *Historical aspects of cataloging and classification* (pp. 3–22). Binghamton, NY: Haworth Information Press.

Brophy, P. (2005). *The academic library*. London, UK: Facet.

Budd, J. M. (2005). *The changing academic library: Operations, culture, environments*. Chicago. IL: Association of College and Research Libraries.

ComDisDome. (n.d.). Retrieved from https://www.proquest.com/products-services/databases/cdd-set-c.html

Guerrero, T. S. (2006). What they don't teach you in library school: Experience is the real teacher. In E. Connor (Ed.), *An introduction to reference services in academic libraries* (pp. 61–76). Binghamton, NY: Haworth Information Press.

Krasner-Khait, B. (2001). Survivor: The history of the library. *History Magazine*, *3*, 47–51.

Library of Congress. (n.d.). *Library of Congress classification outline*. Retrieved from http://www.loc.gov/catdir/cpso/lcco/

Malone, R. (1999). *The first seventy-five years: An oral history of the American Speech-Language-Hearing Association*. Washington, DC: American Speech-Language-Hearing Association.

National Center for Biotechnology Information. (n.d.). *PubMed introduction*. Retrieved from https://www.ncbi.nlm.nih.gov/pubmed/

Online Computer Library Center. (2018). *About OCLC*. Retrieved from http://www.oclc.org/us/en/about/default.htm

Paden, E. P. (1975). ASHA in retrospect. Fiftieth anniversary reflections. *Asha*, *17*(9), 571–572.

Shoffner, R. M. (2002). Appearance and growth of computer and electronic products in libraries. In R. E. Abel (Ed.), *Scholarly publishing: Books, journals, publishers, and libraries in the twentieth century* (pp. 209–256). New York, NY: Wiley.

Shores, L. (1972). *Origins of the American college library*. Boston, MA: Gregg Press.

U.S. Copyright Office, Library of Congress. (2017). *Copyright basics*. Retrieved from http://www.copyright.gov/circs/circ01.pdf

U.S. Department of Education, National Center for Education Statistics. (2005). *The condition of education 2005*, NCES 2005-094, Washington, DC: U.S. Government Printing Office.

Veaner, A. B. (2002). From bibliotheque to omnitheque. In R. E. Abel (Ed.), *Scholarly publishing: Books, journals, publishers, and libraries in the twentieth century* (pp. 163–177). New York, NY: Wiley.

Vickery, B. C. (1970). *Techniques of information retrieval*. Hamden, CT: Archon Books.

Internet Resources

In this chapter, you will be required to:

1. Identify terms and uses of Internet resources.
2. Navigate the Internet to conduct a scholarly search.
3. Identify appropriate Internet sources for citation.

The dot-com boom and bust of the late 1990s into the new century were startling reminders of the blinding speed and mutability of the Internet. Fortunes were won and lost on companies that sometimes appeared to be barely more than dreams. A new English syntax grew in the youth-friendly domains of email and Facebook. Emoticons, such as the colon plus hyphen plus closed parentheses to represent the "smiley-face" (☺) icon, addressed the inherent lack of affect in writing as opposed to speaking. A pair of smart students in California developed a user-friendly means of accessing Internet resources, which led to a new verb form—to Google—and to the former students' new status as billionaires. Search engines replaced trips to the library and bookstore for students writing term papers and clinicians collecting therapy materials. Camera-phones with images and videos later posted on YouTube led to abrupt falls from grace for unprepared and unsuspecting celebrities and politicians.

Welcome to the new way of doing business, meeting your life partner, succeeding in academia, and conducting your clinical practice. There is not much point any more in measuring intelligence by how many things we know, as long as we understand how to access information. Indeed, Guilford's (1967) model of the structure of the intellect should probably be revisited and modified. According to Guilford's theory, intelligence is composed of operations, contents, and products. There are five kinds of operations (cognition, memory, divergent production, convergent production, evaluation), six kinds of products (units, classes, relations, systems, transformations, and implications), and five kinds of contents (visual, auditory, symbolic, semantic, behavioral). These dimensions interact, producing 150 different components of intelligence.

There is less of a need for convergent behavior, characterized by logical conclusions and logical necessities, when silicone chips can do the hunting and gathering for us. There is more of a need for divergent behavior, characterized by logical alternatives and logical possibilities. We have the time and the non-silicone abilities of creativity and imagination, which permit original synthesis of the avalanche of information coming through our computers.

What is the Internet?

The interconnected network of networks is a worldwide collection of cooperating institutions. No corporation, not Microsoft or Google, no government, no university or library, no individual or group of individuals owns all or any part of the Internet.

A history of the Internet (Leeper & Gotthoffer, 2001) usually begins with the U.S. Defense Department in the mid-1960s, which sought to protect the nation against Cold War enemies. The recently completed interstate highway system was to have had an analogy in computing resources, linking information rather than transportation, but the projected cost was prohibitive. The Advanced Research Projects Agency (ARPA) was the funding arm of the Defense Department, having invested large sums in computing hardware, graphics programs, and artificial intelligence. The next project, involving networking, would permit sharing of information so that computer systems could communicate with each other. The resultant ARPANET was used for preliminary research, the first emails, and, inevitably, games.

By the 1980s, a time when young people carried transistor radios the size of photocopy machines on their shoulders, the government had eased out of the Internet in favor of business and institutional applications. An early academic use familiar to one of the authors (RG) was BITNET, developed at the City University of New York (CUNY), which permitted electronic mail and transfer of data between select CUNY centers and other academic institutions. Early transfer of data and emails between coauthors in New York and California was exhilarating, leading to a new and more efficient way of doing research with multiple authors and sites. There were similar "Eureka" moments with respect to software. One humanities software application analyzed word usage in literature. After RG dutifully analyzed Alexander Pope's poem, *The Rape of the Lock*, and found that, of the total number of words used, about 70% were not duplicated, it was a short logical step to apply the program to a spontaneous language sample in order to obtain a type-token ratio. The sophistication level of current software is about as far removed in speed and size from the old programs as an iPod Touch is from the old boombox.

Syntax, Semantics, and Jargon

The authors had two problems in writing this section:

1. Most readers will be as familiar with the Internet as members of the authors' generations were with the typewriter and rotary telephone. Some will adapt with more or less difficulty than others to successive generations of electronic advances. New generations of scholars are needed about every ten years; electronic generations seem to turn over about every five years.
2. Information provided here may be out of date by the time the book goes to print. The authors have attempted to include information that is as enduring as possible, but some topics may appear dated, even quaint, by the time this book is published.

Internet Glossary: An Exercise in Futility

Although some reference terms will likely continue to be useful, there is no substitute for a personal glossary of Internet terms. As noted in Chapter 2, most professions develop jargon using abbreviations, acronyms, terms based on other languages, and code words, and the computer science profession is no exception.

1. *Domain:* The three letters after the dot, of which there are six common categories:
   a. com (commercial)
   b. edu (educational)
   c. gov (government)
   d. mil (military)
   e. net (network)
   f. org (organization)
2. *Email:* Electronic Internet mailbox. The computer of the selected Internet Service Provider represents the post office, and the user accesses a mailbox through a combination of letters and numbers (password).
3. *FTP:* File Transfer Protocol, which allows the user to send (also called *uploading*) and receive (also called *downloading*) files across the Internet.
4. *http://:* HyperText Transfer Protocol, which identifies the way that the file or document will be transferred. Another version is https:// where the last letter (s) indicates *secure*. The protocol indicates the method that Internet software uses to exchange data with a file server.

5. *Hypertext:* A technology enabling combinations of text, graphics, sound, video, and links on a single web page.
6. *ISP:* Internet Service Provider, or your Internet account. Most students have an account through a college or university or by a commercial provider.
7. *Netiquette:* Net etiquette, of which there are several types:
   a. *Emoticon:* The body language of the Internet, consisting mostly of variations on Smiley, including frowning (☹) and winking (;-)) versions.
   b. *Flame:* To insult, hurt, and offend another user in a debasing message.
   c. *Lurk:* To refrain from immediately posting a message on a newsgroup, in order to become more familiar with the style, tone, and content of the messages.
   d. *SHOUT:* To type in ALL CAPS.
   e. *Spam:* The junk mail of the Internet.
8. *URL:* Universal Resource Locator, which enables the user to locate a web page. For example, http://www.pluralpublishing.com is a URL that will connect the user to the publisher of this book. The American Psychological Association (APA, 2010) offers a useful diagram of a URL (Figure 6–1). The host name is often the address for a home page. Test the URL before submitting a paper, because two problems are common:
   a. The URL may be copied incorrectly; or,
   b. The site may have moved.
9. *User name:* Also called user ID, account name, or account number. The authors can be reached at serpanos@adelphi.edu and goldfarb2@adelphi.edu. The numeral in the second user name acknowledges that there are two (or more) faculty members with the same name.
10. *Viruses, worms, Trojan horses, and ransomware:* Dangerous programs designed to perform an undesired task, such as erasing the hard disk, through deception. Ransomware refers to software created to prevent access to a computer until the victim pays a certain sum of money by a certain time.
11. *Educational platform (also called learning platform, e-learning platform, managed learning platform, or virtual learning platform):* An information system used by colleges and universities that enables students to participant in their education. Instructors often post audio- and videoclips, web links, announcements, and tutorials, and invite virtual class participation. Two widely used examples of these platforms are Blackboard and Moodle.
12. *Blended/hybrid or online course:* Definitions vary, but a hybrid or blended course usually has 30% to 70% of the course meeting virtually, or off-campus, and the rest of the course takes place in a traditional, face-to-face classroom. An online course is 80% to 100% off campus. Instructors provide expert guidance and make use of educational platforms in virtual meetings. Some blended courses use a "flip" model, where much of the classwork is done at home, and much of the homework is done in class.

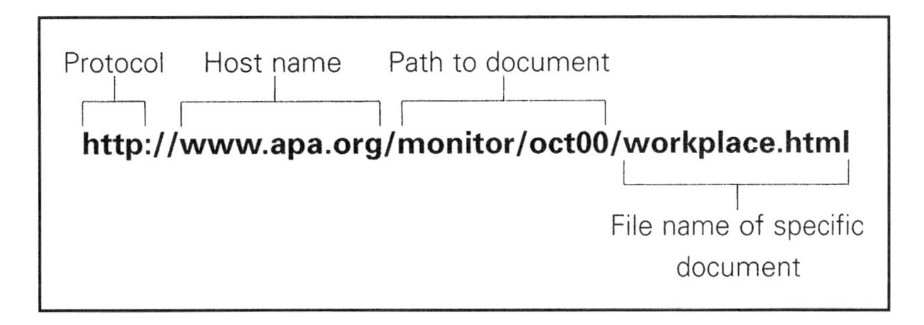

Figure 6–1. Sample URL. From the 6th edition of the *Publication Manual of the American Psychological Association* (APA, 2010, p. 188), by the American Psychological Association

13. *Virtual collaboration:* Expands the four walls of the course. For example, students can collaborate anytime, anywhere; faculty can bring in guest speakers from around the world; and faculty and students can have office hours from home or away from campus.
14. *Podcast:* May be a verb, as in making a digital audio file available, or a noun, referring to a digital audio file that is available on the Internet. Course instructors may podcast lectures, especially in a class that is blended/hybrid or online.
15. *www:* The World Wide Web, developed in the 1990s by the European Laboratory for Particle Physics.

Uses and Abuses

Research resources on the Internet may or, more frequently, may not be peer reviewed. Evaluation by a panel of experts before publishing is an accepted process in the scholarly community to reduce error, fraud, and prejudice. Many peer-reviewed professional journals, including those published by ASHA, require electronic submission of articles, and appear online as well as in hard copy. A member of the American Speech-Language-Hearing Association (ASHA) or NSSHLA (the student organization) can access peer-reviewed journal articles in electronic form as follows: Go to http://www.asha.org → click on ASHA journals → Log in with email address and password → select one of the ASHA Journals Online.

The editor of the *American Journal of Speech-Language Pathology* (AJSLP; Hoit, 2005) addressed some ethical issues that relate to the writing process. She noted that manuscripts available on an individual's website are considered published (but not peer reviewed). AJSLP requires authors to state in a cover letter that the submitted work has not been published elsewhere, which includes publication in electronic form. The journal also includes a letter of instructions to reviewers indicating that a submitted manuscript is a confidential document, not to be shared with anyone else.

As a general rule of scholarship, only references from peer-reviewed publications should be included in research reports. For electronic articles or Internet-only journals, find a publisher's statement, such as the following: *The Journal of Speech-Language Pathology and Applied Behavior Analysis* (JSLP-ABA), ISSN: 1932-4731, is published by Joseph Cautilli. It is a peer-reviewed, electronic journal intended for circulation in the scientific community.

Human participants in research, particularly those children and adults with communication disorders, need special protection (Schwartz, 2006). In most types of peer-reviewed published research, there are two and often three gatekeepers. The first review, before humans may participate in research, comes from the Institutional Review Board (IRB), which must comply with federal regulations and ethical guidelines set forth in DHHS Regulations US CFR 46, NSF Regulations US CFR 690, and The Belmont Report. The IRB, generally including peers and a volunteer member from the broader community, reviews the proposal or research design as well as completion of required IRB forms. These forms require a description of the project's purposes, methods, and design; initiation and completion dates; characteristics and number of participants; recruitment method; and any potential risks, discomforts, or stresses, and precautions taken to minimize them (Goldfarb, 2006). The second gatekeeper is the funding agency. Although many studies are completed without external funding, many papers in ASHA journals will cite the funding source in the acknowledgments section at the end of the article. For example, recognition of support from NIH means that the National Institutes of Health provided funding, usually in the form of new-investigator support (a number beginning with RO3) or as multiyear major funding (a number beginning with RO1). Grants of any type are very competitive, and funding will be provided only after a careful review, similar to but more stringent than that of the IRB, above. The final gatekeeper is the scholarly journal, which has its own peer-review process, but generally includes an editor and several associate editors with expertise in the topic of the submitted manuscript. Erroneous, fraudulent, and prejudicial papers still occasionally find their way into print, but such an event is so rare as to be newsworthy.

Beginning in 2000, anyone submitting a grant proposal to NIH was (and still is) required to complete a computer-based training course on the protection of human research participants. This free course on research ethics is available (subject to change) at http://ohsr.od.nih.gov or for those who are not employees of NIH, https://humansubjects.nih.gov/resources. A student who completes the course is permitted to print a certificate of completion. Students and researchers should also visit the Belmont Report Historical Archive at https://www.hhs.gov/ohrp/regulations-and-policy/belmont-report/index.html to see interviews with members of the National Commission for the Protection of Human Subjects of Biomedical and Behavioral Research in a 9-minute video. Among other websites offering information or tutorials on ethics are the following:

1. Go to the site and click "Health topics" to learn about ethics and health at http:www.who.int
2. Information on human subject research is available from http://www.cdc.gov. Scroll along the alphabetical listings for a wealth of information. We found fascinating reports under the headings of "Diseases & Conditions" and "Healthy Living."
3. In 1994 President Clinton established the Department of Energy's Advisory Committee on Human Radiation Experiments. Of particular interest is "Part I. Ethics of Human Subjects Research: A Historical Perspective" at http://www.hhs.gov/ohrp/education/index.html#materials
4. In the National Library of Medicine's "Current Bibliographies in Medicine" there are 500 references in "Ethical Issues in Research Involving Human Participants." The site, including President Clinton's 1997 apology to the survivors of the Tuskegee syphilis study, is at http://www.nlm.nih.gov/archive//20061214/pubs/cbm/hum_exp.html
5. The "World Medical Association Declaration of Helsinki Ethical Principles for Medical Research Involving Human Subjects," adopted 1964 and amended most recently in October 2000, is at http://www.nihtraining.com/ohsrsite/guidelines/helsinki.html

Now that you have learned some of the history and ethical behavior in conducting research with individuals who have communication disorders, you are ready to use the Internet to study these disorders.

University libraries have access to a variety of databases in specialized areas. Table 6–1 lists some sites of interest to those undertaking research in audiology and speech-language pathology, based on a sample university listing.

Citing References from the Internet

For specific style questions that may not be addressed in this section, refer to electronic reference formats recommended by the American Psychological Association (http://www.apastyle.org/elecref.html).

A reference to an entire website is cited within text, but not in the references section, as in the following example:

> The ASHA website provides links to the code of ethics (http://www.asha.org).

An individual web page should be considered the same as a print reference in terms of citation of author, date, and title. The variety of material available on the Web, and the variety of ways in which it is structured and presented, can present challenges for creating usable and useful references. Although both Modern Language Association (MLA) and American Psychological Association (APA) styles are used widely, our professions favor APA style. Following are guidelines for authors using and citing Internet sources, based on APA (2010) style:

Table 6–1. Sample Database Search

Comdisdome	
(Proquest)—includes topics in audiology and speech-language pathology, covering journal articles, books, dissertations, grants, websites, and information on relevant authors and institutions. Journal coverage, 1949 to the present, includes citations and abstracts with some full text available.	Database
Dissertations and Theses Global	
(Proquest)—offers comprehensive collection of dissertations and theses worldwide, with full texts of graduate work since 1997. Areas of interest to CSD students and professionals include the Health & Medicine and Science & Technology topics.	Database
Linguistics and Language Behavior Abstracts	
(Proquest)—provides abstracts and bibliographical citations from 1973–present in the study and use of language, including topics such as psycholinguistics, special education, nonverbal communication and hearing and speech physiology.	Database
Medline	
(Pubmed)—includes citations and abstracts for articles in biomedical journals.	Database
Medline with Full Text	
(Ebscohost)—provides full text for nearly 1,200 journals indexed in MEDLINE, including more than 1,400,000 full-text articles dating back to 1965.	Full-text database
MedlinePlus	
(free on the web)—offers extensive information from the National Institutes of Health and other trusted sources on over 650 diseases and conditions. Includes lists of hospitals and physicians, a medical encyclopedia and dictionary, information on prescription and nonprescription drugs, health information from the media, and links to thousands of clinical trials.	Database

Note. Edited from Adelphi University. Retrieved from http://libguides.adelphi.edu/az.php?s=65250

1. Direct readers as closely as possible to the information being cited; whenever possible, reference specific documents rather than home or menu pages.
2. Provide references that work.

What kinds of documents are available on the Internet? They may be articles in periodicals (e.g., newspaper, newsletter, or journal); they may stand on their own, not as part of a volume (e.g., research paper, government report, online book or brochure); or they may be uniquely web based (e.g., web page, newsgroup). Internet references should include document title or description, date (either the date of publication or update or the date of retrieval), and the URL. Identify the authors of a document when possible.

Following are examples of APA (2010) style for Internet referencing.

Electronic Article

This is the same as for the print version, but if you have viewed the article only in its electronic form, you should add in brackets the phrase "electronic version."

Reference:

Ambrose, N. G., & Yairi, E. (2002). The Tudor study: Data and ethics. [Electronic version]. *American Journal of Speech-Language Pathology, 11*, 190–203.

In-text:

(Ambrose & Yairi, 2002)

Electronic Article (where the format is modified from the print version)

Author, A. A., Author, B. B., & Author, C. C. (2000). Title of article. *Title of Periodical, vol. no.*, page numbers. Retrieved from URL

In-text:

(Author et al., year)

Specific Internet Document

Reference:

American Psychological Association (APA). (2010). *The basics of APA style* [Tutorial]. Retrieved from http://www.apastyle.org/learn/tutorials/basics-tutorial.aspx

In-text:

(American Psychological Association [APA], 2010)

In-text (subsequent references):

(APA, 2010)

Article in an Internet-Only Journal

Reference:

Goldfarb, R. (2006). Operant conditioning and programmed instruction in aphasia rehabilitation. *The Journal of Speech-Language Pathology and Applied Behavior Analysis, 1*, 56–65. Retrieved from http://www.baojournal.com/SLP-ABAWEBSITE/SLP-ABA-VOL-1/SLPABA-1-1.pdf

In-text:

(Goldfarb, 2006)

Evaluating Internet Sources for Professional Writing

Anyone can post anything on a personal website or to a news group. A particularly intriguing, entertaining, or controversial story has the potential to "go viral," a process whereby the posting in the morning circumnavigates the globe during the day and appears on CNN that evening. The extraordinary number of hits on the site, distribution via electronic mailing lists, and downloads can impose a sense of authority or gravitas to the posting. Not all of these postings are frivolous, nefarious, or sexual; some represent the best efforts of well-meaning people. For example, the notion that a preservative used for vaccines had a direct link to the development of autism has circulated the Internet for years. There have been no double-blinded randomized clinical trials (the gold standard of research) in support of a causal relationship between vaccines and autism, but some parents, through fear or lack of adequate critical evaluation, have put their young children at risk by refusing to have them vaccinated against preventable childhood diseases. Indeed, one of our doctoral students, at the beginning of her studies, submitted a research proposal (not accepted by her mentor) based on the vaccine-autism link "proven" in Internet reports.

Following are some strategies for educated consumers of Internet research:

1. Read the URL. As noted above, the host name (e.g., asha.org) tells you the source or sponsor of the site. Be sure of the domain, though. Entering whitehouse.gov will take you to the residence of the U.S. President,

but whitehouse.com would have taken you to a porn site. (The name was sold to a real estate firm in 2004.) If the source is a major newspaper, the website should be given the same weight as the print version. If the source is not familiar, search for verifiable data, rather than vague or generic terms, such as "most people" or "leading scientists."
2. Establish a comfort level. Lurk in newsgroups or listservs before posting. Avoid sites where boasts, generalities, and flames are common. Use a search engine to verify the host. Of course, evaluate the style and competence of the writing. Be aware that the test of comfort is not part of the scientific method (see "Evidence-Based Writing," Chapter 3).
3. Verify, using independent sources. The same information is represented on the Internet via different paths. Newsgroups often skew the information to the direction of their political or cultural agendas, so visit other newsgroups with compatible as well as opposing points of view. Try to follow cited information back to their sources or contact the writer of the posting for reference material. Remember that, just as an author of a book may misunderstand or misrepresent information gleaned from other sources, the person posting in a newsgroup may not be correct in interpreting source material (even more likely, as newsgroup postings do not undergo peer review).
4. Be skeptical. The vastness of the Internet permits topics to be analyzed in fair and balanced or very narrowly focused ways. The nonprejudicial nature of the Internet requires that all websites, from megacorporations to garage-level start-ups, be delivered to the end user with the same speed and quality. On December 14, 2017 the U.S. Federal Communications Commission (FCC), voted to overturn requirements for net neutrality. In essence, the FCC has told Internet service providers such as AT&T, Comcast, and Verizon that they no longer have to treat all websites and online content equally. We oppose this as scholars who support the ready and equal availability of information of all types. The Internet does not need owners or masters, and it is the job of critical thinkers to separate the wheat from the chaff.
5. Be curious. Following links in websites is similar to reading the articles and books listed in the bibliography section of a journal article. In both cases, the reader's own determination to understand original source material may yield information that supports or refutes the author's claims. Either way, the reader will be performing the non-silicone tasks of original synthesis and divergent thinking.

We have not discussed MUDs (multiuser dimensions), MOOs (multiuser object orienteds), or IRCs (Internet relay chats), because we do not consider them to be useful research venues. Similarly, chat programs such as ICQ ("I seek you") networks and web-based programs are fine for buddies but not for scholarly pursuits.

Peer-Reviewed Journals

A peer-reviewed electronic journal must have some form of publisher's statement (see below; used with permission), which indicates that articles will be evaluated by editors for content and accuracy before they are published. For example, the following is used, with permission, from the *Journal of Speech-Language Pathology and Applied Behavior Analysis* (JSL P-ABA), a peer-reviewed electronic journal:

Peer-Review Process

All submitted manuscripts are reviewed initially by the Lead Editor. Manuscripts with insufficient priority for publication will be rejected promptly. Other manuscripts will be sent to the Senior Associate Editor, who will distribute them to editorial consultants with relevant expertise. The editorial consultants will read the papers and evaluate:

(1) the importance of the topic addressed by the paper; (2) the paper's conformity to standards of evidence and scholarship; and (3) the clarity of writing style. Comments provided by the editorial consultants will then be provided to the author(s) for follow up.

There also may be a disclaimer for what is not intended, an example of which appears in JSLP-ABA: "The information contained in this journal is not intended to create any type of patient–therapist relationship or representation whatsoever." The electronic journal also might include a mission statement, and certainly should include submission information for authors. One way to differentiate commercial from educational sites is that the domain (the three letters after the dot) will be .com for the former and .org or .edu for the latter.

However, there are some perfectly respectable peer-reviewed journals, including medical journals, that use the .com domain.

The Journal of Speech-Language Pathology and Applied Behavior Analysis

Authors' note: Use *JSLP-ABA* after writing the full version of the journal title, followed by the abbreviated title in parentheses, as seen above.

VOLUME NO. 5, ISSUE NO. 1
Authors' note: In most cases, the volume number increases by one every year. However, some journals publish two volumes per year. In addition, most journals produce some four to six issues for every volume.

ISSN: 1932–4731
Authors' note: The ISSN is the international identifier for serials and other continuing resources, in the electronic and print world. ISSN assignment is free of charge. For more information, go to http://www.issn.org

Published: January 12, 2010
Authors' note: Both electronic versions of print journals and purely electronic journals may release papers ahead of the actual publication date, sometimes several months ahead.

Publisher's Statement (reprinted with permission)

The *Journal of Speech-Language Pathology and Applied Behavior Analysis (JSLP-ABA)* is published by Dr. Joseph Cautilli and BAO Journals. It is a peer-reviewed, electronic journal intended for general circulation in the scientific community.

The mission of this journal is to provide a forum for SLP and ABA professionals to exchange information on topics of mutual interest. These topics may include, but are not necessarily limited to, support for disorders of prelinguistic communication, speech perception/production, oral language and literacy, speech fluency, and voice. They may also address issues pertaining to accent reduction, culturally based language variations, and augmentative-alternative communication. *JSLP-ABA* welcomes articles describing assessment and treatment efficacy research based on detailed case studies, single-subject designs, and group designs. Also encouraged are literature reviews that synthesize a body of information, highlight areas in need of further research, or reconsider previous information in a new light. Additionally, this journal welcomes papers describing theoretical frameworks and papers that address issues pertaining to *SLP-ABA* collaboration.

Which Internet Resources Should We Use (And Which Should We Avoid)?

Do Use

1. Electronic versions of such respected peer-reviewed print journals as *Journal of Speech, Language, and Hearing Research*; *Brain and Language*; *Ear and Hearing*; *Journal of the American Academy of Audiology*
2. Peer-reviewed e-journals, such as JSLP-ABA; *SpeechPathology.com*; *Journal of Experimental Stroke and Translational Medicine*
3. Websites of our professional organizations, such as http://www.asha.org for the

American Speech-Language-Hearing Association, or http://www.audiology.org for the American Academy of Audiology
4. National organizations such as http://www.cancer.org for the American Cancer Society or http://www.americanheart.org for the American Heart Association
5. U.S. government websites such as http://www.nih.gov for the National Institutes of Health or http://www.cdc.gov for the Centers for Disease Control and Prevention

Don't Use

1. The free encyclopedia, Wikipedia (http://www.wikipedia.org). Note that even though the domain is .org, we do not recommend a site that is not peer-reviewed or overseen by a respected governing board or a learned society.
2. Social networks, such as Facebook, Twitter, or Instagram.
3. Chat rooms.
4. Political action committees, because, by definition, they are one-sided in their focus.
5. Sites devoted to brand names, pharmaceutical companies, or trade magazines. There is a difference between independent research, which is designed to report either favorable or unfavorable results, and research and development (R & D), which is designed to advertise, sell, or advance a product.

Should We Use These Internet Resources? Why or Why Not?

1. http://www.merck.com: This is tricky. Going to the Merck pharmaceutical website will certainly reveal advertising for medications that Merck wants to sell, and which cannot be trusted to be an unbiased source of information. On the other hand, the site will also take you to the Merck Manuals, a respected source of medical books.
2. http://www.whitehouse.com: Don't go there. It is currently a clearing house for financial aid, but it is not a source of information about 1600 Pennsylvania Avenue.
3. http://www.ees.elsevier.com: Even though the domain is .com, this link will take you to some of the most respected medical and professional journals that exist.
4. http://www.sciencedirect.com: This is an information source for scientific, technical, and medical research, and is highly recommended. A subscription is required for some sections.
5. http://www.linkedin.com: You may find this site useful for job searches and professional contacts, but it is not reliable for research related to speech-language pathology and audiology.

In the exercises that follow, conduct a search and identify appropriate web-based scholarly references.

Final Note

The anonymity of the Web makes it tempting to think that emails and group postings will never be traced back to the sender. There are many people who are awaiting trials, named in lawsuits, or worse, because they were laboring under this misconception. The general rule is to write anything you want, but think long and hard before clicking the "Send" button. To that good advice we would add that you proofread carefully.

Exercises

Exercise 6–1. Chapter Review

1. Which of the following is not a domain (the three letters after the dot)?
   a. com
   b. edu
   c. gov
   d. mil
   e. mon

2. The protocol that identifies the way that the file or document will be transferred is:
   a. FTP
   b. http
   c. email
   d. hypertext
   e. ISP

3. The junk mail of the Internet is called:
   a. emoticon
   b. flame
   c. lurk
   d. shout
   e. spam

4. In the 1990s, the European Laboratory for Particle Physics developed the:
   a. URL
   b. username
   c. viruses
   d. www
   e. Trojan horses

5. What are some strategies for educated consumers of Internet research?
   a. Read the URL.
   b. Establish a comfort level.
   c. Verify, using independent sources.
   d. Be curious but be skeptical.
   e. All of the above.

Exercise 6–2. Navigate the Internet to conduct a search on autism and then answer the questions below.

1. Indicate the database used: ____

2. Write the URL for a link to a source for scholarly information.

   ____

3. Explain why this is a resource that we should use.

   ____

   ____

   ____

4. Write the URL for a link to a source for nonscholarly information.

   ____

5. Explain why this is a resource we should not use.

   ____

   ____

   ____

Exercise 6–3. Navigate the Internet to conduct a search on cochlear implants and then answer the questions below.

1. Indicate the database used: ____________________

2. Write the URL for a link to a source for scholarly information.

   ____

3. Explain why this is a resource that we should use.

   ____

   ____

   ____

4. Write the URL for a link to a source for nonscholarly information.

   ____

5. Explain why this is a resource we should not use.

   ____

   ____

   ____

Exercise 6–4. Go to https://www.youtube.com/watch?v=LLhXxBC9xYk and view the first author's TEDx talk, "An aphasiologist has a stroke." Answer the questions below.

1. What does TEDx mean?

____

____

____

2. How many people viewed this talk?

____

____

____

3. What is the mission of this TEDx talk?

____

____

____

4. View another TED or TEDx talk and explain why you chose to see it.

____

____

____

Exercise 6–5. Go to the following websites and answer the questions.

1. https://www.youtube.com/watch?v=JJ4umcBKKNQ&feature=youtu.be
   a. Is this peer-reviewed? Y N
   b. How do you know?

   ____

   ____

   ____

2. https://www.journals.elsevier.com/journal-of-communication-disorders/
   a. Is this peer-reviewed? Y N
   b. How do you know?

   ____

   ____

   ____

3. http://journals.lww.com/ear-hearing/pages/default.aspx
   a. Is this peer-reviewed? Y N
   b. How do you know?

   ____

   ____

   ____

4. http://blog.asha.org/2013/07/30/what-does-a-fulbright-specialist-do/?utm_source=feedburner&utm_medium=feed&utm_campaign=Feed%3A+ASHAsphere+%28ASHAsphere%29
   a. Is this peer-reviewed? Y N
   b. How do you know?

   ____

   ____

   ____

5. http://aja.pubs.asha.org/article.aspx?articleid=2277739
   a. Is this peer-reviewed? Y N
   b. How do you know?

   ____

   ____

   ____

References

American Psychological Association. (2010). *Publication manual of the American Psychological Association* (6th ed.). Washington, DC: Author.

Cautilli, J. (Ed.). (2007). *The Journal of Speech-Language Pathology and Applied Behavior Analysis*. Retrieved from http://www.slp-aba.net/Pub-Statement.html

Goldfarb, R. (2006). An atheoretical discipline. In R. Goldfarb (Ed.), *Ethics: A case study from fluency* (pp. 117–137). San Diego, CA: Plural.

Guilford, J. P. (1967). *The nature of human intelligence*. New York, NY: McGraw-Hill.

Hoit, J. (2005). Write right. *American Journal of Speech-Language Pathology*, *17*, 171.

Leeper, L. H., & Gotthoffer, D. (2001). *Communication sciences and disorders on the net*. Boston, MA: Allyn & Bacon.

Schwartz. R. G. (2006). Would today's IRB approve the Tudor study? Ethical considerations in conducting research involving children with communication disorders. In R. Goldfarb (Ed.), *Ethics: A case study from fluency* (pp. 83–96). San Diego, CA: Plural.

Writing for Oral Presentation

In an "On Language" column in the *Chicago Tribune* on November 8, 2006, Nathan Bierma related an anecdote about a visiting professor giving a speech at Columbia University. The speaker reported that two negatives often make a positive, but no language used two positives to make a negative. Another professor in the audience shot back, "Yeah, yeah."

Oral presentations fall into four methods of delivery: impromptu, memorized, manuscript, and extemporaneous. With the exception of the impromptu or spontaneous speech, oral presentations do require some level of preparation in a written form of the speech and in practice of the delivery. A memorized delivery is one where the speech has been committed to memory from a prepared script, and the manuscript delivery is one that is read word for word. The extemporaneous method, the most common form used in classrooms and general public speaking, is a combination of the three styles where notes or an outline are used with a high level of spontaneity in the delivery (Seiler & Beall, 1999). Because it is probable that the student of communication sciences will use this format in presentations conducted in the classroom, clinical setting, or professional conferences, this chapter will focus on strategies in the written preparation and execution of an extemporaneous style of oral presentation.

In this chapter, you will work with samples of posters, platform presentations, short courses, and PowerPoint™ presentations located on the website. You will be required to:

1. Create a poster.
2. Review and practice delivery of a platform presentation.
3. Comment on a short course.
4. Prepare a PowerPoint presentation.
5. Create a computer-generated slide presentation.

Preparing the Oral Presentation

In any effective oral presentation except the impromptu style, some level of research, writing, and preparation of the delivery is required. The extent of the research, writing, and preparation depends on various factors such as the speaker's style, comfort with and knowledge of the content, and the length and depth of the presentation itself.

Knowledge of a particular topic is required in order for anyone to be able to speak comfortably and convincingly to an audience. The first step in preparing the presentation is to determine how much information needs to be gathered, which is dependent upon the speaker's expertise or knowledge on the specific topic. The research involved in an oral presentation should follow the same guidelines used in writing a research paper. Statements made by the speaker should be supported by facts either stated in the presentation or in a printed reference list. In other words, orally presented information is bound by the same principles of ethics and plagiarism as the written form (see Chapter 3: Evidence-Based Writing; Chapter 4: Ethics of Professional Writing; and Chapter 5: Referencing Resources).

Developing the Speech

Although topics vary widely, there is a uniform organization and precise order of the components in all speeches—the introduction, body, and conclusion. A proper speech must follow this sequence; however, this is not necessarily the order in which you will prepare it. After you have identified the topic, the next step is to create a *statement of purpose*, which will clarify the objective of the speech or the information the audience should receive. The purpose statement also helps to give focus to the development of the talk. Before you begin writing, it is necessary to know the level of familiarity your audience has with the topic and plan the information to be presented accordingly. For example, if the audience has little or no knowledge of the topic, the speaker may need to spend time providing definitions or modifying technical language so that it is readily understood. Alternatively, if the audience presents with a specific level of knowledge of the topic, it would be wasting time, and possibly insulting, to define or explain professional terms.

To write the body of the speech, it is necessary to identify the *main points*, or major subdivisions, and organize them in a logical sequence. There may be subpoints to the main ones, and there must be support provided for each main point, which is essentially the "filling" of the speech. Forms of support may be reported by the speaker by providing examples, references, or statistics, presented visually by tables, figures, or other images, or in audio-video format. It is helpful first to organize the main points, sub-points, and supporting points in the form of an outline (see below).

When the body of the speech has been created, the introduction should be written. Depending on the nature of the presentation and whether there are preceding introductory remarks given by another, the introduction serves to direct the audience to the topic, relate the main points, and motivate listening. The introduction should be brief and should set the tone for what is to come. For reasons similar in importance to making a good first impression, experienced speakers attempt to create an attention-grabbing start. Several strategies may be used to stimulate listeners, such as presenting an analogy, question, quotation, or statement, or humor in the form of a short story or joke. It is important to note that not all strategies work on every occasion, and an introduction must be chosen carefully so that it is appropriate for the nature of the topic, composition of the audience, and comfort level of the speaker.

Finally, the conclusion of the presentation should be prepared. The goal is to end the talk by concisely summarizing the main points as reinforcement of the message and providing final thoughts or suggestions. New information should not be added in this section. Similar to the introduction, the strategies for gaining audience attention may also be used in ending remarks.

Outlining the Presentation

Using an outline for the speech is helpful in two ways. First, the outline is used in the development stage to help the speaker organize the body of the speech. This outline, using complete sentences, serves to define the main, sub-, and supporting points and assists the writer in keeping on track with the topic. Additionally, during the presentation the complete sentence outline can be reduced to a *topic outline* using key words or phrases, which can serve as a visual display to guide the speaker and the audience through the speech.

A common outline style is known as the Harvard outline format, which alternates indented numbers with letters to distinguish main points from supporting points (as many as needed), with at least two at each level (O'Hair, Friedrich, Wiemann, & Wiemann, 1997). From general to specific, the outline uses uppercase Roman numerals, followed by indented capital letters, Arabic numbers, lowercase letters, and lowercase Roman numerals. This style is based on the idea that breaking something results in at least two pieces. For example, supporting a main point requires that there be at least two subpoints, as follows:

I. First main point
  A. First subpoint
    1. First support point
      a. First sub-support point
        i. First sub-sub-support point
        ii. Second sub-sub-support point
      b. Second sub-support point
    2. Second support point
  B. Second subpoint
II. Second main point

After the speech has been written in its entirety, a speaker may find it additionally helpful to create a *speaker's outline*, by writing key words and phrases onto index cards that can be referred to during the speech. The goal of writing the speech is to allow you to set out the complete points of information that you wish to convey. Your goal should be not to read the speech word for word, but to know it so well that you can relay it by referring to abbreviated segments projected on screen or printed onto notes.

Delivering the Oral Presentation

Computer-Generated Presentations

Visual aids such as graphics in the form of charts, diagrams, graphs, photographs, or tables, tangible items such as objects or models, and text are extremely effective in strengthening an oral presentation. Research indicates that information presented orally together with visual support is retained longer by listeners (APS, 2011; OSHA, 1996). Today, with the wide acceptance and availability of computers in personal, educational, and professional use, the computer-generated presentation (a visual counterpart to the speech) is recognized as a standard presentational form.

In this type of presentation, computer-generated or imported images or text are arranged onto individual slides of information created onto a background selected from a variety of color and layout schemes, which are saved into a file. Additionally, audio and video clips can be downloaded from cameras, movies, or other multi-media to be incorporated into the slides. Several software programs are available that provide users with the tools to create computer-generated presentations, the most popular of which is PowerPoint.

The visual presentation uses a computer interfaced with a video projector to display the slides of information on a screen viewed by the audience and is typically accompanied by an oral narration. A handout of the presentation slides can also be provided, giving listeners a tangible, additional visual aid to follow and take notes on during the presentation. For a PowerPoint handout, we recommend using a layout of three slides on the left side of the page, with lines for note-taking on the right side.

Creating Computer-Generated Presentations

Among the more frustrating experiences for students, as well as graduates attending professional presentations, is the computer-generated presentation characterized by:

the presenter reading the slides to you;

slides with so much information that you can't focus on what the presenter is saying, much less get through it all before it clicks ahead;

images or texts that are not clearly or easily seen from far seating;

"bells and whistles" in the form of animation and sound effects that fail to mask a presentation devoid of content or interest, or so many effects that they distract attention from the speaker.

The journal *Computers & Graphics* presents research on cutting edge technology, including virtual reality. Here are a few rules for preparing your computer-generated presentation (Preim & Saalfeld, 2018; Zarefsky, 2002):

1. Use color to contrast the slide background with text to make the slides interesting, or to add emphasis by highlighting key sections of text or images. Keep the color schemes and background layout similar throughout the presentation for uniformity and keep it simple; too much color can create a busy-looking slide.
2. Refer to the information on the slide, but never read it to your audience.
3. Try for a limit of seven words per line and seven lines per slide; use bulleted sentences or phrases to separate thoughts.
4. Verify that images are not distorted when enlarged and that graphs or tables are clearly labeled. Use basic fonts (avoid using "fancy" fonts such as script or decorative types or all capitalized letters in text, as they are visually more difficult to read) and use large font sizes for text to ensure visibility from a distance, e.g., title: 44 point type, subtitle: 32 point type, text: 28 point type.
5. Use pictures, cartoons, jokes, racing car noises, and other "enhancements" sparingly, so that their effect will be magnified when you do use them. Remember that animation and sound may not work on a computer with a different operating system than the one you used to program your presentation, so plan accordingly. Make sure to reference all copied or downloaded materials.

Factors in Effective Speech Delivery

In addition to thorough content and knowledge of the topic, vocal and physical characteristics and self-confidence in the speaker will affect audience attention, interest, and perception of the speaker's credibility, and therefore must be considered for an effective speech delivery.

Listeners will judge the *quality* of the speaker's voice in terms of tone (e.g., nasal, harsh, melodic, etc.) and manner (arrogant, bored, excited). Speaking with enthusiasm is contagious; if you radiate energy, your audience will likely be more interested and responsive to the topic. The *intelligibility* of the speaker's voice, the extent to which the spoken message is heard and understood, is defined by aspects such as appropriate vocal rate, volume, articulation, correct use of pronunciation and grammar, and limited use of fillers (e.g., "uh," "um," "like," "ok," etc.) and pauses. *Vocal variation*, such as altering pitch, rate, or volume, and pausing at appropriate points in the speech can add emphasis to a particular word or thought and assists in avoiding a monotonous, boring delivery.

Physical or nonverbal aspects of the speaker such as appearance, eye contact, facial expressions, and gestures are equally important to a successful presentation. Attire and grooming should be appropriate for the audience or may create distraction or loss of speaker credibility. Although tasteful "student apparel" may be suitable for speaking in front of classmates, professional wear is proper for more formal presentations. Direct eye contact with audience members is likely the most important of the physical characteristics of speech delivery. As in interpersonal communication, looking at individual members of the audience while speaking helps to maintain attention and create connections with the listeners. Varying facial expressions and gestures with the head, arms, and hands can add emphasis or further define the spoken message, in addition to enlivening what would otherwise be a statue-like presenter.

Surveys show that the top fear reported by Americans—even greater than the fear of dying —is public speaking (Bovee, 2001).

Self-confidence and maintaining poise through the delivery are key qualities for an effective speaker and are most influenced by anxiety issues. Almost everyone, including the most experienced speaker, is likely to feel some form of nervousness before speaking publicly. It is reassuring to know that you are not alone in feeling this type of discomfort. Understanding the cause and knowing the symptoms of public speaking anxiety can help you deal with it in a positive way.

Fears of inadequacy (in physical appearance or knowledge), of stating incorrect information, of criticism by the audience, or of something "going wrong" during the presentation are typical causes of apprehension when speaking in front of others. A variety of physical symptoms may be experienced by the speaker who is apprehensive, some of which may or may not be apparent to listeners: accelerated heart beat, queasiness, stomach "butterflies," sweating, flushing of the face, dryness of the mouth, heavy breathing, excessive swallowing or clearing of the throat; speech that is rapid, shaky, low in volume, or monotonous; disfluent speech such as stuttering, blocking, pausing inappropriately, or excessively using fillers; restricted head or body movement, lack of hand or arm gestures, pacing, wringing of hands, tapping of fingers; and lack of eye contact.

Speech anxiety will be a likely occurrence, so it is useful to learn strategies to help control the effects.

Preparation

A common cause of speech apprehension is the fear of unanticipated situations that may arise during the presentation. Being prepared for the environment in which the speech is to take place and for possible mishaps during the delivery will help alleviate this concern. If possible, it is very helpful to view the room in which you will be speaking beforehand to familiarize yourself with the physical aspects of the room setting such as size, lighting, the speaking location, and placement of audiovisual equipment. It is very unsettling to think that a technical problem may make a computer-generated presentation undeliverable after all the effort put into the preparation. Make sure you are familiar with the equipment to be used and that you can quickly summon technical assistance if a problem arises. Although it is unlikely, be prepared for the possibility of a complete equipment malfunction and the need to deliver the speech without audiovisual assistance. For this scenario, bring a complete copy of the slides from the computer-generated presentation as your reference. If isolated audio or video segments fail without resolution of the problem, you can summarize the content to the audience or have substitute material ready. Send your computer-generated presentation to yourself in an email attachment, so that you have a backup if your disk or flash drive is lost or malfunctions. Also, arrive early and install your presentation onto the desktop of the computer, as both access to and advancing/reversing your slides will be faster.

Practice

This is probably the most significant aspect of speech preparation in terms of strengthening and polishing the delivery. A bonus is that practice leads to familiarity and comfort with the presentation, building confidence that can help to reduce stress. Although there is no magic number as to how many times you should practice, do so until you have learned and can speak unassisted about the main components of the presentation. Ways to practice include speaking the presentation alone quietly or aloud, in front of a mirror or small audience of friends or family, or videotaping and then viewing yourself. Most importantly, be sure to practice on any equipment to be used so that you are sure of the operation and compatibility of any special effects that you plan to use.

Confidence

Don't underestimate the power of positive thinking. If you are prepared and have practiced your speech, you have every reason to believe you will deliver a good one. Also, remember that if you do feel nervous, most often audience members will not notice, so relax.

Tips for Delivering the Speech

Be confident and enthusiastic. A positive attitude and energetic tone will *motivate the audience to listen.*

Speak clearly. Make sure you are not speaking rapidly and that your vocal volume is appropriate. If a microphone is used, check that it is working and not producing a booming or distorted sound.

Dress and groom appropriately. "Clinic dress" is a good rule of thumb. You want your audience to listen to you, not to be distracted by your outfit, hairstyle, or accessories.

Establish eye contact with the audience. This shows that you are confident and are welcoming your audience to listen. Try to vary your eye contact among different listeners rather than focusing on the same few individuals.

Use facial expressions and body gestures. Avoid being stiff; being animated maintains the audience's attention and can add emphasis to your statements.

Don't read the presentation or information projected onto slides. You should be able to talk comfortably about the material in your presentation when prompted by a main or subpoint listed on index cards or on computer-projected slides. The spoken text is more casual and informal than written text. In oral presentation it is appropriate to use the first-person pronouns *I*, *we*, and *you*, rather than *the speaker* and *the audience*. Spoken presentation is more redundant, and generally has shorter sentences than written text.

Sample Computer-Generated Presentation

Following is the introduction to an all-day symposium, delivered by the first author. The slide is followed by the oral text, which is roughly equivalent to the extemporaneous presentation. A reminder, in the form of XX, is used to indicate that it is necessary to move forward to the next slide. (Begin with Figure 7–1.)

Welcome to the symposium. Some preliminary announcements: XX (Figure 7–2).

1. Make sure you have Continuing Education forms if you want ASHA CEUs. Partial credit (0.3 CEUs) will be available for those attending only the morning or afternoon session.
2. Lunch break from 12:30 to 2:00. There is a restaurant list on the registration desk. Coffee and snacks are available on this level at 365 Express.
3. There is a display case of historical books on stuttering and original letters from Wendell Johnson and others in the

Symposium on Ethics and The Tudor Study: Implications for Research in Stuttering

Friday, December 13, 2XXX
Baisley Powell Elebash Recital Hall
The Graduate Center, CUNY

Figure 7–1. Sample PowerPoint™ slide 1.

registration area, thanks to Prof. Emeritus Robert Rieber.

4. Restrooms are located in the back of the hall.

5. There are microphones on stands on both sides of the room. We will invite you to ask questions after each presentation, as time permits. XX (Figure 7–3)

Announcements

- ASHA CEUS (0.3)
- lunch break from 12:30–2:00
- display case on stuttering in registration area
- rest rooms located in the back of the hall
- questions welcome !!

Figure 7–2. Sample PowerPoint™ slide 2.

SPONSORS

- Ph.D. Program in Speech and Hearing Sciences, The Graduate Center, CUNY
- Continuing Education and Public Programs, The Graduate Center, CUNY
- The Malcolm Fraser Foundation
- Lehman College, CUNY (for CEUs)

Figure 7–3. Sample PowerPoint™ slide 3.

We are grateful to our sponsors for supporting this symposium. Please let me know at the break if you would like more information about our PhD program.

It is tempting and dangerous in a conference dealing with ethics to seize the moral high ground. XX (Figure 7–4)

Cicero warns us about the dangers of hubris. It is probably better if we think of this symposium more as an academic exercise than as a forum to respond to all the ethical issues posed by the Tudor study. That said, we will be looking in detail at Wendell Johnson's diagnosogenic or semantogenic theory, which most of us learned in our undergraduate study.

The theoretical physicist Stephen Hawking, who as you may know suffers from ALS and severe dysarthria, proposed a definition of a good theory. XX (Figure 7–5)

If the predictions agree with the observations, the theory survives that test, though it can never be proven to be correct. On the other hand, if the observations disagree with the predictions, we have to discard or modify the theory. XX (Figure 7–6)

If we think of theories as somewhat sacred, the reality of those charged with testing them is rather more profane.

We are about to begin a critical review not only of the Tudor study, which is, after all, no more or less than a 63-year-old master's thesis, but also a critical look at the issues of diagnosis in stuttering and ethics in scientific research.

Notes:

1. Simple slide design and color scheme, uniform throughout the presentation.
2. Minimal use of images to complement the slide text.
3. Use of short phrases with few lines of text per slide; thoughts separated by use of bullets, line spacing, or contrasted font sizing.
4. Text information on the slide was referred to, but not read verbatim in the oral presentation.

Professional Presentations

There are three ways to present research at our local, state, and national (ASHA) conventions: poster session, platform session, and short course. All three types are described here, with supplementary materials available on the website (http://www.pluralpublishing.com/pwslpa3).

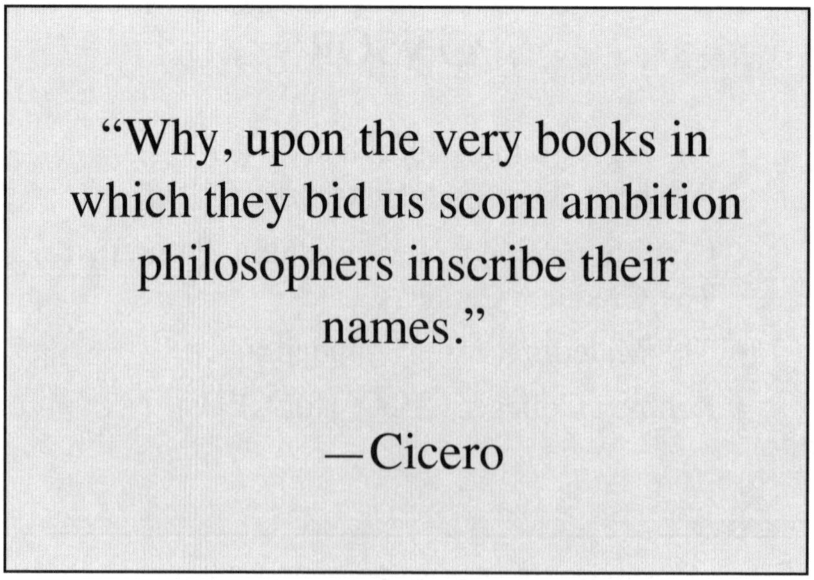

"Why, upon the very books in which they bid us scorn ambition philosophers inscribe their names."

—Cicero

Figure 7–4. Sample PowerPoint™ slide 4.

Stephen Hawking's definition of a good theory

- Describe a large range of phenomena on the basis of a few simple postulates.
- Make definite predictions that can be tested.

Figure 7–5. Sample PowerPoint™ slide 5.

"(At least, that is what is supposed to happen. In practice, people often question the accuracy of the observations and the reliability and moral character of those making the observations.)"

Hawking, S. *The universe in a nutshell*. New York: Bantam, p. 31

Figure 7–6. Sample PowerPoint™ slide 6.

I. The Poster Presentation

The poster session is a popular format for student presentations, although many seasoned professionals also prefer it. The presenter prepares a large poster (convention instructions for submitting posters indicate size limits) and remains by the poster for an hour or so while visitors stop by for Q & A and informal chats. A well-done poster usually should be organized in research paper style, with enough visual interest in the form of graphs, figures, and tables to attract the eye of the visitor. Experimental research should be displayed, generally, as follows:

Top of poster, centered

1. Author's name and professional affiliation or sponsor of research
2. Title of poster
3. Name of professional association (e.g., American Speech-Language-Hearing Association); city, state, country (if international); date of presentation

Top left side of poster

1. Explanation in first sentence of the purpose of the study
2. Brief review of relevant literature
3. Research questions or hypotheses

Bottom left, center, top right

1. Description of participants
2. Materials
3. Procedures
4. Results

Bottom right side of poster

1. Conclusions
2. Discussion
3. Clinical implications
4. References

Wherever appropriate, but centered is best

1. Graphs
2. Figures
3. Table

Figures 7–7 and 7–8 provide samples of posters used in presentations.

II. The Platform Presentation

The platform presentation generally runs from 15 minutes to one hour. The basic rules for use of PowerPoint or other electronic visual aids apply:

1. Don't read the slide.
2. Limit words on the slide (in general, use no more than 25 words).
3. If you read from a manuscript that corresponds to slides, cue yourself (e.g., "comment") to encourage spontaneity.

III. The Short Course

Conventions offer short courses for professionals and students who hope to gain detailed information about a topic of interest. They also provide professionals with an opportunity to earn continuing education credits. The PowerPoint on Ethics on the website at https://www.asha.org/policy/ET2016-00342/ would be of interest to professionals interested in the areas of fluency and professional practice in speech-language pathology and to students taking graduate courses in research methods and fluency disorders.

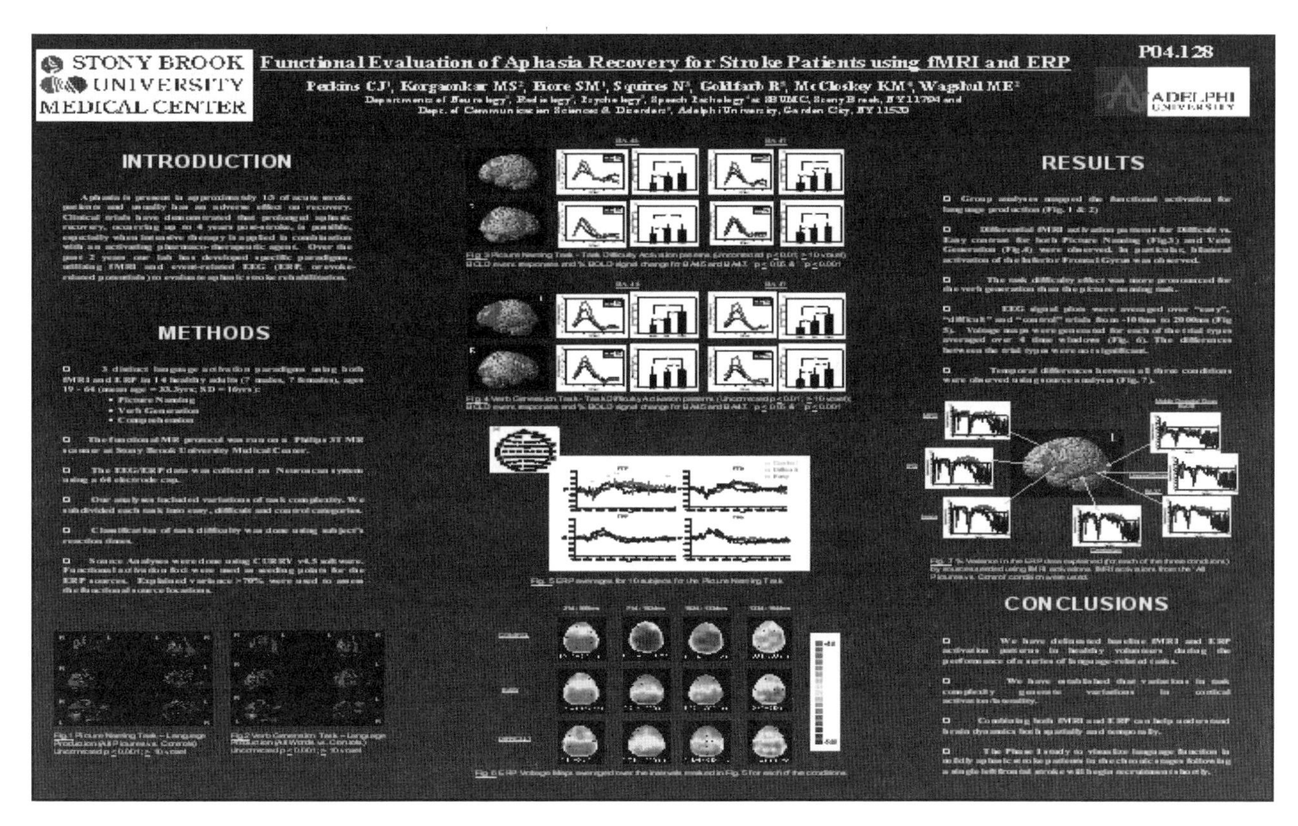

Figure 7–7. Sample speech-language pathology poster.

Auditory Function Following Aerobic Exercise and Music Listening

Authors: Brenna Bynum, B.S. & Yula Serpanos, Ph.D.

Long Island Au.D. Consortium

AAA, San Diego, CA, April 2XXX

BACKGROUND

Hearing acuity may be temporarily reduced following exposure to high level noise, and the physiological effects that occur during exercise may enhance this effect. There is limited research and no consensus in the literature as to whether listening to music during exercise enhances a noise-induced temporary threshold shift (NITTS). [1,3]

In recent years the term music-induced hearing loss has been used to refer to the noise-induced hearing loss resulting from listening to excessively loud levels of music. Both noise- and music-induced hearing loss are characterized by a sensorineural hearing loss (notch) in the 4000 to 6000Hz region on an audiogram. [2,5]

The hair cells in the cochlea are particularly dependent on oxygen. Acute cardiovascular responses to exercise in combination with noise may deplete the oxygen supply to the cochlea.

During physical exercise, such as in occupational or recreational (exercise) activities there is a decrease in circulation to the stria vascularis of the inner ear, which is associated with hemodynamic (blood movement) shifts caused by changes in heart rate associated with exercise. [1,4]

Yokoyama, Osaka, and Yamamoto, (1974) [6] found the growth of NITTS is caused by the effects of noise on the blood circulation in the inner ear, specifically the organ of Corti, or the structure of the walls of the blood vessels.

With cardiovascular changes that occur during aerobic exercise it has been suggested that the cochlea may be more susceptible to NITTS during simultaneous music listening, perhaps by depleting the oxygen supply to the cochlea. [1,4]

PURPOSE

Given the prevalence of exercise and simultaneous music listening in present society and the potential effect on hearing, further studies are needed to determine the NITTS effects in the various forms of exercise and music listening.

The purpose of this study is to determine the auditory effects of moderate intensity aerobic exercise while listening to a typical, high-level of music that is typically played during a professional aerobics exercise class.

METHODS

Participants

Five female and five male volunteers in good cardiovascular health with no previous history of hearing loss or middle ear disease served as participants.

Procedures

Pure tone hearing thresholds (.5, 1, 2, 3, 4, 6, 8 kHz) and distortion product otoacoustic emissions (DPOAEs) (2, 3, 4 kHz) were tested on each participant before and after each of two experimental conditions, while listening to a typical high-level music as played in an aerobics studio for a period of 30 minutes:

Condition 1: at rest in a seated comfortable position.

Condition 2: while performing a moderate intensity aerobic exercise routine at a 70-80% maximum heart rate as determined by cardiovascular intensity measures using a heart rate monitor.

REFERENCES

1. Alessio & Hutchinson (1991).
2. Chesky (2008).
3. Feuerstein (2002).
4. Manninen (1984).
5. Santos, Morata, Jacob, Albizu, Marques, & Paini (2007).
6. Yokoyama, T., Osaka, S., Yamamoto, K. (1974).

RESULTS

Average music levels of 79.7 dBA (Condition 1) and 79.85 dBA (Condition 2) were recorded at the ear level of participants. A two-way ANOVA revealed no significant differences in the pure tone thresholds of the right [$F(1,139) = 0.19$, $p = 0.66$] or left ears [$F(1,139) = 0.79$, $p = 0.38$], or the DPOAE amplitudes of the right [$F(1,59) = 0.26$, $p = .61$] or left ears [$F(1,59) = 1.4$, $p = .24$] between Condition 1 and 2.

DPOAE RESULTS

	CONDITION 1						CONDITION 2					
	R			L			R			L		
Subj #	2k	3k	4k	2k	3k	4k	2k	3k	4k	2k	3k	4k
1	18.6	17	15	10	6.1	8	23	16	10	8.2	5.2	4.8
2	8.7	8.1	10	13	9.3	11	11	3.6	5.8	7.1	7.7	8.1
3	3.7	12	15	18	14	18	13	8	8.2	9.2	18	8.3
4	16.4	17	15	20	7	13	13	19	12	17	13	11.6
5	14.6	14	6.8	16	6.3	9.1	14	13	15	8.4	11	6.2
6	9.1	5.6	6.2	12	6.1	11	1.9	3.2	6.1	11	5.8	11.7
7	4.5	6.8	7.2	4.6	11	18	4.5	6	6	4.9	12	14.9
8	18.8	23	11	18	15	10	18	25	9.3	16	13	12.3
9	2.2	12	17	6.5	0.6	17	6.6	0.6	17	12	16	12.6
10	13.4	8.7	9	7.3	9.2	13	13	8	8.6	6.1	8.1	10.2

CONCLUSION

- Outcomes revealed no significant differences between the pure tone thresholds or DPOAE amplitudes of participants listening to high-level (~80 dBA) free-field music as measured in a seated (resting) position (Condition 1) and while performing moderate intensity aerobic exercise (Condition 2).
- The results of this study suggest that listening to free-field high-level music during moderate intensity aerobic exercise, at least for a 1 hour duration, may not affect auditory function.

Figure 7–8. Sample audiology poster.

EXERCISES

Exercise 7–1. Chapter Review

1. Which of the following is *not* one of the four methods of delivery of oral presentations?
   a. impromptu
   b. choral
   c. memorized
   d. manuscript
   e. extemporaneous

2. The research involved in oral presentation:
   a. is the same for all types of speeches.
   b. does not require a reference list.
   c. has looser rules for ethics and plagiarism.
   d. should follow the same guidelines used in the writing of a research paper.
   e. should not contain too many facts, which may be boring to the listener.

3. In developing a speech:
   a. prepare the introduction, body, and conclusion in that order, because that is the order of presentation of the speech.
   b. identify the *main points*, or major subdivisions, and organize them in a logical sequence for the introduction.
   c. prepare forms of support by providing examples, references, or statistics, presented visually by tables, figures, or other images or in audio-video format.
   d. always start with humor in the form of a short story or joke, as the main purpose of the introduction is to gain the attention of the audience.
   e. conclude by saying, "The end" or "That's it," so the audience knows you are finished.

4. In outlining the presentation:
   a. use sentence fragments in preparing and delivering the speech.
   b. supporting a main point requires that there be at least two subpoints.
   c. create a *speaker's outline*, using complete sentences.
   d. use a Harvard outline, alternating Roman numerals and Arabic numbers.
   e. use only main points and subpoints, because more detail will be too hard to follow.

5. In delivering the oral presentation:
   a. always use computer-generated stimuli.
   b. read the information on the PowerPoint (or other software program) slide.
   c. keep the number of words per slide at 100 or fewer.
   d. use as many "bells and whistles" in the form of animation and sound effects as possible, to maintain the audience's attention.
   e. refer to the information on the slide, but never read it to your audience.

6. The following outline is an example of:

   I. First main point
      A. First subpoint
         1. First support point
            a. First sub-support point
               i. First sub-sub-support point
               ii. Second sub-sub-support point
            b. Second sub-support point
         2. Second support point
      B. Second subpoint
   II. Second main point

   a. a topic outline.
   b. a Harvard outline.
   c. a teacher's outline.
   d. a speaker's outline.
   e. a graded outline.

7. To deliver a speech effectively, be sure to follow this rule:
   a. Wear heels and hose (ladies) or jackets and ties (gentlemen).
   b. Keep facial expressions and gestures to a minimum.
   c. Visualize everyone in the audience in their underwear.
   d. Make direct eye contact with audience members.
   e. Limit variation in vocal pitch, rate, and volume.

8. In creating and presenting computer-generated presentations:
   a. read the slides aloud, so that the audience will not miss important points.
   b. use as many animations and sounds as you can to sustain audience interest.
   c. aim for between 50–100 words per slide.
   d. insert pictures, jokes, and cartoons often to sustain audience interest.
   e. ensure images and texts are clear and easily seen from far seating.

9. Which of the following is likely to lead to speech apprehension?
   a. Viewing the room in which you will be speaking beforehand
   b. Having substitute material in case of audiovisual malfunction
   c. Sending the computer-generated presentation to yourself in an email attachment before the presentation
   d. Not being told where technical assistance can be found if a problem arises
   e. Being familiar with the size, lighting, and speaking location in the room

10. What is a good tip for delivering a speech?
    a. Speak clearly.
    b. Don't be too confident.
    c. Don't be enthusiastic.
    d. Be animated without using gestures.
    e. Understand that spoken text is the same as written text.

Exercise 7–2. Create Your Own Poster

Use the poster template and presentation information contained in the website at http://www.pluralpublishing.com/pwslpa3 to create your own poster, either with your own information or with the information provided. Copy the text and table and then paste and arrange it to conform to the organizational structure for posters outlined in Section I above. Modify the layout, headings, and so forth, as needed.

Exercise 7–3. Review and Practice Delivery of a Platform Presentation

Upload the presentations for Speech-Language Pathology and Audiology on the website.

There are two platform presentations contained on the website at http://www.pluralpublishing.com/pwslpa3, one each from speech-language pathology and audiology. Please upload the presentations, and review and compare with the organizational recommendations above. Choose one to practice delivery of a platform presentation.

A. Platform Presentation in Speech-Language Pathology: "What Nouns and Verbs Say: Neurotypical and Disordered Adult Brains." Goldfarb, R. ASHA Convention, November 2XXX, New Orleans.

Following is the manuscript for a recent one-hour platform presentation at ASHA. Please upload the PowerPoint of the same title from the website at http://www.asha.org/Events/convention/handouts/2009/1784_Goldfarb_Robert/ to compare the manuscript with the slides.

"He saw her slip on the floor." Did you think he saw her fall, or that he saw her petticoat? (SLIDES 3–4; COMMENT ON 4–5) This presentation will focus on our recent studies, using noun-verb ambiguity tasks, with typical adults ages 50 to 80, adults with fluent and non-fluent aphasia, and adults with chronic undifferentiated schizophrenia. Results address localizationist, neurolinguistic, and psycholinguistic theories. Finally, the results provide evidence for differential diagnosis of adults with neurogenic communication disorders. (TEST AUDIENCE ON SLIDES 7–19)

The distinction between nouns and verbs is a fundamental property of human language, beginning with acquisition, demonstrated in normal usage, and often revealed in language breakdown. Neurologic studies indicate that there are different anatomic substrates for nouns and for verbs. There may be separate neural systems for the different categories, the temporal lobe for nouns, the frontal lobe for verbs. (SLIDE 20)

The disparity between the two grammatical classes is clearly displayed in English homonyms, where the same word can serve as both noun and verb, depending on context. In this subset is another dichotomy, systematic versus unsystematic homographs. In systematic homographs, the noun/verb connection is transparent: "to kiss" [verb]/"the kiss" [noun]); unsystematic homographs have no apparent connection between noun and verb forms: squash/squash (action and vegetable) or steer/steer (action and animal). With systematic homographs, both forms, noun and verb, may be stored as a unit. In an alternative model for unsystematic homographs, the verb meaning and the noun meaning of a homograph are stored separately.

As frequency of occurrence has been repeatedly demonstrated to be a robust variable in lexical ambiguity tasks, there were an equal proportion of N < V, N > V, and N = V stimuli.

(SLIDES 21–24) Two competing psycholinguistic theories on decoding lexical ambiguity relate to context and frequency of occurrence (COMMENT). (SLIDES 25–26) Neurolinguistic evidence suggests that there might be different storage of noun-verb homographs based on systematicity (COMMENT). (SLIDES 27–28) In several studies, frequency of occurrence has been shown to be the most robust of word characteristics (COMMENT).

(SLIDES 29–31) Now let's talk about some areas of the brain that are involved in resolving lexical ambiguity (COMMENT)

(SLIDES 32–40) Some of our research has involved neural imaging techniques, including fMRI and ERP (DESCRIBE; COMMENT ON STRENGTHS AND WEAKNESSES; HIGHLIGHT "BRAINS VS. VEINS")

(SLIDES 38–39) For neurotypical adults, group analyses revealed differential fMRI activation patterns for difficult vs. easy contrast for both picture naming and verb generation. In particular, bilateral activation of the inferior frontal gyrus was observed. EEG signal plots were averaged over "easy," "difficult," and "control" trials from −100 ms to 900 ms.

Subtraction maps were generated for the difficult-to-easy stimuli. ERP results revealed an early parietal (300 to 400 ms) and late temporal-frontal activation (500 to 600 ms) similar to the fMRI activation patterns observed. (SLIDE 41) Based on the putative frontal lobe storage for verbs and temporal lobe storage for nouns, the prediction was that those individuals with nonfluent aphasia would overselect the noun form of the homograph, and that those with fluent aphasia would overselect the verb form.

Now let's review what we know about nouns and verbs (COMMENT ON SLIDES 42 to 44). We compared adults with fluent (n = 15) and nonfluent (n = 16) aphasia, as well as other groups of adults (SLIDE 45). Tasks included ambiguous words in phrases (e.g., Time: the race, to relax) (SLIDE 46); sentences (e.g, Stoop: We stoop in the doorway./We sit on the stoop) (SLIDE 46); and in an ambiguous sentence (e.g., Flag: The coach saw her flag at the finish line) (SLIDE 47).

(SLIDES 48–50) Although adults with fluent aphasia were consistent in selecting verb meanings over noun meanings, those adults with nonfluent aphasia were less consistent in selecting noun meanings over verb meanings. The fluent subjects preferred verbs more strongly than the nonfluent subjects rejected them (COMMENT ON SLIDES).

(SLIDE 51) Although adults with aphasia might point to the phrase, "cut of veal" (a noun choice) and say, "Cut the veal" (a verb choice), there were no examples of ambiguity of this type in schizophrenia. Typical adults overselected verbs, but generally followed the pattern of frequency of occurrence. In conversational language, adults use a small number of verbs frequently and a larger number of nouns less frequently.

(SLIDE 52) Regarding individuals with chronic undifferentiated schizophrenia, both frontal deficit and temporal overactivation models predict that there would be an overselection of nouns. Because verbs are a more closed class and nouns a more open class, meaning that fewer verbs are used more frequently than the more numerous nouns, it was predicted that neurotypical adults would overselect the verb form. Findings may contribute to differential diagnosis among adults in these groups. (COMMENT ON SLIDES 53–54).

(SLIDE 55–56) That adults with chronic undifferentiated schizophrenia demonstrated noun preference in ambiguous noun-verb homographs supported the frontal deficit and temporal overactivation models. The design of the study was not adequate to permit differentiation between the two models. Noun preference was stronger than effects of frequency of occurrence and systematicity. Because the experimental group chose more nouns than verbs in all four conditions where N = V, noun preference did not depend on frequency of occurrence. Findings supported the psycholinguistic model of suppression of alternative meanings when one meaning is selected, and did not support the model of selection according to relative meaning frequency. (SLIDES 57–60) Let's close with a look at how this information can be used in differential diagnosis of diagnostically related groups (COMMENT).

Any questions?

B. Platform Presentation in Audiology: "Growth of Loudness Assessment in Children Using Cross-Modality Matching (CMM)." Serpanos, Y., Phonak International Pediatric Conference, November 2XXX, Chicago.

Following is the manuscript for a 20-minute platform presentation at an international conference. Please upload the PowerPoint of the same title from the website at http://www.pluralpublishing.com/pwslpa3, in order to compare the manuscript with the slides.

[SLIDE 2] Loudness judgments serve an important role in the hearing aid selection and fitting process. They can be used to prescribe output levels and to set compression characteristics to avoid loudness discomfort

[SLIDE 3] Loudness judgments may be obtained at discrete points (e.g., levels of comfort/discomfort), or over a range of stimulus levels (e.g. loudness growth curves [functions] where the magnitude of loudness judgments are plotted by stimulus level)

[SLIDE 4] There are several ways in which loudness growth can be measured (i.e., methods of loudness scaling): **magnitude estimation**: use of numbers to scale loudness; **magnitude production**: loudness produced to match number; **categorical scaling**: use of a bounded range of categories (either numbers, words, or pictures); **cross-modality matching (CMM)**: substitution of another sensory modality to judge loudness, for example, vision

[SLIDE 5] Categorical Scaling is the most popular clinical method for assessing loudness growth for purpose of hearing aid fitting. In this procedure, loudness magnitude is matched to one item in a restricted range of categories such as numbers (e.g., 1 to 100); words (e.g., loud, too loud); or pictures (e.g., smiley face to represent a comfortable level, frowning face to represent an uncomfortable level). There are limitations for use in a pediatric population, however: continuum of number to reflect stimulus magnitude is unreliable less than 8 years of age; word descriptors may be problematic for below average language age; recent study on pictorial representation of loudness descriptors showed poor reliability in children with normal hearing, 7 to 12 years (Ellis & Wynne, 1999)

[SLIDE 6] Cross-Modality Matching (CMM) is a psychophysical procedure where loudness is matched to another sensory modality, for example, vision. CMM between visual of line length & loudness is most popular, where loudness magnitude is matched to line length. The psychoacoustic literature supports that with normal hearing, children as young as 4 years can provide reliable matches of loudness to length, similar to adults

[SLIDE 7] Serpanos and Gravel, 2000 conducted a study on CMM between Line Length & Loudness to determine the clinical feasibility, validity and reliability of CMM between loudness and line length in pediatric population. Participants were 16 children, 4 to 12 yrs of age with normal hearing or sensorineural hearing loss.

[SLIDE 8] The procedure was modified from the literature for use with a pediatric population. The visual stimuli were eight graphics of varying line lengths (0.52 to 65 cm; ratio of 125:1) A graphic was chosen to capture the interest of young children (i.e., face of a smiling caterpillar, called "Katie the Caterpillar"). Each graphic of varying line length appeared on separate cards. The acoustic stimuli were narrow bands of noise (NBN) centered at 500 Hz and 2000 Hz, generated by a clinical audiometer (Grason-Stadler 16) and presented monaurally via EAR-3A foam tips to the test ear. One ear was chosen as the test ear; randomized R/L ear selection. Prior to the loudness tasks, a behavioral threshold and a threshold of uncomfortable loudness to the stimuli was obtained for each individual subject. Loudness growth functions were defined separately for 500-Hz and 2000-Hz narrowband noise signals.

[SLIDE 9] Summary of Findings:

Validity: CMM was found to be a valid procedure of assessing loudness in children with normal hearing or sensorineural hearing loss.

Clinical Efficiency: CMM shows potential for clinical efficiency, except for the length of time for task completion. Children seemed to enjoy the task; however, the time to complete the task was lengthy (20 minutes on average to complete one frequency per ear).

Reliability: A subset of adults (n = 4) and children with normal hearing (n = 4) and sensorineural loss (n = 4) were retested 1 month later. Children with normal hearing or sensorineural hearing loss displayed reliable test-retest data; significant correlations were found in all groups.

[SLIDE 10] Recently, Serpanos and Gravel conducted an investigation into a computerized CMM task in order to standardize the generation and presentation of stimuli, and to determine whether test time to complete the task could be reduced. Twenty children with normal hearing, 4 to 9 years of age were tested.

[SLIDES 11–12] Loudness growth functions for the children in the 4 to 6 and 7 to 9 year age groups were similar to those obtained from adults with normal hearing.

[SLIDE 13] The reliability of the procedure was investigated within the same day of testing, and a week after the first test. Each procedure was repeated three times (with breaks as needed) within the same day of testing for children (n = 17) and adults (n = 6). No significant differences were found when loudness functions from run 1 were compared to run 2 and run 3.

A subset of participants was repeated within one week of testing (total n = 11; children: n = 7, adults: n = 4). No significant differences were found when loudness functions from week 1 were compared to week 2.

[SLIDE 14] Computerized CMM Task Summary of Findings:

Validity: As outlined above, the computerized task showed similar loudness growth functions between children (4 to 9 years old) and adults with normal hearing.

Clinical Efficiency: The test time for obtaining a single loudness growth function with the computerized CMM task was half as long compared to the manual method (10 minutes versus 20 minutes, respectively).

Reliability: The computerized CMM task was found to be reliable within the same day of retesting and following a one-week separation.

[SLIDE 15] CMM: Future Studies

Exercise 7–4. The Short Course

Upload sample short course PowerPoint on the website at http://www.pluralpublishing.com/pwslpa3

Individuals attending short courses who desire continuing education credits often are required to write three learning outcomes. These outcomes should be phrased in the active (not passive) voice, avoiding such verbs as "learn," "understand," or "remember" and using such verbs as "treat," "diagnose," or "implement." The presenter of the short course should have listed three similarly phrased course objectives in the course description.

Provide three responses to the following:

After viewing the PowerPoint of the short course on Ethics, I can:

1. ______________________________

2. ______________________________

3. ______________________________

Exercise 7–5. Submit Notes for a PowerPoint Presentation of a Content Area in Speech-Language Pathology or Audiology

The website at http://www.pluralpublishing.com/pwslpa3 includes short PowerPoint stimuli for 5-minute presentations of a content and professional area in speech-language pathology or audiology. Choose one in each area to develop notes for a presentation.

1. "Brain Imaging in SLP"
2. "Pediatric Hearing Tests"

In the spaces below, submit notes for one of the PowerPoint presentations above.

____

____

____

____

____

____

____

____

Exercise 7–6. Submit Notes For a PowerPoint Presentation of a Professional Issues Topic

From the website at http://www.pluralpublishing.com/pwslpa3, choose one of the following topics for in-class practice of a professional issues area:

1. "Council on Academic Accreditation"
2. "Disorientation." We provide an orientation to all entering graduate students, and a review at the end of the program which, according to our language toy, is called a disorientation.

In the spaces below, submit notes for one of the PowerPoint presentations above.

Exercise 7–7. Create a Computer-Generated Slide Presentation

Topic: Anatomy of the Ear

SLIDE 1

The human auditory system is the most complex of our sensory systems. It is composed of five parts; the outer ear, middle ear, inner ear, auditory nerve, and central auditory system.

SLIDE 1

SLIDE 2

The function of the outer ear (OE) is to collect sound waves through air vibrations and transmit them to the middle ear (ME). The major divisions of the OE include the pinna and ear canal.

SLIDE 2

SLIDE 3

The ME transmits sound vibrations from the OE to the inner ear (IE), and overcomes the loss of energy that results when sound passes from an air medium to a fluid medium. The ME is an air-filled space composed of the tympanic membrane, ossicular chain, and eustachian tube.

SLIDE 3

Exercise 7–8. Create a Computer-Generated Slide Presentation

Topic: Hearing Disorders

SLIDE 1

Not all disorders of the ear will necessarily cause hearing loss. Hearing loss depends on the location and extent of the auditory disorder. The audiologist's role is to identify a potential disorder of the ear and to make a referral to a physician for diagnosis.

SLIDE 1

SLIDE 2

Microtia is a malformation of the pinna, which may be congenital or acquired by trauma. This condition in isolation should not cause hearing loss, but it often co-occurs with atresia (malformation of the ear canal) which can cause conductive hearing loss (CHL). Microtia can be treated surgically.

SLIDE 2

SLIDE 3

External otitis is an inflammation of the skin of the OE (ear canal and/or pinna), which can lead to infection. Symptoms may include redness, swelling, itchiness, and pain accompanied by discharge. The cause is bacteria that arise from water trapped in the ear canal, and it therefore is often referred to as "swimmer's ear."

SLIDE 3

Exercise 7–9. Create a Computer-Generated Slide Presentation

Topic: Hearing Aids

SLIDE 1

There are several common removable styles of electronic hearing aids which can be grouped into behind-the-ear (BTE), in-the-ear (ITE), and in-the-canal (CIC).

SLIDE 1

SLIDE 2

Components of electronic hearing aids include the receiver, amplifier, microphone, and battery.

SLIDE 2

SLIDE 3

Device selection is individualized for each patient to include considerations such as the extent of the hearing loss, cosmetic preference, cost, lifestyle, and dexterity.

SLIDE 3

Exercise 7–10. Create a Computer-Generated Slide Presentation

Topic: Types of Hearing Loss

SLIDE 1

Hearing loss can cause difficulty with the detection and/or processing of sound. Hearing loss can be categorized into three types: conductive, sensorineural, or mixed (a combination of conductive and sensorineural).

SLIDE 1

SLIDE 2

Conductive hearing loss (CHL) is caused by disorder in the outer (OE) and/or middle ear (ME). In CHL, there will be detection loss. As there is no effect to the portions of the auditory system beyond the ME, there is no processing difficulty of the signal. CHL is often medically treatable.

SLIDE 2

SLIDE 3

Sensorineural hearing loss (SNHL) is caused by disorder in the sensory (cochlea) or neural (auditory nerve or central auditory pathways) portions of the ear. In SNHL, there will be detection loss often accompanied by auditory processing difficulty. SNHL typically is not medically treatable, but patients may benefit with amplification.

SLIDE 3

References

Association for Psychological Science. (2011, May 28). Miracle fruit and flavor: An experiment performed at APS 2010 [Video file]. Retrieved from http://www.psychologicalscience.org/index.php/publications/observer/obsonline/miracle-fruit-and-flavor-an-experiment-performed-at-aps-2010.html

Bovee, C. L. (2001). *Contemporary public speaking* (2nd ed.). San Diego, CA: Collegiate Press.

O'Hair, D., Friedrich, G. W., Wiemann, J. M., & Wiemann, M. O. (1997). *Competent communication* (2nd ed.). New York, NY: St. Martin's Press.

Preim, B., & Saalfeld, P. (2018). A survey of virtual human anatomy education system. *Computers & Graphics 71,* 132–153

Seiler, W. J., & Beall, M. L. (1999). *Communication: Making connections* (4th ed.). Boston, MA: Allyn & Bacon.

United States Department of Labor. (1996). *Presenting effective presentations with visual aids.* Retrieved from http://www.osha.gov

Zarefsky, D. (2002). *Public speaking: Strategies for success* (3rd ed.). Boston, MA: Allyn & Bacon.

The Diagnostic Report

The diagnostic report represents a comprehensive written account of the clinical assessment/evaluation and serves two general purposes. First, the report is a professional document (and thus a legal document; see discussion below) and written evidence of the clinical service. Second, the diagnostic report is often sent to other professionals involved with the case, as the source of or for referral. As such, diagnostic reports, although they may differ among clinics, are generally written in formal, professional language. We begin this chapter with rules for diagnosis and end with strategies for writing the diagnostic report, with guidelines specific to speech-language pathology or audiology.

Diagnostic Labeling

The New York Times (Carey, 2007) reported a 40-fold increase in the number of American children and adolescents who were treated for bipolar disorder in the decade from 1994 to 2003. Almost certainly, the number has increased further since then. There is little concern about the likelihood of a vast increase in incidence of bipolar disorder, as the consensus is that doctors currently use the diagnosis more aggressively than before. The startling magnitude of the increase in diagnosis intensifies the debate over the validity and reliability of the diagnosis. If the term *bipolar disorder* is applied as a catchall for any child exhibiting explosive or aggressive behaviors, then far too many children are being treated with powerful psychoactive drugs with few demonstrable benefits and many potentially serious side effects.

The field of communication sciences and disorders is hardly exempt from faddish behavior in applying diagnostic labels. The term *cluttering* was widely used in the 1960s and 1970s to describe rapid-fire, indistinct speech with some word-finding difficulty and lack of awareness of difficulty by the speaker. This may be a result of adopting the theories of Deso Weiss (1964), but the term subsequently fell into disuse. It may be reviving currently, in part because of new research efforts (see, for example, St. Louis & Myers, 2007).

Similarly, the term *central auditory processing disorder* (CAPD) has frequently been misused to label individuals, particularly children, who present with listening problems in the absence of apparent hearing loss. Though true CAPD is a deficit of the auditory modality, comparable listening difficulties may be noted in children with attention deficit hyperactivity disorder (ADHD), language impairment, or learning disability, rendering a possible misdiagnosis of CAPD. Following decades of inconsistency on the definition, assessment, and remediation of CAPD, ASHA organized a Task Force on Central Auditory Processing in 1993, which arrived at consensus on the issues (ASHA, 1996; 2005).

Threats to Accurate Diagnosis

Problems in written diagnostic reports may be traced to the following two threats:

- *Polytypicality:* Schwartz (1984) noted shortcomings in the descriptors for aphasia. She noted that adults with aphasia commonly display language characteristics that cross diagnostic boundaries. That is, they are polytypic in nature. It is not unusual for a patient with Broca's aphasia, for example, to have difficulty in auditory comprehension, an impairment listed among the principal diagnostic characteristics of Wernicke's aphasia. As noted in Diagnostic Rule 1 below, it is appropriate to write about the speech, language, and hearing characteristics of the individual, rather than merely assigning a label, especially if the diagnostic category is not obvious.
- *Dumping it in the chocolate:* One of the authors (RG) supported himself through college by working in an ice cream factory. As an interesting aside, he had firsthand experience with homeostasis, or the body's tendency to maintain itself in an essentially healthy state. Alternating half-hour shifts in the ice box, where the temperature was −42°, with half-hour shifts outside, where the temperature was as high as 90° in the summer, his internal temperature stayed at 98.6°. Occasionally, at the end of the workday there was excess ice cream mix. The next day's run would start with chocolate, and the excess mix would be blended in. Chocolate was strong enough in flavor and color to absorb the leftover.

There are frequent instances in our professions where we metaphorically dump the diagnosis in the chocolate (Goldfarb, 2012). Some gratuitous examples occur in the diagnosis of "quirky" children. Catch-all terms begin at birth, where the diagnosis of FLK (for *funny-looking kid*; see Chapter 2) has only recently been discontinued. Children whose language impairment is presented in the absence of other disorders are classified as having *specific language impairment* (SLI). Not so many years ago, *aphasia in children* was the preferred classification. In the Middle Ages, the medical diagnosis for quirky children was *humors of the liver*; more recently, the children were diagnosed with brain fever, minimum brain damage, and minimal cerebral dysfunction. Currently, the chocolate into which these children's problems are dumped is the reticulolimbic complex.

Rules for Diagnosis

Rule 1

Say what the client does, not what the client is. In other words, report behaviors and limit the number of diagnostic labels.

Nobody likes to read an overlong diagnostic report. Efforts at brevity are laudable, and a strategy for summarizing case history information appears later in this chapter. However, a haphazard use of diagnostic labels often does more harm than good. A general application of Rule 1 is to follow any diagnostic label with the phrase, *characterized by* . . . Although this rule may seem similar to the signing statements of a U.S. President, indicating the applications and limitations of a new law (which may or may not be constitutional), the rule addresses the need of school districts and third-party payers for a diagnostic label, and summarizes the areas of deficit to be addressed in therapy.

A diagnostic report is a legal document. In the following trial transcriptions, the first author was employed by the defense as an expert witness, to counteract claims put forth by the plaintiff that were supported by a speech-language pathologist. Although trial transcriptions are a matter of public record, names and identifying information were changed here. Certifying a witness as an expert allows that individual to offer opinions; a witness who is not certified as an expert can offer only facts. Certification as an expert may be based on academic standing (a rank of full professor, not adjunct instructor), publications (which have been peer-reviewed), or experience (many years in positions of high responsibility).

The judge is indicated as *the court*; the first author is *the witness*.

The Court: In your opinion, using these two documents [Exhibit H and Exhibit RR], has Ms. B been misdiagnosed?

The Witness: Yes. Let me give two examples in the speech-language evaluation report where Ms. B was misdiagnosed.

The first diagnostic term that was used in error was *paragrammatism*. That is on page 2. Here we have, "Paragrammatisms and superfluous words were noted in writing and speech." We have as an example that sentence beginning, "Lee Atwater was a tumor."

The definition of paragrammatism is that it occurs in Wernicke's aphasia, and that it is characterized by substitutions of functors. A functor is what might be called a helping word as opposed to a substantive or a lexical word. So under functors we look at things like prepositions, articles, conjunctions, auxiliary verbs. And what I am interpreting here is that the justification for the diagnosis of paragrammatism is the word "was" after "Lee Atwater" when the word should have been "had." "Lee Atwater had a tumor," as opposed to, "Lee Atwater was a tumor."

The problem is that paragrammatism, as I said, occurs in posterior aphasia. There was no evidence and no claim in this diagnostic report that the patient had any kind of posterior aphasia. To the contrary, there is significant evidence that the aphasia was an anterior type, that is, the kind of aphasia that is characterized by halting, effortful speech, by problems with articulation. For example, the apraxias that are referred to do not accompany posterior aphasias or Wernicke's aphasia. These apraxias accompany anterior or Broca's aphasia, as it was referred to here.

So the problem that I see with paragrammatism is that it doesn't belong as a diagnostic classification with this kind of patient.

Furthermore, the one example here, the word "was" which follows "Lee Atwater," was an example of a functor substitution. However, if we can look for a moment at Exhibit RR—I am going to try and find it; this is another large document here—we have an example where a paragrammatism was described—if I don't find it, let me explain it to you—where a paragrammatism was described, and the example given was the substitution of a substantive word rather than a functor word.

What I am saying is that a paragrammatism has to be a grammatical or a syntactic error. The example which had something to do with the organization of the government in the City of New York, I believe it was on 6/8—I am just not getting it here—the example was one of a semantic error rather than a syntactic error.

So the term "paragrammatism" was used incorrectly and was also used to describe a symptom that would occur in a different kind of aphasia.

The other misdiagnosis has to do with, again, going back to Exhibit H, the bottom of page 2: "Impression. Presenting persistent aphasia is Broca and conduction in type." Let me speak to that.

This cannot be. The aphasia cannot be Broca and conduction in type. Broca's aphasia is nonfluent aphasia. Conduction aphasia is fluent aphasia. A person can't be fluent and nonfluent at the same time.

Conduction aphasia is characterized by, among other things, a disproportionately large number of errors in repetition, as opposed to other language modalities tested.

Now, the references to repetition, again in Exhibit H, top of the page, page 2,

"Repetition (sentences) was impaired and variable." Going back, bottom of the page under "Impression," we have "manifested and mildly impaired repetition."

Repetition, according to these notes, even if it was mildly impaired, was not impaired in a disproportionately significant way to other modalities tested.

Furthermore, in Exhibit RR, the first page, dated 5/14, we have a note: "Repetition intact."

The last thing I want to say about conduction aphasia is that classically Broca's area, if Ms. A was following the model of the localizationist, Broca's area is classically associated with the third frontal convolution on the left side of the brain, and Broca's aphasia then would presumably follow a lesion in that area. Conduction aphasia would presumably follow a lesion in the arcuate fasciculus, which is the neural pathway connecting Wernicke's area to Broca's area. There was no evidence and no claim that there was any damage to the arcuate fasciculus.

What I am troubled by is the tendency to form diagnostic categories or label diagnostic categories based on skimpy evidence and done in an illogical manner.

As a final note to Rule 1, all of the above criticisms might have been avoided if the speech-language pathologist, Ms. A, had described the characteristics of Ms. B's language disorder, rather than the labels that she used in error. There is no shame in using the term *nonfluent aphasia* if you are not sure of such terms as *Broca's aphasia*, *conduction aphasia*, or *paragrammatism*. In fact, describing aphasia as nonfluent is probably more useful, because it describes an aspect of the communication disorder that needs to be addressed in therapy.

Rule 2

Be an educated consumer of tests and measures. Although the doctorate is generally seen as the degree associated with the production of research, all audiologists and speech-language pathologists must understand research methodology.

The authors recall discussions with the late Ira Ventry when he was developing ideas for a book on research methods in communication sciences and disorders. The current edition of the book (Orlikoff, Schiavetti, & Metz, 2015) provides the basis for the information that follows.

Reliability means precision of measurement. It is assessed by examining the consistency or stability of a test or measure. *Validity* means generalizability of the data. It means the degree to which a test measures what it purports to measure. It means truth or correctness or reality of measurement. A butcher's scale may consistently and precisely weigh meat at ½ pound over the true or correct weight. It is reliable, but not valid. On the other hand, it is not possible for a test to be valid without being reliable.

There are three ways to check reliability of a test or measurement.

1. *Test-retest reliability:* Completely repeat the test. If the test is repeated with the same client after a latency period (to avoid the practice effect or learning to learn), but within a reasonable period of time (to avoid effects of maturation or spontaneous recovery), the score should be pretty much the same as it was in the first administration of the test.
2. *Parallel or equivalent form:* Examine consistency of the results across the two equivalent forms. These forms are used when testing two different modalities or two different conditions (see, for example, time-altered word association tests by Goldfarb & Halpern, 2013).
3. *Split-half:* Subdivide the test or measure into two equivalent parts (usually odd-even) to examine consistency of these parts. This is similar to parallel or equivalent forms, where one half may be used at the beginning of therapy as a baseline measure, and the other half at the end of therapy for baseline recovery.

Another type of reliability, called inter-rater or interscorer reliability, is used in experimental research, to ensure that there are no significant differences in scores assigned, and is based only on how people score the data.

There are also three ways to establish the validity of a test or measure.

1. *Content validity:* Logically or rationally evaluate items on a test to see how well they reflect what the tester wishes to measure, using subjective procedures.
2. *Criterion validity:* See how well the test or measure correlates with some outside validating criterion. There are two types of criterion validity.
   a. *Concurrent validity:* Administer a test or measure and an outside validating criterion at the same time. For example, the first edition of the *Peabody Picture Vocabulary Test* used an IQ test as a measure of concurrent validity, and indicated an equivalent IQ score based solely on this test of receptive vocabulary. (It no longer has a space to report an IQ score.) A key concept is that an *outside* validating criterion is used. Hildred Schuell (1966, 1973) assessed concurrent validity using two versions of the same test (the short and long forms of the *Minnesota Test for Differential Diagnosis of Aphasia* [MTDDA]), a questionable strategy also used to compare the third and fourth editions of the *Clinical Evaluation of Language Functioning*. However, Schuell determined that the short form of the MTDDA was not valid.
   b. *Predictive validity:* Use a test or measure to predict some future behavior. Administer the test, allow time to elapse, and then administer the criterion measure. For example, use the *Boston Naming Test* (BNT) as a baseline measure and the *Porch Index of Communicative Ability* (PICA) to predict word retrieval following therapy for aphasia, and then give the BNT at the final therapy session. See how the differences in the BNT correspond to the "HOAP slope" (high overall prediction method) predicted on the PICA. Note that IQ tests, such as the *Stanford-Binet* or the *Wechsler Intelligence Scale for Children*, are predictive tests. An IQ score is properly used to predict how well a child may be expected to perform in school.
3. *Construct validity:* Assess the degree to which a test or measure reflects some theory or explanation of the characteristic to be measured. The test or measure should confirm the theory if the test is valid *and* if the theory is correct. For example, a theory might predict that post-stroke and typical adults might use vocabulary differently. If the test or measure confirmed this, then the measure would have construct validity with respect to that aspect of the theory. However, if the theory has been discredited, as has Osgood's notion that language is based on the sum of a set of specific abilities, then no manner of validity in the content of the *Illinois Test of Psycholinguistic Ability* (short of attempting to confirm another theory) will yield construct validity.

Rule 3

Beware of "clinicese." Clients may exhibit behaviors in the clinic that they do not generalize outside of the speech and hearing center.

Young children, particularly those with disfluencies, may present dramatically different patterns of communication disorders, depending on context. For example, a child may stutter more when evaluated by "Dr. Goldfarb," who is wearing a tie and a lab coat, than when "Bob" conducts the same evaluation wearing casual clothing.

Yaruss, LaSalle, and Conture (1998) recommended a three-part evaluation to determine quantitative and qualitative differences in arriving at a diagnosis of stuttering:

1. Conversational interaction between child and caregiver(s) (20 to 30 minutes);
2. Evaluation of the child's speech, language, and related behaviors (60 to 90 minutes); and

3. An interview of the child's caregiver(s) (45 to 60 minutes).

This 3-hour procedure may be unrealistic in many work settings. However, the traditional method of assessing a wide variety of interacting psychosocial, psycholinguistic, and physiologic variables will likely take longer and may not differentiate among children at risk for stuttering.

Yaruss et al. (1998) used measures of speech fluency, measures of speech and language development, and other measures, including the child's diadochokinetic rate and parents' speaking rates to determine presence of a pathological condition. There was still considerable overlap between children recommended for reevaluation and those who received neither treatment nor reevaluation. "It would seem essentially impossible to develop absolute criteria for determining which children should receive which diagnostic recommendation" (Yaruss et al, 1998, p. 72).

Rule 4

Do differential diagnosis when appropriate. Diagnostically related groups (sometimes abbreviated as DRGs) often present similar audiometric and/or language profiles.

Our research has proceeded from the premise that linguistic data can aid in the differential diagnosis of diagnostically related groups. The following case study (Goldfarb, 2006b) illustrates the need for differential diagnosis, and assumes the reader to be a physician, nurse, or social worker at University Hospital:

> An elderly homeless man, identified as Mr. X because he cannot say his name, has been admitted with what the emergency room physician described as "disorganized language." The patient has no identification, no documented medical history, and has not yet had brain imaging studies. You have been asked to determine if the disorganized language represents fluent aphasia, the language of schizophrenia, or the language of dementia.

The patient is referred to a speech-language pathologist at University Hospital. Evaluation of Mr. X's language reveals preservation of prosody, phonology, morphology, and syntax, with disturbances in semantics and pragmatics. This still fits the pattern of the diagnostically related groups of fluent aphasia, the language of Alzheimer and multi-infarct dementia, and the language of chronic undifferentiated schizophrenia.

In a standard diagnostic audiologic evaluation, several subtests within the complete battery of testing provide information on a patient's middle ear and hearing status (degree, configuration, and type of hearing loss). However, several auditory or vestibular pathologies may exhibit similar audiometric profiles, warranting further differential diagnosis before an appropriate treatment plan can be implemented. Characteristics such as a report of sudden hearing loss and dizziness along with audiometric findings of unilateral sensorineural hearing loss and normal middle ear function may be associated with disorders such as Ménière's disease, acoustic neuritis, or acoustic tumor. In this case, the audiologist may need to perform further diagnostic tests such as auditory brainstem response testing (ABR) or electronystagmography (ENG) in order to assist the physician in a medical diagnosis.

Rule 5

Obey the limits of our scope of practice. Provide diagnostic labels that relate to the communicative disorder, not the medical cause.

It is no wonder patients frequently assume audiologists are physicians; given recent changes in ASHA certification standards (Council for Clinical Certification in Audiology and Speech-Language Pathology of the American Speech-Language-Hearing Association, 2007) most now hold the "doctor" title, typically work in a medical setting, and perform many "medical-like" tasks such as otoscopy, ABR, ENG, and cerumen removal. It is also logical that the audiologist, who upon otoscopic examination detects fluid bubbles and redness of the tympanic membrane and finds conductive hearing loss following audiometric testing with reduced tympanometric peak admittance, will conclude *otitis media* as the underlying cause of pathology. Nonetheless, however obvious the disorder, it is not within the audiologist's scope of practice to provide a medical label. Similarly, the speech-language pathologist who evaluates an adult with imprecise articulation, word-finding deficits, and right facial droop may diagnose aphasia and dysarthria, but not the underlying stroke. The role of the communicative disorders specialist, audiologist or speech-language pathologist is to describe and identify the disorder and to refer the patient for medical diagnosis of the cause (in these examples, middle ear pathology and brain damage).

Writing the Diagnostic Report

A generation ago, Dr. Aaron Smith used to highlight his presentations to the Academy of Aphasia by noting that, "The patient doesn't lie." Conversely, the television incarnation of Sherlock Holmes, Dr. Gregory House, tended to tell his Dr. Watson (Dr. Wilson on TV) that the patient always lies. In Dr. House's case the resolution between the received wisdom and the awful truth involved a heavy dose of misogyny as well as breaking and entering, and it took one hour. In Dr. Smith's case, the differences between the patient's language behavior and the population norms described in professional literature were not resolved.

The large-sample studies reported in our journals are essential to provide the theoretical bases for our professions and to permit generalization of the findings to untested populations. However, there are two problems in using clinical data to support or disconfirm hypotheses. The first is that language, speech, and hearing are incredibly complex processes. The underlying basis for the disorder is often debatable, especially in speech-language pathology (see Goldfarb, 2006a, for a description of the atheoretical discipline of stuttering). Our tendency toward reductionism in thinking and writing works better in audiology, which is a more mature science, but is still a reflection of what we may call *physics envy*. Boiling down cascades of data into a more manageable size is typical of the natural sciences, but it does not work very well in the behavioral sciences. The second problem is that clinical data reflect the client's, not the population's language, speech, and hearing. As we have learned in the discussion of diagnostic labeling above, the client's communication disorder may cross typical categorical boundaries, and may be uniquely the individual's own, in terms of type and severity of disorder. That is why we always put the individual first in our descriptions; an individual who stutters, rather than a stutterer. It is also why we must be logical in our report writing.

The Logic of Report Writing

If only fools are kind, Alfie,
Then I guess it's wise to be cruel.

Although Burt Bacharach is to be commended for the excellence of his song writing, his logic is flawed. Beginning with the thesis of "if p, then q," there are four constructions, only two of which are logical. Accordingly,

Statement: if p then q

Converse: if q then p

Inverse: if not p then not q

Contrapositive: if not q then not p

In the *Alfie* song, the logical thesis, which is accepted here for argument's sake, is, *If a person is kind (p), then that person is a fool (q)*. The actual lines of the song represent the inverse of the argument, which is not logical. Examples from our discipline follow.

Thesis: If there is a lesion in Broca's arca (p), then there will be a word retrieval deficit (q). This statement is accepted as logical.

Inverse: If there is not a lesion in Broca's area, then there will not be a word retrieval deficit. This statement is not logical.

Converse: If there is a word retrieval deficit, then there will be a lesion in Broca's area. This statement is not logical.

Contrapositive: If there is not a word retrieval deficit, then there will not be a lesion in Broca's area. This statement is logical.

Curiously, the patient Broca described in 1861 (called Tan or Tant because that was his stereotypic utterance) probably did not have Broca's aphasia. Broca described Tan as having *aphémie*, or aphemia, which corresponds to apraxia of speech, rather than having *aphasie*, the French word that corresponds to aphasia. In addition, Tan's lesion was in the anterior portion of the third frontal convolution in the left hemisphere, rather than the posterior portion described as Broca's area. Damasio (2008) reviewed the case of Tan and concluded that he must have suffered from global aphasia. So Broca's patient didn't have Broca's aphasia, nor did he have a lesion in Broca's area.

The Diagnostic Report Format

Though the specific format and subheadings of the diagnostic report may differ among clinics, most follow a commonly used medical organizational outline known as *SOAP* (S = *subjective*; O = *objective*; A = *assessment*; P = *plan*).

The subjective section (a.k.a. referral, background information, or history) includes the client's biographical information, reason for referral, and relevant developmental (with a pediatric client), medical, and communicative history. The objective part (a.k.a. assessment information; *note*: this term differs from the SOAP definition of assessment; see below) incorporates all the information obtained during the session, including observed behaviors and elicited test procedures and outcomes. The information obtained from the subjective and objective sections is synthesized to formulate a diagnostic statement, often headed in a section entitled, "Clinical Impressions." (In the SOAP format this section is referred to as assessment.) Finally, a plan (a.k.a. recommendations) for treatment, further recommendations, and follow-up are indicated.

Guidelines for Writing Diagnostic Reports in Speech-Language Pathology and Audiology

Writing Aspects

1. Always write in complete, grammatically correct sentences. Use professional books, not a dictionary, to make sure you are using the appropriate terminology and that terms are spelled correctly.
2. Write clearly and present the information accurately.
3. Be concise; state only the relevant information of the case. Reports that are too lengthy will typically not be read thoroughly.

Format

Follow the diagnostic report format of the institution. Although the format may vary according to site, the following specifics are usually considered:

1. Include all section headings (using boldface, underline, and italics as indicated by the institution; see headings below).
2. Adhere to the format regarding positioning, lettering, and underlining of the section headings (e.g., some may be centered, some flush with the left margin; the report title is usually all capitals; section headings may be underlined).
3. Include the names of students (designated as *clinical interns*), as well as the name and credentials of the clinical supervisor.

Sections of the Diagnostic Report

Referral Information[1]

Include full name, age, and gender of client; name of treatment center; referral source; name of person accompanying client to evaluation; name of informant; reliability of informant to provide background information; reason for referral; and statement of problem.

Background Information

Document case history information pertinent to the disorder and appropriate to the client.

For a child:

1. Child's prenatal and birth history, including maternal health; medications during pregnancy, labor, and delivery; length of pregnancy, indicating pre- or post-term; type of delivery (using *C-section* as an abbreviation for cesarean section, but not *SVD* as an abbreviation for spontaneous vaginal delivery); complications; neonatal health.
2. Child's developmental history for motor and speech-language development, indicating if ages of developmental milestones are within normal limits.

For a child or an adult:

1. Child's or adult's medical history, such as pertinent illnesses or injuries, hospitalizations, respiratory infections, allergies, ear infections and how treated, and medications.
2. Other pertinent evaluations and therapies, such as speech-language, audiologic, psychological, and neurologic.
3. Family, social, educational, and occupational history, indicating with whom client resides, primary language spoken if not English, peer relationships, and history of speech, language, hearing, and learning problems in family.

Assessment Information

Include information obtained during the diagnostic session, both observed and measured.

1. Report formal test scores in a table format.
2. Use narrative sections to *describe behaviors*, not to reiterate test scores (see above).

Clinical Impressions

Formulate a diagnostic statement of the problem. Provide a summary of relevant findings from the previous sections of the report, highlighting problem areas, etiology, and prognosis.

1. Do not report new information in this section.
2. Use behaviors and test scores previously reported as evidence to substantiate a diagnosis.

Recommendations

Recommendations may include a plan of treatment, further testing (continuation or follow-up), additional evaluations, and referral to other specialists. List the appropriate recommendations in order of importance. For example, if a medical referral is warranted, that should be indicated first.

Report Drafts

1. *Double-space report drafts* to facilitate editing and correcting by the supervisor.
2. *Maintain client anonymity*. Identify the client only by initials in drafts of reports, whether in email, diskette, compact disc, or hard copy form. Remember that all these

[1]In some report formats, as is typical in audiology, *Referral* and *Background Information* may be combined into a *History* section.

versions contain privileged and confidential information.

3. *Place final drafts of reports*, with the supervisor's signature, in the appropriate tray on the office administrator's desk. Sign in all reports in the log book.

Writing the History

In "Notes for Contributors" for the journal *Aphasiology*, submissions including reports of research with human participants should include the descriptive data identified by Brookshire (1983). These data include the following:

Age	Hemianopia	Lateralization of damage
Type	Hemiparesis	Localization of damage
Sex	Time since onset	Handedness
Mood	Education	Participant source
Severity	Etiology	
Hearing	Natural speaker	
Vision		

These descriptors may not all be relevant to individuals who do not have brain damage, or to children, and the list should be expanded when writing a diagnostic report for an individual with hearing loss.

With so much information recommended, the first part of the diagnostic report can go on for several pages, so it is important to be concise. For example, consider the following summary:

> This 67-year-old, right-handed, English-speaking former construction worker with 12 years of education presented with a history of L CVA (3 mo. post-onset) with resultant R hemiparesis and R homonymous hemianopia. He appeared alert and oriented × 3, wore corrective lenses and bilateral hearing aids, and appeared to be a reliable informant.

Some of the shorthand used, identified in Chapter 2, included *L* and *R* for *left* and *right*, *CVA* for *cerebrovascular accident*, *mo.* for *months*, and *oriented × 3* for *oriented to time, place, and person*. The two sentences (51 words) above provided 17 relevant pieces of case history information:

1. Age (67 years old)
2. Handedness (right-handed)
3. Natural speaker (English-speaking)
4. Previous employment (construction worker)
5. Education (12 years)
6. Medical diagnosis (CVA)
7. Localization of damage (L hemisphere)
8. Time since onset (3 mo.)
9. Lateralization of damage (R side of body)
10. Hemiparesis (present)
11. Hemianopia (present)
12. Sex (male, indicated by "he" to begin the second sentence)
13. Mood (alert)
14. Orientation (oriented to time, place, and person)
15. Vision (corrective lenses)
16. Hearing (bilaterally aided)
17. Reliability of information (reliable informant)

Diagnostic Report Format—Speech and Language

Name

Date of Evaluation

Date of Birth

Age (years: months for age <18)

Address

Address (2nd line)

Telephone Number (Specify home, work, or cell, and include area codes.)

Email

Referral Information

Include full name of client, age, gender, name of treatment center, referral source, name of person accompanying client to evaluation, name of informant, reliability of informant to provide background information, reason for referral, and statement of problem.

Background Information

Document information pertinent to the disorder and appropriate to the client.

For a child:

1. Child's prenatal and birth history, including maternal health; medications during pregnancy, labor, and delivery; length of pregnancy, indicating pre or post-term; type of delivery (using *C-section* as an abbreviation for caesarian section, but not *SVD* as an abbreviation for spontaneous vaginal delivery); complications; neonatal health.
2. Child's developmental history for motor and speech-language development, indicating if ages of developmental milestones are within normal limits.

For a child or an adult:

1. Child's or adult's medical history, such as pertinent illnesses or injuries, hospitalizations, respiratory infections, allergies, ear infections and how treated, and medications.
2. Other pertinent evaluations and therapies, such as speech-language, audiological, psychological, and neurological.
3. Family, social, educational, and occupational history, indicating with whom client resides, primary language spoken if not English, peer relationships, and history of speech, language, hearing, and learning problems in family.

Assessment Information

Write an introductory paragraph, citing behavioral observations, such as willingness to separate from the accompanying person; cooperation and participation during assessment; attention span, eye-gaze, head and trunk orientation; activity level, remembering that *very active* is not the same as *hyperactive*; imitation of motor and speech behaviors, remembering that *echoic* is not the same as *echolalic*; and interaction behaviors.

Formal Testing (in table format)

Name of Test	*Results*
(use italics for test names)	Raw Score Age Equivalent Percentile Rank Standard Score

Pragmatics of Communication

Document form of communication, such as vocal, gestural, graphic; conversational skills, such as initiation, maintenance, elaboration, and termination of discourse topics; body posture and eye contact; turn-taking skills; requesting (action, information, clarification); comprehension/use of indirect requests involving modals, such as, *Would you close the door?*); contextual appropriateness of responses. Document level of demand for creativity, or communicative responsibility, when assessing disfluency.

Language Comprehension

Document responses to *yes-no*, *either-or*, and *wh* questions; vocal and written directives (one-step and multistep, with simple and complex syntax); receptive vocabulary tasks, including sequential, confrontation, and associative naming; and reading comprehension tasks.

Language Production

Assess expressive vocabulary, and differentially diagnose word retrieval impairment from vocabulary deficit; mean length of utterance as a word-morpheme index (the average of number of words plus number of morphemes per utterance, divided by 2, for at least 50 utterances); encoding of questions; syntax of constructions; narrative abilities; and written language skills.

Speech Production

Assess phonetic inventory, including sound substitutions, omissions, and distortions; phonemic inventory, including syllable shapes, and phonological processes used, with examples; overall intelligibility, comprehensibility, and stimulability.

Orofacial Examination and Feeding

If swallowing is not a primary concern, assess diadochokinesis in alternating and sequential motion rate tasks; facial symmetry, structure, and function; response to isometric and counter-resistance tasks for lips, tongue, cheeks, and mandible; tongue bulk and presence of fasciculations; velopharyngeal closure for speech and swallowing; self-feeding of liquids and solids.

If swallowing is a primary concern, assess frequency and percentage of swallowing characteristics on a clinical/bedside instrument such as the 28-item *Northwestern Dysphagia Patient Check Sheet*. Be prepared with liquid, puree, and solid bolus samples; be prepared to refer for videofluoroscopic swallowing evaluation.

Voice and Fluency

If voice and fluency are not primary concerns, report perceptual judgments of fluency, as well as vocal quality, resonance, pitch, and loudness.

If voice is a primary concern, in addition to the perceptual judgments above, report laboratory findings, such as fundamental frequency, maximum phonation time, s/z ratio, vital capacity, phonation quotient, and ability to shift from vegetative breathing to speech breathing. If fluency is a primary concern, in addition to the perceptual judgments above, report types, frequency, duration, and loci of disfluency; part-word and whole-word (or whole-phrase) repetitions; syllables stuttered divided by syllables spoken; secondary or associated behaviors; linguistic and situational behaviors affecting fluency; client's perceptions of fluency; and stimulability to modify fluency.

Cognition and Play

Include play only for young children. Assess parallel play, representative or symbolic play, and cooperative play; object permanence; means-to-an-end causality; conservation of continuous quantity; decentration from color to shape, size, and orientation; and problem-solving skills.

For older children and adults, assess cognitive tempo and cognitive style, and categorize as immediate-accurate, delayed-accurate, immediate-inaccurate, and delayed-inaccurate. Assess primacy (first stimulus) and recency (last stimulus) effects.

Audition

Report results of hearing screening or complete audiological evaluation, as well as response to sound at conversational levels.

Motor Skills

Include assessment of fine and gross motor skills, such as full-fist versus pincer grasp for young children, and writing with the nondominant hand for adults with aphasia poststroke.

Clinical Impressions

Justify your recommendations. Do not present new information in this section, but refer statements to prior assessment sections. Begin with full name of client and diagnosis (e.g., *Jane Doe, age 6:1, presents with a language production disorder, characterized by . . .*). Provide a summary of relevant findings, highlighting problem areas, etiology, and prognosis.

Recommendations

Indicate type (e.g., individual and group), frequency (e.g., three times per week for 9 weeks), and duration (e.g., 45-minute sessions) of therapy, as well as additional evaluations needed (e.g., audiological, psychological, educational). If you recommend speech-language therapy, end this paragraph with, *Initial goals of therapy should include . . .*

Clinical interns
(Names of students participating in evaluation)

Supervisor's name, degree, CCC-SLP

Speech-language pathologist

Institutional title (professor, clinical supervisor)

Diagnostic Protocol Worksheet— Speech and Language

Client's Name

Date of Evaluation

Referral Information

Referral source

Informant

Informant reliability

Reason for concern

Background Information

For a Child

Prenatal and birth history

Speech-language developmental milestones

Motor development milestones

Medical history

For a Child or Adult

Other evaluations

Prior and current therapies

Client resides with

Primary language spoken at home

Family history of speech-language, hearing, learning problems

Educational and occupational information

Peer relationships

Favorite foods, TV shows, activities, best friend

Assessment Information

Behavioral observations

Is today's performance typical?

Pragmatics

Form of communication

Conversational skills

Eye contact and body orientation

Functional use of language

Communicative demand

Language Comprehension

Receptive vocabulary

Response to questions

- Yes-no
- Either-or
- Wh-

Ability to follow directions

- One-step commands
- Multiple-commission commands
- Reading comprehension

Language Production

Expressive vocabulary

Encoding of questions

Content categories

Word-morpheme index for MLU

Morpho-syntactic skills

Word retrieval skills

Narrative abilities

Written language skills

Speech Production

Phonetic inventory

Sound substitutions, omissions, distortions

Phonemic inventory and syllable shapes

Phonological processes and examples

Speech intelligibility and comprehensibility

Stimulability

Orofacial Examination and Feeding

Facial symmetry

Structure of mandible, lips, teeth, tongue, palate, velum

Function of articulators

Diadochokinesis. Alternating motion rate. Sequential motion rate

Feeding for liquids, purees, solids

Drooling, dribbling

Voice

Quality

Resonance

Pitch (or *frequency*, if a laboratory measure)

Loudness (*volume* or *amplitude displacement*, if a laboratory measure)

Fluency

Blocks

Whole-word or phrase

Part-word repetitions prolongations

Associated/secondary mannerisms; Fluency ratio; Linguistic/environmental triggers

Cognition and Play

For a Child

Object permanence

Decentration

Conservation

Means/end

Play skills

Parallel

Representative/symbolic

Cooperative

For an Adult

Imitation skills

Problem solving

Orientation to time, place, person, direction

Cognitive tempo/style

Audition

Testing results

Response to conversational levels

Motor Skills

Fine motor

Gross motor

Use of nondominant hand

Sample of Diagnostic Report Writing in Speech-Language Pathology

Following are professional reports in original (with errors in writing form) and revised versions.

Speech-Language Evaluation Report—Original

Name: J.K. Date of Evaluation: 7/1/18

Date of Birth[1]: 4/1/2004

Address: 123 Fourth Road
Montauk, NY 11954

Telephone: 631-668-8888

Background Information

J.K. is a 14 year old[2] female who was evaluated at the Hy Weinberg Center for Communication Disorders. She was accompanied by her mother,[3] Mary, who served as a reliable informant. Jane reportedly has no significant birth/medical history. Her mother reported that Jane suffered from frequent ear infections the first 2 years[4] of her life. PE tubes were not inserted because antibiotics always resolved the infection. [5]Mary stated that J. did not have any feeding or swallowing difficulties at any time. Her developmental milestones were achieved at or before [6]appropriate ages. She sat at 7 months, crawled at 8, walked at 11 months, and stood alone at 10 months of age. She babbled "very early," spoke her first words "early," and put 2 to 3 words together at 12 months. She spoke in sentences soon after her first birthday and was described as being "very verbal." [7]Jane and Mary reported that Jane was evaluated for a lisp [8]that she always had but just became more aware of within the last year. She is an active, friendly young lady who engages in basketball, track, and [9]hanging out with her friends. Jane said she has trouble producing her [10][s] sounds and said it doesn't really bother her but other people are aware of it. [11]She went to speech therapy in fourth grade for 2 to 3 months, but no progress was seen. She was given exercises to do at home but they were not successful.

Jane's father has a slight lisp but has never had speech therapy. [12]She is entering high school in the fall and is motivated to retrain her mouth to improve articulation. She has normal interactions with peers and adults but is looking forward to speaking without a lisp.

Assessment Information

An assessment was performed on July 1, 2018. J.K. was cooperative [13]throughout the entire evaluation process. She quickly became comfortable with the clinicians. J.K. was friendly and interacted well with the clinicians, laughing and conversing with each of them. She had an appropriate attention span and was able to comprehend and complete all tasks given to her by the clinicians.

Formal Testing[14]

The Goldman Fristoe 2 Test of Articulation (GFTA-2) was used to evaluate J.K.'s speech production. The results from the GFTA-2 revealed an interdental lisp on [15][s] and [z] phonemes in [16]all positions of words and sentences.

Pragmatics

J.K.'s pragmatic skills were informally assessed throughout the evaluation. She demonstrated adequate conversational skills, as she was able to appropriately initiate, maintain, and terminate interactions with the clinicians. She appropriately used and maintained eye contact when engaged in conversation [17]throughout the assessment.

Language Comprehension

J.K.'s language comprehension abilities were judged to be within functional limits, as she appropriately responded to questions asked by the clinicians. She was able to understand and follow instructions given by the clinicians and was able to maintain conversation.

Language Production

A formal language assessment was not performed because it was observed that J.K's expressive language abilities are within functional limits. She demonstrated [18]a large repertoire of vocabulary and appropriate syntactic abilities. [19]Overall, she was able to formulate complex sentences using correct grammatical morphemes, sentence structure, and [20]appropriate vocabulary.

Speech Production

J.K.'s articulation skills were assessed by the [21]GFTA-2. Although J.K. demonstrated an interdental lisp, her overall intelligibility was not affected. Her errors were typical of speakers who demonstrate an interdental lisp, as she produced the [22][θ] phoneme for the [23][s] and [z] phonemes in all word positions. However, J.K. was stimulable for correct production of her error sounds. [24]She was able to correct her errors with the clinician's assistance.

Oral Facial Examination

An oral peripheral examination revealed typical facial symmetry of the jaw, lips, and tongue. Tongue range of motion, lip closure, and diadochokinetic rate appeared to be within normal limits. J.K. demonstrated good oral–nasal shifting and adequate closure of the velopharyngeal port. [25]J.K. did exhibit a tongue thrust when asked to swallow.

Voice and Fluency

Perceptual judgments indicated vocal quality, resonance, pitch, and loudness were within normal limits. Fluency was within normal limits.

Cognitive Tempo

Rapid alternating questions were used to assess cognitive tempo. J.K.'s cognitive tempo was immediate and accurate.

Audition

On 7/1/18 J.K. demonstrated hearing in both ears to be within normal limits. [26](Both ears were tested at 20 dB at 1000 Hz, 2000 Hz, 3000 Hz and 4000 Hz).

Motor Skills

J.K.'s fine and gross motor skills were deemed to be within normal limits.

Clinical Impressions

J.K. presented with a mild interdental lisp. Her language production and comprehension skills appeared to be within functional limits. J.K.'s [27]pragmatic skills, language skills, motor skills, voice, fluency, and audition were all within [28]normal limits. J.K. would benefit from speech therapy focusing on her articulation errors.

Recommendations

Individual speech therapy is recommended once a week for thirty minutes [29]along with an eight-week myofunctional therapy program to address the tongue thrust.

Initial goals of therapy should focus on:

[30]-The correct production of [s] starting from the interdental [t] position

[31]-Producing a backward swallow to reduce the tongue thrust

K.K., C.C., H.H.
Clinical Interns

[32]Dr. Robert Goldfarb, PhD, CCC-SLP
[33]Speech/Language Pathologist Clinical Supervisor

Speech-Language Evaluation Report—Revised Version

(Note revisions are highlighted in bold.)

Name: J.K. Date of Evaluation: 7/1/18

Date of Birth[1]: **4/1/04**

Address: 123 Fourth Road
Montauk, NY 11954

Telephone: 631-668-8888

Background Information

J.K. is a **14-year-old**[2] female who was evaluated at the Hy Weinberg Center for Communication Disorders. She was accompanied by her mother, [3]**(deleted "Mary")** who served as a reliable informant. Jane reportedly has no significant birth/medical history. Her mother reported that Jane suffered from frequent ear infections the first [4]**two** years of her life. PE tubes were not inserted because antibiotics always resolved the infection. [5]**Ms. K.** stated that J. did not have any feeding or swallowing difficulties at any time. Her developmental milestones were achieved at or before [6]**typical** ages. She sat at 7 months, crawled at 8, walked at 11 months, and stood alone at 10 months of age. She babbled "very early," spoke her first words "early," and put 2 to 3 words together at 12 months. She spoke in sentences soon after her first birthday and was described as being "very verbal." [7]**Ms. K.** reported that Jane has become more aware of a lisp [8]**(deleted extraneous verbiage)** within the last year. She is an active, friendly young lady who engages in basketball, track, and [9]**socializing** with her friends. Jane said [10]**her trouble producing /s/ sounds does not bother her**, but other people are aware of it. She [11]**had speech therapy** in fourth grade for 2 to 3 months, but no progress was seen. She was given exercises to do at home but they were not successful.

Jane's father reportedly has a slight lisp but has never had speech therapy. [12]**As Jane is entering high school in the fall, she is motivated to improve articulation**.

Assessment Information

An assessment was performed on July 1, 2018. J.K. was cooperative [13]**throughout the evaluation**. She had an appropriate attention span, and was able to comprehend and complete all tasks given to her by the clinicians.

Formal Testing

The [14]**Goldman Fristoe 2 Test of Articulation (GFTA-2)** was used to evaluate J.K.'s speech production. The results from the GFTA-2 revealed an interdental lisp on [15]**/s/ and /z/** phonemes [16]**in pre- and postvocalic positions** in words and sentences.

Pragmatics

J.K.'s pragmatic skills were informally assessed throughout the evaluation. She demonstrated adequate conversational skills, as she was able to appropriately initiate, maintain, and terminate interactions with the clinicians. She appropriately used and maintained eye contact when engaged in conversation 17**(deleted extraneous language)**.

Language Comprehension

J.K.'s language comprehension abilities were judged to be within functional limits, as she appropriately responded to questions asked by the clinicians. She was able to understand and follow instructions given by the clinicians and was able to maintain conversation.

Language Production

A formal language assessment was not performed, because it was observed that J.K's expressive language abilities are within functional limits. She demonstrated [18]**age-appropriate vocabulary** and appropriate syntactic abilities. [19]**(deleted "Overall")** She was able to formulate complex sentences using correct grammatical morphemes and sentence structure [20]**(deleted "appropriate vocabulary," which is redundant)**.

Speech Production

J.K.'s articulation skills were assessed by the [21]***GFTA-2***. Although J.K. demonstrated an interdental lisp, her overall intelligibility was not affected. Her errors were typical of speakers who demonstrate an interdental lisp, as she produced [22]**/θ/ for /s/** and [23]**/ð/ for /z/** in all word positions. However, J.K. was stimulable for correct production of her error sounds [24]**(deleted redundant sentence)**.

Oral Facial Examination

An oral-peripheral examination revealed typical facial symmetry of the jaw, lips, and tongue. Tongue range of motion, lip closure, and diadochokinetic rate appeared to be within normal limits. J.K. demonstrated good oral-nasal shifting and adequate closure of the velopharyngeal port. J.K. [25]**exhibited a unilateral tongue thrust when performing a dry swallow. She was stimulable for reduction of tongue thrust via myofunctional therapy techniques.**

Voice and Fluency

Perceptual judgments indicated vocal quality, resonance, pitch, and loudness were within normal limits. Fluency was within normal limits.

Cognitive Tempo

Rapid alternating questions were used to assess cognitive tempo. J.K.'s cognitive tempo was immediate and accurate.

Audition

On 7/1/18, J.K. demonstrated hearing in both ears to be within normal limits. Both ears were tested at 20 dB at 1000 Hz, 2000 Hz, 3000 Hz and 4000 Hz [26]**(deleted parentheses)**.

Motor Skills

J.K.'s fine and gross motor skills were deemed to be within functional limits.

Clinical Impressions

J.K. presented with a mild interdental lisp. Her language production and comprehension skills appeared to be within functional limits. J.K.'s [27]**syntactic, semantic, and pragmatic language skills**; motor skills; voice; fluency; and audition were all within [28]**functional** limits. J.K. would benefit from speech therapy focusing on her articulation errors.

Recommendations

Individual speech therapy is recommended once a week for thirty minutes. [29]**Initial goals of therapy should focus on:**

[30]**1. Correct production of /s/ starting from the interdental /θ/ position; and**
[31]**2. Elimination or reduction of the tongue thrust.**

K.K., C.C., H.H.
Clinical Interns

[32]Robert Goldfarb, PhD, CCC-SLP
[33]Speech-Language Pathologist Clinical Supervisor

Diagnostic Report Format—Audiology

See Martin and Clark, 2012; Northern, 1995; Stach, 2010.

Name

Date of Evaluation

Date of Birth

Age (years: months for age <18)

Address

Address (2nd line)

Telephone Number (Specify home, work, or cell, and include area codes.)

Email

History

Include full name of the client, age, gender, referral source, name of person accompanying client to evaluation, name of informant (if not the client), reliability of informant to provide background information, reason for referral, and statement of problem. State whether this is a first or reevaluation. If this is a reevaluation, summarize the findings from the last session.

Document only information pertinent to the disorder and appropriate to the client.

1. For a child:
   a. Child's prenatal and birth history, including maternal health; medications during pregnancy, labor, and delivery; length of pregnancy, indicating pre or post-term; type of delivery; complications; neonatal health.
   b. Child's developmental history for motor and speech-language development, indicating if ages of developmental milestones are within normal limits.
   c. Educational history including class grade, academic difficulties, special services.
   d. Behavioral issues such as hyperactivity, attention difficulty, etc.

2. For a child or an adult:
   a. Medical history, such as pertinent illnesses or injuries, hospitalizations, surgeries, respiratory infections, allergies, dizziness, medications, ear infections, ear pain, drainage.
   b. Hearing history, with description of current hearing status, hearing loss (if any) including onset, known cause, stability, and affected ear(s), amplifica-

tion use, family history of hearing loss, tinnitus, noise exposure.
c. Previous hearing tests and other pertinent evaluations and therapies, such as speech-language, psychological, and neurological.

Assessment Information

1. Write an introductory paragraph, citing only relevant behavioral observations, such as cooperation and participation during assessment; attention span, eye-gaze; reliability of testing.
2. If this is a reevaluation, compare findings to previous outcomes, noting whether or not there has been any change (improvement or decrease) in test outcomes in the appropriate assessment section of the report.
3. List all tests performed and the results obtained.

Ear Examination and Otoscopy

Audiologists perform the external ear examination and otoscopy to describe and identify, not diagnose abnormalities of the pinna, periauricular structures, ear canal, and tympanic membrane. When reporting ear examination results absent of apparent disorder, it is best to indicate that results are *unremarkable* rather than *normal*, because the latter term may fall within the confines of diagnosis.

1. Pinna and periauricular structures
   Note any malformations, growths, lesions (cuts or scabs) of or around the pinna, including the mastoid bone region.

2. Ear canal
   Document narrowing or obstructions of the ear canal (cerumen, excessive hair, foreign objects, growths); discharge (blood or other; describe consistency, e.g., color, thickness, etc.), or lesions along the canal wall.

3. Tympanic membrane
   Describe atypical findings such as clarity and color (cloudiness, redness, or yellowness), discharge, fluid bubbles, perforation, retraction, or bulging. Note the presence of a pressure-equalizing (PE) tube.

Pure-Tone Audiometry

1. Describe the test technique used (e.g., standard audiometry, play, visual reinforcement audiometry [VRA], etc.). If sound-field testing is conducted, results reflect the hearing of the better ear, if there is a difference. A rationale for using sound-field testing should be provided (e.g., child would not allow earphone placement), and earphone assessment should be attempted (and documented) in order to obtain ear-specific information. Indicate whether using a screening or diagnostic procedure.
2. The interpretation statement on hearing other than that which is normal should indicate the degree (amount), configuration (shape), and type (conductive, sensorineural, or mixed) of hearing loss for each ear if different, or indicate *bilaterally* if the hearing for both ears is the same (e.g., a moderate sloping to severe sensorineural hearing loss bilaterally). Categorize the degree of hearing loss as slight, mild, moderate, moderately severe, severe, or profound. Note the configuration of hearing loss other than flat (e.g., rising, gradually or sharply sloping). If there is hearing loss in specific frequency regions, also report the range that is normal (e.g., normal hearing up to 1000 Hz sloping to a mild mixed hearing loss for the right ear). If the type of hearing loss differs within the same ear (i.e., conductive in the lower frequencies but sensorineural in the higher frequencies), specify each type rather than using the combined term *mixed*.
3. Indicate whether there is any asymmetry in pure tone findings between ears.
4. Report the two- and three-frequency pure-tone averages (PTAs).

Speech Audiometry

1. Report the speech recognition thresholds (SRTs) and consistency with the two or three frequency PTAs.
2. Report the speech recognition scores (SRSs), the presentation levels used, and consistency of the SRS with the degree and type of hearing loss. Classify the SRS as excellent, good, fair, poor, or very poor. Indicate if the SRS findings were poorer than expected or asymmetric between ears.

Immittance

1. Indicate whether using a screening or diagnostic procedure.
2. Note whether results of tympanometry, ipsilateral and/or contralateral acoustic reflex thresholds (ARTs), and acoustic reflex decay (ARD) are within normal limits, which is suggestive of normal middle ear functioning.
3. With tympanometric findings outside of normal range, describe aspects of the tympanogram such as peak admittance (abnormally low or high), middle ear pressure (excessively negative or positive), and ear canal volume (abnormally low or high) in addition to the classification (e.g., A, B, C), if used.
4. Ipsilateral or contralateral ARTs outside of normal range may be elevated or absent; specify frequencies tested; report results relative to the stimulus ear.
5. Classify ipsilateral or contralateral ARD as either positive or negative, and frequencies at which performed; report results relative to the stimulus ear.
6. Depending on the findings, indicate whether results are suggestive of a specific pathology. For example, reduced peak admittance, abnormally low ear canal volume, and absent ARTs would support impacted cerumen, particularly if observed on otoscopic examination. There is a fine line between *identifying* and *diagnosing* abnormality. Be careful to use phrasing of potential pathology in hypothetical rather than actual terms. For example, reduced peak admittance, excessively negative middle ear pressure, and absent ARTs coupled with otoscopic findings of redness of the tympanic membrane *may be suggestive of middle ear pathology such as otitis media*, but may not be stated as *indicating otitis media*. With PE tube placement, comment on function based on the ear canal volume reading. For example, an abnormally high ear canal volume reading would be suggestive of a patent (and normally functioning) PE tube. In the presence of normal tympanometry and sensorineural hearing loss, ART and ARD outcomes may be interpreted to support either cochlear or retrocochlear pathology.

Behavioral Site-of-Lesion Tests

When site-of-lesion is of concern in patients with sensorineural hearing loss, several behavioral tests may be useful in providing further information to the standard audiometric battery in addition to electrophysiologic tests. Report findings from tone decay, short increment sensitivity index (SISI), or performance-intensity function for phonetically balanced (PI-PB) word tests as either positive or negative (the term *rollover* may be used with PI-PB outcomes). Indicate whether results support cochlear or retrocochlear pathology.

Electrophysiologic Tests

1. Report the purpose of the electrophysiologic test.
2. Indicate whether using a screening or diagnostic procedure.
3. In hearing estimation, ABR can be used to estimate hearing thresholds to a specific degree, frequency (with tonal ABRs), and type (with bone conduction ABR).
4. ABR conducted in neurologic assessment should be classified as normal or abnormal (which would be indicative of retrocochlear pathology).

5. Present otoacoustic emissions (OAEs) support normal cochlear outer hair-cell function, whereas absent OAE s may suggest abnormal cochlear, outer, or middle ear disorder.
6. Vestibular function is assessed by tests such as (video-) electronystagmography (V/ENG), rotational chair, or posturography.

Clinical Impressions

Provide a summary of relevant findings. Do not present new information in this section, but refer to statements in prior assessment sections.

Recommendations

In cases where no significant hearing loss or other audiometric outcomes were noted, no further audiologic recommendations are indicated. Further recommendations may include the following, and should be indicated in order of importance:

1. Further testing
   a. Re-evaluation to complete the hearing test, as is often required in pediatric populations
   b. Electrophysiologic tests (e.g., ABR, OAE, ENG)
   c. (Central) auditory processing tests
2. Follow-up testing
   a. To monitor hearing in patients with potential late-onset or progressive hearing loss, occupational or recreational noise exposure, or those taking ototoxic medications
   b. Following medical treatment
   c. Annual retesting
3. Rehabilitative options
   a. Amplification assessment, dispensing, verification, and follow-up of a new fitting
   b. Hearing aid checks for an existing fitting
   c. Cochlear implant evaluation
4. Hearing conservation
   a. Use of hearing protection
   b. Monitoring use of ototoxic medication
   c. Counseling regarding hearing preservation
5. Referral to other professionals
   a. Speech-language pathologist
   b. Otologist or other medical specialist (i.e., pediatrician, general practitioner)
   c. Educational specialist
   d. Social worker
   e. Psychologist
   f. Genetic counselor

Clinical interns (Names of students participating in evaluation)

Supervisor's name, degree, CCC-A

Audiologist

Institutional title (Professor, Clinical Supervisor)

Diagnostic Protocol Worksheet—Audiology

Client's Name

Date of Evaluation

History

Referral source

Informant

Informant reliability

Reason for concern

For a Child

Prenatal and birth history

Speech-language developmental milestones

Motor development milestones

For a Child or Adult

Medical history

Hearing history

Other evaluations

Prior and current therapies

Family history of hearing problems

Assessment Information

Behavioral observations

Reliability of testing

Changes from prior testing

Ear Examination and Otoscopy

Pinna and periauricular structures

Ear canal

Tympanic membrane

Pure-Tone Audiometry

Test technique

Degree, configuration, type of hearing loss

Hearing asymmetry

Two- and three-frequency pure-tone averages (PTAs)

Speech Audiometry

Speech recognition threshold (SRT)

SRT consistency to PTA

Speech recognition score (SRS)

Presentation level of SRS

Consistency of SRS to pure tones

Immittance

Tympanometry

Ipsilateral, contralateral acoustic reflex thresholds (ARTs), acoustic reflex decay (ARD)

Behavioral Site-of-Lesion Tests

Tone decay

Short increment sensitivity index (SISI)

Performance-intensity function for phonetically balanced (PI-PB)

Electrophysiologic Tests

Auditory brainstem response (ABR)

Otoacoustic emissions (OAEs)

(Video) electronystagmography (V/ENG)

Rotational chair

Posturography

Sample of Diagnostic Report Writing in Audiology

Following is a professional diagnostic audiology report, with errors in writing form noted in superscript in the original; the corrections follow in a revised version.

Audiologic Evaluation Report—Original

Name:	Aaron Stone
Date of Evaluation:	11/23/18
Date of Birth:	01/19/15
Age:	3yr.(1)
Address:	88 Sunset Terrace Long Beach, CT 87654
Telephone:	(651) 999-9999

History

Aaron Stone, a 3-year-old male(1), was seen at the University Audiology Center on November 23, 2018 for an audiologic re-evaluation.(2) Aaron's previous results revealed normal hearing between 500 Hz and 2000 Hz, in at least one ear.[3] He was accompanied by his mother, who acted as the informant. Aaron's mother reported that the speech therapist[4] indicated that he has had more speech and has been putting together longer sentences.[5] She also reported that he has been receiving speech therapy twice weekly. Aaron will be attending a preschool in the fall and will receive 1:1 speech therapy[6] three times weekly. He has no significant medical history. There is no family history of hearing loss.

Assessment Information

Otoscopy

Otoscopic examination was unremarkable.[7]

Pure-Tone Audiometry

Pure-tone test results are considered to be good in reliability.[8] In sound field and under headphones in each ear, responses to pure tones were obtained from 5 to 15 dB HL at frequencies from 500 Hz-2000 Hz.[9]

Speech Audiometry

A speech detection threshold in sound field was obtained at 15 dB HL for the right ear. A speech detection threshold for the left ear could not be obtained.

Immittance

Acoustic immittance measures revealed normal admittance and middle ear pressure (type A tympanograms bilaterally).

Clinical Impressions

Audiologic results revealed normal hearing between 500 to 4000 Hz, bilaterally.[10] Acoustic immittance measures indicate normal middle ear function, bilaterally.

Recommendations

1. Retest at an older age[11] in order to obtain a complete audiogram.

Laura Hanes, BS
Clinical Intern

Dara Sratton[12]
Audiologist
Clinical Supervisor

Audiology Evaluation Report—Edited

1. Age is incorrectly indicated, Aaron is almost 4 years old; should be written as 3:10 years
2. Should indicate the purpose of the re-evaluation.
3. Should indicate when the previous evaluation was conducted.
4. Correct term is "speech-language pathologist,"
5. Wording is awkward and information is incomplete; would be clearer to indicate that his vocabulary increased, and the word length of his sentences.
6. Better to use words rather than a numeric ratio to indicate that the speech therapy is individualized.
7. Need to clarify which ears; "Otoscopic examination was unremarkable bilaterally."
8. Indicate the procedure used
9. For consistency with the range "5 to 15 dB HL" reported in the sentence, use word "to" instead of the hyphen to indicate the frequency range "500 to 4000 Hz".
10. The statement "between 500 to 2000 Hz" does not match the reported range of "from 500 to 2000 Hz" indicated in the pure-tone audiometry section
11. Specify the time frame for the retest
12. Specify the credentials

EXERCISES

Section A: Speech-Language Pathology

Phonetic Transcription Review

One of the basic skills to be acquired in our undergraduate study is phonetic transcription. It is an essential skill for representing speech in diagnostic reports. As with the mastery of any technical skill, continued practice is required. A good way to "shake off the rust" is by creating simple crossword puzzles in phonetics, including the clues as well as the answers. In the exercises below, first make sure you can read the clues and the answers in the puzzle, and then use the blank template to create your own.

Exercise 8–1. Phonetic Transcription Review

1 p	2 ɛ	3 n
4 oʊ	k	ei
5 p	oʊ	m

Clues (in Phonetic Symbols)	Transcribe the Clues	Answer the Puzzle
əkrɔs		
1. sʌmθɪŋ tə raɪt wɪθ		1.
4. əpruv		4.
5. laɪnz əv vɜs		5.
daʊn		
1. tʃɝtʃ lidɚ		1.
2. saʊnd ðæt baʊnsiz ɔf wɔlz		2.
3. haʊ juɚ ədrɛst		3.

Exercise 8–2. Phonetic Transcription Review: Create Your Own Phonetic Puzzle

naʊ tʃraɪ ə fənɛtɪks pʌzl jɚrsɛlf

1	2	3
4		
5		

raɪt ðə kluz

Clues (in Phonetic Symbols)	Transcribe the Clues	Answer the Puzzle
əkrɔs		
1.		1.
4.		4.
5.		5.
daʊn		
1.		1.
2.		2.
3.		3.

Exercise 8–3. Edit the Speech-Language Pathology Diagnostic Report

In the worksheet below, edit bolded items 1–10, followed by a number in parentheses.

Speech-Language Evaluation

Name: Jane Jones

Address: 123 Articulation Road
Garden City, NY 11530

Telephone Number: 516-877-4777

Date of Evaluation: 7/19/18

Date of Birth: 1/15/04

Chronologic Age: **14.6**(1)

Background Information

Jane Jones is a **fourteen year old**(2,3) female who was evaluated at the Center for Communication Disorders. She was accompanied by her mother, who served as a reliable informant. Jane reportedly has no significant birth/medical history. Her mother reported that Jane suffered from frequent ear infections the first 2 years of her life. Tubes were not inserted because antibiotics always resolved the infection. Ms. Jones stated that Jane did not have any feeding or swallowing difficulties at any time.

Jane's developmental milestones were achieved at or before typical ages. She sat at 7 months, crawled at 8 months, walked at 11 months, and stood alone at 10 months of age. She babbled "very early," spoke her first words "early," and put 2 to 3 words together at 12 months. She spoke in sentences soon after her first birthday and was described as being "very verbal."

Ms. Jones reported that Jane has become more aware of a lisp within the last year. She is an active, friendly child who engages in basketball, track, and socializing with her friends. Jane said her trouble producing /s/ sounds does not bother her but other people are aware of it.

She(4) had speech therapy in 4th grade for 2 to 3 months, but no progress was seen. She was given exercises to do at home but they were not successful. Jane's father reportedly has a slight lisp but has never had speech therapy. She is entering high school in the fall and is motivated to improve articulation.

Assessment Information

A speech and language assessment was performed at the Center on July 19, 2018. Jane was cooperative throughout the evaluation. She had an appropriate attention span and was able to comprehend and complete all tasks given to her by the clinicians.

Formal Testing

The ***Goldman Fristoe II***(5) *Test of Articulation* (GFTA-2) was used to evaluate Jane's speech production. The results from the GFTA-2 revealed an interdental lisp on **[s] and [z]**(6) phonemes in all positions of words and sentences.

Pragmatics

Jane's pragmatic skills were informally assessed throughout the evaluation. She demonstrated adequate conversational skills, as she was able to appropriately initiate, maintain, and terminate interactions with the clinicians. She appropriately used and maintained eye contact throughout the assessment when engaged in conversation.

Language Comprehension

Jane's language comprehension abilities were judged to be within functional limits, as she appropriately responded to questions asked by the clinicians. She was able to understand and follow instructions given by the clinicians and was able to maintain conversation.

Language Production

Formal language assessment was not performed because it was observed that Jane's expressive language abilities **are**[7] within functional limits. She demonstrated age-appropriate vocabulary and appropriate syntactic abilities. She was able to formulate complex sentences using correct grammatical morphemes and sentence structure.

Speech Production

Jane's articulation skills were assessed by the GFTA-2. Although she demonstrated an interdental lisp, her overall intelligibility was not affected. Her errors were typical of speakers who demonstrate an interdental lisp, as she produced the /θ/ for the /s/ and /ð/ for the /z/ phonemes in all word positions. However, Jane was stimulable for correct production of her error sounds.

Oral Facial Examination

An oral peripheral examination revealed **normal**[8] facial symmetry of the jaw, lips, and tongue. Tongue range of motion, lip closure, and diadochokinetic rate appeared to be within normal limits. Jane demonstrated good oral-nasal shifting and adequate closure of the velopharyngeal port. Jane exhibited a unilateral tongue thrust when performing a dry swallow. She was stimulable for reduction of tongue thrust via myofunctional therapy techniques.

Voice and Fluency

Perceptual judgments indicated vocal quality, resonance, **pitch, and loudness**[9] were typical for age and gender. Fluency was within normal limits.

Audition

On 7/19/18 Jane demonstrated hearing in both ears to be **within normal limits.**[10] Both ears were tested at 20 dB HL at 1000 Hz, 2000 Hz, 3000 Hz, and 4000 Hz.

Clinical Impressions

Jane Jones presented with a mild interdental lisp. Her language production and comprehension skills appeared to be within functional limits. Jane's language skills, voice, fluency, and audition were all within normal limits. Jane would benefit from speech therapy focusing on her articulation errors.

Recommendations

Individual speech therapy is recommended once a week for 30 minutes. Initial goals of therapy should focus on:

1. Correct production of /s/ starting from the /t/ position; and
2. Eliminating or reducing the tongue thrust.

Hildred Schuell Clinical Intern	Robert West, PhD, CCC-SLP Speech-Language Pathologist Clinical Supervisor

Exercise 8–3 Worksheet

1	
2	
3	
4	
5	
6	
7	
8	
9	
10	

Exercise 8–4. Edit the following portion of a speech-language pathology diagnostic report.

In the worksheet below, edit bolded items 1–10, followed by a number in parentheses.

(assume report heading is correct)

Referral information

AB, a **20 year old**(1) female, was seen at the Center for Communicative Disorders for a speech/language evaluation, due to her concerns regarding articulation secondary to a **Trinidad**(2) accent. **She is concerned with how others understand her speech, she is interested in speech therapy to remediate the articulatory difficulty.**(3)

Background Information

AB was born in Trinidad and has lived in the United States for seven years. Her only language is English, **however**(4) she stated that she speaks in **Patwa**(5). AB works in Helping Hands Hospital as a health aide and is currently enrolled in an online bachelor's degree program.

Assessment

Formal as well as informal measures were used to assess AB's proficiency in English in a variety of areas. AB remained an active participant during formal testing procedures as she followed directions, listened to the clinicians, **as well as answering questions asked of her**(6).

Formal Testing

The **Proficiency in Oral English Communication: An Assessment Battery of Accented Oral English (POEC)**(7) was used to assess the client's speech and language. The *POEC* assesses the extent and the source of accent issues in non-native speakers of American English. Accents can be influenced by many factors, **therefore**(8) the POEC measures a wide range of oral abilities **including:**(9) articulation, intonation, auditory discrimination, and pragmatics. AB was asked to read the words and/or sentences presented to her on stimulus cards as a response to a comment or question posed by the clinician. For example, the clinician stated, **"I'll meet you after work,**(10) and AB responded, "Fine" (the word on the stimulus card).

Exercise 8–4 Worksheet

1	
2	
3	
4	
5	
6	
7	
8	
9	
10	

Exercise 8–5. Edit the following portion of a speech-language pathology diagnostic report.

In the worksheet below, edit bolded items 1–10, followed by a number in parentheses.

(Assume sections on heading, referral, background, and assessment information are correct.)

CD is a **6 year-, 10 month old**(1) male who was referred by his mother, Ms. RD, due to concerns regarding his language deficits secondary to his diagnosis of an autism spectrum disorder.

Testing

No formal testing was administered during this evaluation due to lack of **verbal**(2) language and AB's diagnosis (nonverbal autism spectrum disorder).

Pragmatics: **During the moments that CD wanted access to items during the evaluation, he preferred to communicate this by either using the signs for *give me* or *more*, or by grabbing the hand of his mother, or a clinician, and guiding it to the item that he wanted instead of using his PECS.**(3) Ms. RD reported that he also does this when he needs help opening or accessing a preferred item at home. When the clinicians prompted CD to use his PECS to request items, he used **them**(4) efficiently. **Ms. RD reported that CD uses his PECS to communicate at school, however she does not prompt him to use it at home, instead, she asks for an approximation of verbal speech.**(5) Although CD used his PECS to request, he did not use it to respond to simple questions **(i.e.,**(6) **what**(7) color is this?) or to refuse items. For example, when presented with food, he pushed it away rather than using his PECS to express that he did not like or want the food.

He demonstrated his frustration by biting his arms and hands various times throughout the session. His mother reported that she responds by either ignoring the behavior or redirecting CD to **biting**(8) a chewing tube**, which**(9) was not brought to the evaluation.

CD made fleeting eye contact when using the signs **give me** and **more**,(10) but did not make eye contact when using his PECS. His mother reported that he responds to his name about 60% of the time and that he nods his head for *yes* inconsistently. During the evaluation, he responded to his mother saying, "C, let's go eat," by looking at and walking toward his mother.

Ms. RD also explained that CD understands when she is upset. For example, he will give her a hug when she pretends to cry.

Exercise 8–5 Worksheet

1	
2	
3	
4	
5	
6	
7	
8	
9	
10	

Exercise 8–6. Edit the following portion of a speech-language pathology diagnostic report.

In the worksheet below, edit bolded items 1–10, followed by a number in parentheses.

Background Information

EF attends the Early Learning Center at the University where this evaluation was conducted. His parents did not attend the evaluation; **however**(1) his classroom teachers served as reliable informants and background information was obtained from their perspective, **but his parents should verify the accuracy of the report.**(2) EF resides with his mother, father, and **5 year old**(3) sister. EF understands that his mother is pregnant with her third child. English is the only language spoken in the home.

EF's teachers indicate that he enjoys playing with building blocks, shares with his peers, and **helpful to his peers.**(4) During classroom activities, EF attends to structured tasks (**i.e.,**(5) listening to a story). However, EF reacts negatively to being redirected when his attention is limited. EF's teacher expressed her concern regarding his speech production. **It was also reported by his teacher**(6) that EF becomes easily frustrated when he is not understood. EF's teacher indicated that strategies (e.g., reminding him to slow down) have been identified as helpful for increasing his speech intelligibility.

Assessment Information

EF was willing to participate in the activities presented to him (**i.e.,**(7) puzzles and books). Due to his young age and limited attention span, EF required verbal prompting from the evaluators to maintain focus on particular tasks **thru-out**(8) the evaluation. Although his attention to the formal diagnostic tasks **were**(9) limited, he enjoyed engaging in informal play with the evaluators. Due to EF's young age and limited attention span, a formal test was not administered in its entirety: **therefore**(10) a formal overall score was not generated.

Exercise 8–6 Worksheet

1	
2	
3	
4	
5	
6	
7	
8	
9	
10	

Exercise 8–7. Edit the following portion of a speech-language pathology diagnostic report.

In the worksheet below, edit bolded items 1–10, followed by a number in parentheses.

Background Information

GH is one of a set of fraternal twins who were born **6**(1) weeks prematurely. GH was born with a cleft palate that was repaired when she was 13 months old. GH's motor milestones were reportedly delayed, and sitting, standing, and walking **within**(2) two years of age. Speech and language milestones were also reported to be delayed. It was reported that she said her first word at **2½ years of age;**(3) started combining words and speaking in complete sentences at 3½ years of age. It was also reported that GH experiences **recurrent**(4) nasal and respiratory infections, as well as fluid buildup in her ears. She has an Individualized Education Plan (IEP) and is classified with having a speech and language impairment. The primary language spoken in the home is English.

Clinical Impressions

GH is a **5 year-, 3 month old**(5) female who presents with a severe articulation disorder, as characterized by misarticulations of the **/m, n, ng, y, s, z/**(6,7) phonemes. She presented with delays in her oral motor skills, resulting in lingual protrusion during rest and speech tasks and with decreased coordination of her lips. GH exhibited moderate **hyponasality** that is typical of children with a cleft palate. Velopharyngeal closure is affected due to decreased movement of the soft palate, resulting in **hyponasal**(8) speech. It is recommended that GH receive speech services twice a week for **30 minutes**(9) sessions. Goals should focus, initially, on the nasal **[m], [n]. and [ŋ]**(10) phonemes.

Exercise 8–7 Worksheet

1	
2	
3	
4	
5	
6	
7	
8	
9	
10	

Exercise 8–8. Write Your Own Diagnostic Report in Speech-Language Pathology

Observe a diagnostic evaluation in speech-language pathology, and write your own report following the template for diagnostic report writing, rules for diagnosis, and sample speech-language pathology report provided in the sections above.

Section B: Audiology

Exercise 8–9. Edit the Audiology Diagnostic Report

In the worksheet below, edit items 1–10 highlighted in bold and followed by a number in parentheses.

Audiologic Evaluation

Name: Tyler Frank

Address: 9 Reade Road
Maintown, NY 12345

Telephone: (987) 654-3210

Date of Evaluation: 7/10/18

Date of Birth: 3/1/16

Chronologic Age: 2:4

History

Tyler Frank, a 2:4-year-old male, was seen at the Center for Communication Disorders on July 10, 2008, for an initial audiological evaluation. He was referred for this evaluation by the County Early Intervention program to rule out hearing loss as a cause of his speech and language delay. **Mrs. Frank**(1) reported that Tyler has been receiving speech and language therapy **3**(2) times a week for about 6 months. According to Mrs. Frank, Tyler's motor milestones were **developed in the appropriate time frame**(3); however, his speech and language milestones were delayed. **Mrs. Frank**(4) indicated that there is no familial history of hearing loss. Medical history revealed that Tyler was hospitalized for a severe fever, **but other than that he did not suffer any pertinent illnesses**(5).

Assessment Information

Tyler was cooperative during the audiologic assessment.

Pure-Tone Audiometry

Audiological test results obtained via **VRA**(6) in the sound field were considered to be of good reliability. Responses to warbled tones were obtained at **15 dB**(7) for the frequencies of **500–4k Hz**(8).

Speech Audiometry

A speech detection threshold in sound field was obtained at 20 dB HL.

Immittance

Acoustic immittance measures revealed Type A tympanograms bilaterally.

Clinical Impressions

Audiologic results revealed normal hearing in at least the better ear. Acoustic immittance measures indicated normal middle ear function bilaterally. Based upon these results, hearing loss may be ruled out as a contributing factor to Tyler's speech and language delay.

Recommendations

The results of the evaluation were discussed with Mrs. Frank, and **re-evaluation**[9] in 6 months for **monaural thresholds**[10] was recommended.

Kelsy Masters Clinical Intern	Sara Booth, AuD, CCC-A Audiologist Clinical Supervisor

Exercise 8–9 Worksheet

1	
2	
3	
4	
5	
6	
7	
8	
9	
10	

Exercise 8–10. Edit the Audiology Diagnostic Report

In the worksheet below, edit bolded items 1–12, followed by a number in parentheses.

Audiologic Evaluation

Name: Don Smith

Address: 14 Arlington Road
Newton, NJ 42732

Telephone: (908) 999-9999

Date of Evaluation: 06/10/18

Date of Birth: 04/02/57

Age: 61

History:

Don Smith, a **sixty-one-year-old**(1) male, was seen at the University Audiology Center on June 10, 2018 for an audiologic re-evaluation. He was last seen on **April 28** (2) for an annual evaluation. **His**(3) audiometric findings from the previous evaluation revealed a mild to moderately severe sensorineural hearing loss bilaterally. Mr. Smith continues to report a constant tinnitus in both ears. **Since the last evaluation, he notes a decline in his ears and his understanding and comprehension has decreased.**(4) He also continues to have difficulty hearing in noisy surroundings. Mr. Smith currently has hearing aids, **but never wears his left aid at all.**(5) Medical history includes meningitis as a child and occipital lobe damage from brain injury. Mr. Smith is taking a variety of medications for various reasons, including Trileptal, an anti-seizure medication, and statins for cholesterol.

Assessment Information

Audiologic test results are considered good in reliability.

Otoscopy

Otoscopic examination was unremarkable bilaterally.

Pure-Tone Audiometry

Pure-tone test results revealed a **mild-moderately severe**(6) sensorineural hearing loss bilaterally. Three-frequency pure-tone averages were 43 dB HL and 45 dB HL **for the right and left ears.** (7) Aided testing revealed improvements in pure-tone thresholds by 10 to 30 dB HL.

Speech Audiometry

Speech recognition thresholds were **45dB HL**(8) bilaterally. **SRTs**(9) were consistent with pure-tone findings. Speech recognition scores (SRSs) obtained at 80 dB HL were 80% in the right ear and at 84% in the left ear. SRSs were symmetric and were judged to be good, bilaterally. The aided **SRSs**(10) obtained at 50 dB HL was 96%. Uncomfortable loudness levels were 105 dB HL, bilaterally.

Immittance

Acoustic immittance measures revealed Type As **tympanograms**(11) in the right ear, and a Type A in the left ear.

Clinical Impressions

Pure-tone results revealed a mild to moderately severe sensorineural hearing loss bilaterally. Speech recognition thresholds were consistent with pure-tone findings. Speech recognition scores were symmetric and were judged to be good, bilaterally. Acoustic immittance measures revealed reduced middle ear immittance for the right ear and normal middle ear function for the left. No change in audiometric findings was noted from the last evaluation. Aided sound-field testing indicated Mr. Smith is benefiting from binaural amplification.

Recommendations

1. Continued use of binaural amplification.
2. Return for annual **re-evaluation.**(12)

Ellen Hurst, BS Clinical Intern	Holly Lightly, AuD, CCC-A Audiologist Clinical Supervisor

Exercise 8–10 Worksheet

1	
2	
3	
4	
5	
6	
7	
8	
9	
10	
11	
12	

Exercise 8–11. Edit the Audiology Diagnostic Report

In the worksheet below, edit bolded items 1–12, followed by a number in parentheses.

Audiologic Evaluation

Name: Maria Aresta
Address: 54 Knollwood Drive
Springfield, CT 02345
Telephone: (312) 444-444

Date of Evaluation: 2/24/18
Date of Birth: 2/27/29
Age: 89

History

Maria Aresta, an 89-year-old female, was seen at the University Audiology Center on February 24, 2018 for an audiologic evaluation. Mrs. Aresta expressed that her hearing had decreased in the last **two to four years,**(1) and that she has difficulty in **lots**(2) of different listening situations. Mrs. Aresta(3) reported that she inconsistently hears the doorbell, and uses an amplifier for the telephone and while watching television. Mrs. Aresta indicated that she first noticed a decrease in her hearing after being diagnosed with shingles. She has high blood pressure, arthritis, and has had two hip replacements. She is currently taking **multiple medications.**(4)

Assessment Information

Otoscopy

Otoscopic evaluation was unremarkable bilaterally.

Pure-Tone Audiometry

Pure-tone test results are considered excellent in reliability and reveal a moderate to severe sensorineural hearing loss, bilaterally. Three-frequency pure-tone averages were 57 dB HL for the right ear, and 58 dB HL for the left ear.

Speech Audiometry

Speech recognition thresholds (SRTs) were 55 dB HL for the right ear and **60 dB**(5) for the left. Speech recognition scores (SRSs) obtained at **80 db HL**(6) were 72% in the right ear and 68% at 95 dB HL in the left ear. **Most comfortable listening level was**(7) 70 dB HL in the right ear and 80 dB HL in the left ear. Uncomfortable listening levels were obtained at 100 dB HL in the right ear and 105 dB HL in the left ear.

Immittance

Acoustic immittance measures revealed **Type A sub S**(8) tympanograms bilaterally.

Clinical Impressions

Pure tone results indicated a moderate to severe sensorineural hearing loss bilaterally. **Speech recognition thresholds**[9] were consistent with pure-tone findings. SRS s were fair bilaterally. Acoustic immittance measures revealed reduced immittance, bilaterally. **No change in audiometric findings was noted from the last evaluation.**[10]

Recommendations

1. Amplification of the **right and left ear.**[11]
2. Medical clearance before amplification.

Susan Krane[12]	Donald Saunders, PhD, CCC-A
Clinical Intern	Audiologist
	Clinical Supervisor

Exercise 8–11 Worksheet

1	
2	
3	
4	
5	
6	
7	
8	
9	
10	
11	
12	

Exercise 8–12. Edit the Audiology Diagnostic Report

In the worksheet below, edit bolded items 1–12, followed by a number in parentheses.

Audiologic Evaluation

Name: Lyle Zorros

Address: 765 Highland Road
Northtown, NY 22445

Telephone: (877) 222-2222

Date of Evaluation: 10/15/18

Date of Birth: 5/7/16

Age: **2.5**(1)

History

Lyle Zorros, a 2:5-year-old male was seen at the University Audiology Center on October 15, 2018 for an initial **Audiologic**(2) evaluation. He was referred for this evaluation by the County Early Intervention **program**(3) to rule out hearing loss as a cause of his speech delay. **Lyle was born full term without complications. His mother reported that he is receiving speech therapy and physical therapy.** (4) **Also, she reported that Lyle has kidney problems, Hydronephrosis.** (5) **Lyle is not taking any medications currently.**(6)

Assessment Information

Otoscopy and immittance exams were not obtained due to crying.(7)

Pure-Tone Audiometry

Testing was conducted via Visual Reinforcement Audiometry (VRA) in the sound field. Lyle refused to cooperate for pure-tone testing.(8)

Speech Audiometry

A speech detection threshold and a music awareness level in sound field were recorded at 10 dB HL. **Informal speech recognition testing was conducted and Lyle was not following simple directions at 40 dB HL.**(9)

Clinical Impressions

Incomplete audiologic test information was obtained due to limited cooperation. **Results suggest hearing to be within normal limits in the speech frequencies for both ears.**(10)

Recommendations

1. **Continuation of testing**(11)
2. Otoacoustic **Emmisions**(12) testing

Rosemarie Borden, B.A.
Clinical Intern

Sarah Bell, AuD, CCC-A
Audiologist
Clinical Supervisor

Exercise 8–12 Worksheet

1	
2	
3	
4	
5	
6	
7	
8	
9	
10	
11	
12	

Exercise 8–13. Edit the Audiology Diagnostic Report

In the worksheet below, edit bolded items 1–12, followed by a number in parentheses.

Audiologic Evaluation

Name: Sam Gould
Address: 42 Corporation Drive
Farmingville, NY 11427
Telephone: (631) 333-3333

Date of Evaluation: 2/22/18
Date of Birth: 1/2/09
Age: 9:1

History

Sam Gould, a 9-year, **1 month old**(1) **boy**(2), was seen at the University Audiology Center on February 22, 2018 for an audiologic re-evaluation. **Sam is a Down syndrome, developmentally delayed child**(3) Sam has been coming to this center since 2010. Mrs. Gould, Sam's mother, reported that he has a **pressure equalizing (PE tube)**(4) in his left ear since March 4, 2017. Sam is currently in third grade at a public elementary school in an inclusion classroom. Mrs. Gould reported that her **sons**(5) language is at the emerging level and that he speaks simple sentences. He also uses some sign language and can mimic and point to express his needs. Sam receives **OT and PT**(6) services. Medical history includes optic nerve atrophy and spinal pressure for which he is followed medically.

Assessment Information

Otoscopy

Otoscopic exam revealed a PE tube in the left ear.

Pure-Tone Audiometry

Pure-tone air conduction testing via play audiometry revealed normal hearing at **500 Hz to 2 kHz**(7) for the right and left ears;(8) **he fatigued for further pure-tone testing**.(9) Test results are considered good to fair in reliability.

Speech Audiometry

Speech detection **thresholds in the sound field were**(10) 5 **dBHL**(11) in at least one ear. An informal speech recognition test was conducted, and Sam was able to follow simple directions at 30 dB HL.

Immittance

Acoustic **immitance**(12) measures revealed type B tympanograms bilaterally. Ear canal volume readings were normal (0.7 cc) for the right ear and excessively high (3.5 cc) for the left ear.

Clinical Impressions

Pure-tone air conduction testing via play audiometry revealed normal hearing from 500 Hz to 2000 Hz, bilaterally; further testing could not be obtained as the client fatigued. A speech detection threshold was consistent with the pure-tone findings. Immittance testing is suggestive of middle ear pathology for the right ear; the high ear canal volume reading is consistent with a patent PE tube for the left ear.

Recommendations

1. Otologic exam to rule out middle ear pathology in the right ear.
2. Retest following any medical intervention

Steve Jones, BS
Clinical Intern

Michael Reiner, PhD, CCC-A
Audiologist
Clinical Supervisor

Exercise 8–13 Worksheet

1	
2	
3	
4	
5	
6	
7	
8	
9	
10	
11	
12	

Exercise 8–14. Write Your Own Diagnostic Report in Audiology

Observe a diagnostic evaluation in audiology and write your own report following the template for diagnostic report writing, rules for diagnosis, and sample audiology report provided in the sections above.

References

American Speech-Language-Hearing Association. (1996). Central auditory processing: Current status of research and implications for clinical practice. *American Journal of Audiology*, *5*, 41–54.

American Speech-Language-Hearing Association. (2005). *(Central) auditory processing disorders*. Rockville, MD: Author.

Brookshire, R. H. (1983). Subject description and generality of results in experiments with aphasic adults. *Journal of Speech and Hearing Disorders*, *48*, 342–346.

Carey, B. (2007, September 4). Bipolar soars as diagnosis for the young. *The New York Times*, pp. A1, A15.

Council For Clinical Certification in Audiology and Speech-Language Pathology of the American Speech-Language-Hearing Association. (2007). *2007 Standards for the Certificate of Clinical Competence in Audiology, revised July 2008*. Retrieved from http://www.asha.org/about/membership-certification/certification/aud_standards_new.htm

Damasio, H. (2008). Neural basis of language disorders. In R. Chapey (Ed.), *Language intervention strategies in aphasia and related neurogenic communication disorders* (5th ed., pp. 20–41). Baltimore, MD: Lippincott Williams & Wilkins.

Goldfarb, R. (2012). Problems in diagnosis: Dumping it in the chocolate. *Plural Community*, *27*, 1–7.

Goldfarb, R. (2006a). An atheoretical discipline. In R. Goldfarb (Ed.), *Ethics: A case study from fluency* (pp. 117–137). San Diego, CA: Plural.

Goldfarb, R. (2006b). Differential diagnosis of adults with neurogenic communication disorders. In E. M. Walsh (Ed.), *Topics in Alzheimer's disease research* (pp. 90–108.). Hauppauge, NY: Nova.

Goldfarb, R., & Halpern, H. (2013). Time-altered word association tests. In H. Halpern & R. Goldfarb, *Language and motor speech disorders in adults* (3rd ed., Appendices A, B; website). Burlington, MA: Jones & Bartlett Learning.

Martin, F. N., & Clark, J. G. (2012). *Introduction to audiology* (11th ed.). Boston, MA: Pearson.

Northern, J. (1995). *Hearing disorders* (3rd ed.). Boston, MA: Allyn & Bacon.

Orlikoff, R. F., Schiavetti, N. E., & Metz, D. E. (2015). *Evaluating research in communication disorders* (7th ed.). New York, NY: Pearson.

Schuell, H. M. (1966). A re-evaluation of the short examination for aphasia. *Journal of Speech and Hearing Disorders*, *31*, 137–147.

Schuell, H. M. (1973). *Differential diagnosis of aphasia with the Minnesota test* (2nd ed., revised by J. W. Sefer). Minneapolis, MN: University of Minnesota Press.

Schwartz, M. (1984). What the classical aphasia categories can't do for us, and why. *Brain and Language*, *21*, 3–8.

Stach, B. A. (2010). *Clinical audiology: An introduction*. (2nd ed.). San Diego, CA: Delmar.

St. Louis, K. O., & Myers, F. L. (2007). *Cluttering* (DVD No. 9700). Memphis, TN: Stuttering Foundation of America.

Weiss, D. (1964). *Cluttering*. Englewood Cliffs, NJ: Prentice-Hall.

Yaruss, J. S., LaSalle, L. R., & Conture, E. G. (1998). Evaluating stuttering in young children: Diagnostic data. *American Journal of Speech-Language Pathology*, *7*, 62–76.

Clinical Goals, Reports, and Referrals

The diagnostic report (see Chapter 8) is the most comprehensive account of professional interaction with a patient. Following the diagnosis, the clinician will need to develop a therapeutic plan with specific goals for treatment.

In this chapter, you will review formats for writing therapeutic goals in treatment plans, progress reports in speech-language pathology, audiogram form reports in audiology, and medical chart notes and professional letter formats.

Often, the diagnostic report is sent to other professionals as part of the referral process and may be accompanied by a cover letter along with copies of clinical assessment outcomes, such as an audiogram or speech documents that may be sent. However, the lengthy diagnostic report may not be the appropriate reporting format to document information for all clinical services or practice sites. In this chapter, other clinical report formats will be discussed and presented, in addition to considerations in the correspondence and sharing of written information with other professionals.

Exercises in the chapter will require that you:

1. Practice writing clinical goals in speech-language pathology and audiology.
2. Observe therapy sessions in speech-language pathology and write a treatment plan, progress report, and medical chart note.
3. Write audiogram form reports and medical chart notes in audiology.
4. Write professional cover letters and letter reports for cases provided in speech-language pathology and audiology.

Informed Consent and Permission

Justification

Informed consent is a crucial part of the "Respect for persons" portion of the Belmont Report (1979) that is described in Chapter 4. Respect for persons requires that researchers and practitioners treat participants or patients as autonomous agents, and those with diminished autonomy must be protected. For example, parents are required to give consent for their minor children to participate in therapy. The capacity for self-determination may change during a person's life, because of maturation, illness, mental disability, or circumstances that restrict liberty. Accordingly, some protected classes include children, those who are imprisoned, who are physically sick or mentally ill, and who are pregnant. Belonging to a protected class does not mean that these individuals cannot or should not participate in therapy. Failure to include certain populations in clinical intervention would preclude their ability to benefit from therapy. Regarding the application of informed consent, information must be provided to a person who is competent to comprehend the information in order to make a decision.

Prior to initiating therapy, a speech-language pathologist or audiologist, or the institution that employs them, should obtain a signed informed consent from the consumer of therapeutic services. If the consumer is a minor child or a disabled adult, an adult advocate should provide informed consent. The form specifies terms of treatment and permission for release of information. The clinician should also obtain permission to make audio-visual recordings for therapeutic and educational purposes and permission to use instrumentation and edibles. Where appropriate, as in a medical or educational setting, there should also be permission to permit observation of therapy and diagnostic sessions. Where HIPAA regulations prevail (see Chapter 4, Ethics of Professional Writing), confidentiality of individually identifiable health information must be assured. The following informed consent form, based on the one used at Adelphi University, may be modified to suit the needs of other institutions or individual practitioners.

Informed Consent Form

I consent and request that the following service(s) be performed for (circle)

myself   my spouse   my child

____

(print name)

at the Center for Communication Disorders at State University (check services requested):

_____ Speech-Language Evaluation

_____ Speech-Language Therapy

_____ Audiological Evaluation

_____ Hearing Aid Evaluation

_____ Other Services (specify):

____

I understand and agree to the following:

a. Services will be performed by or under the supervision of an appropriately licensed and certified speech-language pathologist or audiologist;
b. Graduate and undergraduate student interns may participate in the delivery of any and all services;
c. Promises for success of treatment cannot be made;
d. All information will be kept confidential unless written consent to release information is obtained from me;
e. If authorization for services is denied by my insurance company, I will be responsible for all charges incurred;
f. If the Center for Communication Disorders is not a participating provider for my insurance company, I will be responsible for all charges incurred;
g. I give permission for the Center for Communication Disorders to release information required to receive approval and reimbursement for services to the source of reimbursement for such services (e.g., insurance company, Early Intervention Program, school district, etc.).

Please send me a copy of any evaluation or progress report relating to the above services.

Print Name ______________________

Sign Name ______________________

Relationship to Client ______________________

Date ______________________

Primary Insurance ______________________

Secondary Insurance ______________________

Permission Form

I understand and agree to the following:

a. In order to execute certain therapeutic and diagnostic procedures, it is occasionally necessary to use instruments, such as a penlight or tongue depressor, or edibles, such as crackers or juice, in the course of treatment or evaluation. Before using any edible item, the clinician will consult with me to ensure that there are no contraindications, such as allergies, to the use of that item.

b. I consent to the use of any instrument or material within the scope of practice for use by the speech-language pathologist or audiologist in order to conduct effective assessment and treatment.
c. I agree to permit students enrolled in pertinent academic coursework, trainees, or clinical fellows to participate in the evaluation and/or treatment procedures, which will be conducted under the supervision of an appropriately licensed and certified professional.
d. I consent to the use of audio-visual recordings for therapeutic, educational, and research purposes.

Please list any contraindications, such as allergies or other medical conditions, to the use of edibles:

Print Client's Name ________________________

Signature (Client, Parent, or Advocate)

____

Relationship to Client ______________________

Date ___________________________________

Writing Clinical Observations

Goals: accuracy, readability, style

Good reporting enlivens case presentations, term papers, and even your clinical interventions. Following the rules listed below will result in written clinical observations that are clearer, more accountable, and more interesting to read.

1. Use language that is
   a. Active, not passive. Using the active voice makes your writing come alive. Writing does not have to be dull, or in the passive voice, to be professional. Consider this sentence: *The patient used esophageal voice for the first time to say, "I love you" to his wife*. In the passive voice, this powerful message is somewhat deflated: *Esophageal voice was used for the first time by the patient, who said, "I love you" to his wife.*
   b. Behavioral, not mentalistic. We should write about what people do, not what they think. Even when we are working with individuals on the autism spectrum, there are behavioral ways to express theory of mind. In fact, these behavioral goals are used to help the individual "fake it until you make it." How do we know that a child is happy? What does happy look like and sound like? If he is smiling or laughing, write that instead.
2. Avoid
   a. "Dead wood." Writing in a course evaluation that your professor was very nice to you does not convey the same message as writing that the professor met you every week during office hours for individual tutoring. We call terms such as "very nice" *dead wood* because they do not contribute to nuanced understanding. Similarly, avoid generic terms, such as "We did many things in this therapy session." We recognize that an adult with nonfluent or Broca's aphasia and associated difficulty in naming and word finding might use generic terms instead of substantive words (e.g., "the thing with the stuff over there"). However, you are neurotypical, and you must do better.
   b. Trite or slang words and phrases. Develop a keener sense of observation by avoiding overused expressions. Writing that you had trouble fitting the EEG electrode net was difficult because "her hair was all over the place" does not accurately describe the student volunteer whose heavily gelled, spiky hair made electrode contacts with her scalp difficult. Similarly, slang words that have a specific current meaning do not have a place in written clinical observations. For example, writing that a client who

demonstrates excellent orientation to time, place, person, and circumstance is *woke* will soon seem as archaic as if you had written that she is *hip*.

Writing Goals for Therapy

A recent issue of *Perspectives on Neurophysiology and Neurogenic Speech and Language Disorders* (2012, Volume 22, No. 4), the official publication of ASHA's Special Interest Group 2, was devoted to patient-reported outcomes of speech-language intervention. We have reported elsewhere (see, for example, Goldfarb & Santo Pietro, 2012) that an adult with a communication disorder should be included as a partner in developing goals for speech and language rehabilitation. In this section we will explore what clinical interns and professional practitioners need to consider when writing goals for therapy.

Setting Goals

Ask the adult client or the child's caregivers what goals will have the most impact on the speaker's effectiveness as a communicator. Compare these with the goals that the clinician may have in mind, and start with the ones that appear on both lists. Some explanation may be needed when the clinician rejects goals that may be touted in the media or on websites but are unsupported by solid clinical evidence. Cultural sensitivity is very important so that, for example, reducing gaze aversion is not addressed as a goal for a child who has been taught that it is rude to maintain eye contact with an authority figure.

The practice guidelines posted by the Academy of Neurologic Communication Disorders and Sciences (http://www.ancds.org) are based on exhaustive literature reviews. These guidelines indicate that some unresolved but crucial issues in setting goals relate to what might be called dosage of therapy. For example, we still do not have enough hard evidence to answer the following basic questions about many disorders of speech, language, and hearing:

How often should we schedule therapy? Is intensive treatment most effective? How long should each therapy session be? Should treatment tasks be grouped together as massed practice or spread out across the therapy session as distributed practice? What warrants immediate placement, follow-up, or watchful waiting? What are the criteria that motivate discharge from clinical intervention?

We have a long way to go before we can say, with confidence, our equivalent of, "Take two aspirin and call me in the morning."

Setting Criterion Levels

We have noticed a pattern at speech and hearing centers across the United States that 80% correct for 20 trials is overwhelmingly used as a therapy goal. We will deal with the number (80%) in a moment, but we first want to ask some questions. Is the goal met after 4 correct responses out of 5; 8 million correct out of 10 million; or something in between? Is the goal met after a single therapy session or multiple sessions, and do the multiple sessions need to be consecutive? Here is an exercise for setting criterion levels for an adult who stutters (Yairi & Seery, 2011):

> *Compare/contrast these two written therapy objectives:*
>
> John will perform his fluency targets with 95% accuracy.
>
> John will independently apply a slow easy speech initiation on 100 utterances with 95% accuracy during spontaneous conversation with peers across two consecutive group sessions in the therapy room.

It is clear that the second goal is more specific and gives a better indication of what is expected in therapy. It is also clear that Yairi and Seery do not consider 80% correct to be some sort of magical goal.

For tasks where muscle memory must be developed, such as therapy for fluency or articulation disorders, a high number of trials and a high level of mastery are required. Think about it.

Would your piano teacher think you were doing a good job if you played one-fifth (20%) of the notes incorrectly? Should Malcolm Gladwell, who advocated 10,000 hours of practice to become an expert, rewrite *Outliers*: *The story of success* (2008) to indicate that only 20 hours are really needed? On the other hand, many programs accredited by the Council on Academic Accreditation (CAA) permit students to take College-Level Examination Program. (*CLEP*) tests as substitutes for required courses in physical and biological sciences. CLEP indicates a score of 50, or on some exams, 46 out of 80 passes. As ASHA accepts CAA recommendations, it seems that a grade equivalent to D- in biological or physical sciences may be a reasonable goal for students hoping to earn the Certificate of Clinical Competence.

Let's get back to therapy goals and appropriate criterion levels. Sometimes an interval (temporal) goal is more appropriate than a ratio (numerical) goal. For example, in *The Stocker Probe for Fluency and Language* (Stocker & Goldfarb, 1995), a disfluent child ascends to a higher level of demand for creativity (or communicative responsibility) after achieving a criterion of 60 seconds of fluency at the current level for three consecutive sessions.

Principles of Therapy

Client-centered therapy means that we design treatment according to individual requirements. We need to make an early decision about error responses: should we provide correction or should we re-stimulate? What constitutes an adequate stimulus for the individual client? Ideally, in an operant-based program of instruction, there should be a hierarchy that permits the client to succeed at every level, yet provides appropriate challenges along the way. We also need to address antecedent events, or stimuli that set the stage for the occurrence of the target communicative behavior; what the target behavior should be at every level of therapy; and consequent events, or the types of "pay-offs" that follow performance of the target behaviors. Finally, we need to decide on a fixed or variable ratio (number of trials) or interval (period of time) schedule of reinforcement (pay-offs). A therapy goal should be to increase the number of trials or amount of time before reinforcement is delivered.

Write goals for a program of treatment that is arranged hierarchically. For example, structure therapy goals for an articulation disorder to treat the sound in isolation → in CV syllables → in more complex syllables → in words → in phrases → in sentences, gradually increasing utterance length. This should not be confused with increasing mean length of utterance, a language measure that can be used diagnostically, but that should not be a therapy goal. Other client-centered hierarchies can be syntactic complexity of the utterance, communicative responsibility, rate of speech, vocal volume, and cues or support provided by the clinician.

For generalization outside the clinic, sometimes called carryover, we must enable the client to be his or her own clinician. Goals for success entail self-correction as well as its prerequisite, self-monitoring. The compensations and adjustments the client makes may be a lifelong process. The two main parts of self-monitoring and subsequent self-correction are awareness and analysis, where the client develops familiarity with and responsibility for all the features of the communication disability.

Finally, the clinician should evaluate clinical outcomes based on the following:

> Did the treatment work or have the desired outcome? Was it *effective*?
>
> Did the treatment make the best use of the time set aside for it? Did it work faster than alternative treatments? Was it *efficient*?

To what degree did the treatment reflect a combination of the above? The combination of effectiveness and efficiency is called *efficacy*.

Sample Long-Term/Short-Term Goals

1. *Long-Term Goals of Therapy*
    a. The client, AB will demonstrate improved pragmatic/social interaction skills.
    b. AB will improve receptive language skills.
    c. AB will improve expressive language skills.

2. *Short-Term Goals of Therapy*
   a. AB will maintain purposeful eye contact for 3 to 5 seconds during 16/20 consecutive conversational exchanges for three consecutive sessions.
   b. AB will follow two-step directives 16/20 times for three consecutive sessions.
   c. AB will produce transitive verbs in a Picture Exchange Communication System (PECS) 16/20 times in three consecutive sessions.

Types of Professional Reports

I. Treatment (Therapy Session) Format Plan in Speech-Language Pathology

Following the diagnostic evaluation, the speech-language pathologist establishes a written treatment plan in the form of long and short-term goals of the therapy for the client.

University Center for Communication Disorders Therapy Session Plan

Composite plan of clinician intervention strategies based on a female college student, age 19. Identify what you think is well done, and what can be improved.

Client: M.N. Semester: Fall 2018

Clinician: Bea Prepared

Date: 9/9/18 Session #: 9 Room: 2424

Supervisor: Dr. Doctor

Supervisor Signature ______________________

Goals

1. The client will produce the /l/ sound correctly in words with 100% accuracy.
2. The client will produce the phonemes /l/ and /r/ in a paragraph, with no more than 5 articulation errors.
3. The client will engage in a 5-minute conversation with the clinician, making no more than 5 articulation errors.

Techniques/Materials

The client will be instructed to read 20 target words in sentences.

The client will be instructed to read paragraphs with the target sounds.

The clinician will engage the client in a 5-minute conversation about current events, while recording misarticulated phonemes.

Results

The client produced the /l/ sound with 80% accuracy (16/20). She self-corrected and repeated the error three times.

The client produced the /l/ and /r/ sounds correctly when reading aloud from a newspaper.

The client engaged in a spontaneous 5-minute conversation, with 5 errors.

Sample Treatment Plan: Nonfluent Aphasia

1. Warm-ups: massed practice of 25 highly associative open-ended sentences + symbolic gesture + phonemic cue, for example, You wash your hands (clinician provides appropriate gesture) with soap and w____.

   Therapy goal: Delete one (e.g., phonemic) cue when 80% correct criterion (20/25 correct responses) is met.

2. Discuss homework from previous session, where the caregiver indicated the number of times the client initiated, maintained, or elaborated on discourse topics during dinnertime each day.

   Therapy goal: Initiate 1 topic, maintain 5 topics, and elaborate on 3 topics in each of 3 consecutive days.

3. Semantic feature therapy: client and clinician each have the same 10 common objects, with a board between them hiding the objects. Client and clinician take turns describing one semantic feature of form (cue: What does it look like?) and function (cue: What do you do with it?) before guessing the name of the object.

   Therapy goals: 1. Receptive: 10/10 correct responses = 100% for client to guess (or hold up) the object described by the clinician. 2. Expressive: 8/10 correct responses = 80% for client to provide 1 feature each of form and function that is adequate for the clinician to identify the target object. Clinician provides cues as required.

Sample Treatment Plan: Central Auditory Processing Disorder (CAPD)

(with thanks to Donna Geffner, PhD, CCC-SLP/A)

1. The student will be able to process, integrate and discern auditory information in the presence of noise and in a timely manner when presented with multiple auditory events, background noise, and rapid speech.

   Evaluation Criteria: 85% accuracy (17/20 correct responses in 3 consecutive sessions)

   Procedure to Evaluate Goal: Reduced requests for repetition, improved ability to listen in background noise and process rapidly presented information based on baseline measures and performance on a temporal integration skill test.

   Evaluation Schedule: by end of school year

   Primary responsibility: Speech-Language Pathologist and/or Audiologist or classroom teacher

2. Student will improve his ability to understand spoken language and be able to summarize and recall details of the paragraphs read aloud using a visualizing and verbalizing approach.

   Evaluation Criteria: 75% accuracy (15/20 correct responses in 3 consecutive sessions)

   Procedure to Evaluate Goal: Student will demonstrate improved understanding of spoken language by being able to answer questions, follow directions, and provide details about a story read aloud.

   Evaluation Schedule: By the end of the school year

   Primary Responsibility: Classroom teacher as noted in class activities, speech-language pathologist by administering a test of auditory comprehension.

3. Student will improve his auditory short-term memory to recall words in sequence and lengthy sentences accurately, using techniques of auditorization and visualization.

   Evaluation Criteria: 75% accuracy (15/20 correct responses in 3 consecutive sessions)

   Procedure to Evaluate Goal: Speech-language pathologist will re-evaluate the child's auditory short term using a measure of short-term memory.

   Evaluation Schedule: By the end of 6-month intervals.

   Primary Responsibility: Classroom teacher and speech-language pathologist.

4. Student will improve his ability to infer and interpret a message and integrate information by using higher order reasoning skills and cohesion in order to comprehend a spoken message.

   Evaluation Criteria: 75% accuracy (15/20 correct responses in 3 consecutive sessions)

   Procedure to Evaluate Goal: Student will be assessed on a test of inference and nonliteral language.

Evaluation Schedule: At the end of the school year

Primary responsibility: Speech-language pathologist.

II. Progress Report

The progress report documents the client's performance in meeting the objectives of the treatment plan. In addition, the clinician indicates any changes that relate to future treatment goals, and provides a review of the long- and short-term goals and results, as in the following example:

1. The first goal was to have AB demonstrate improved pragmatic/social interaction skills. Tasks included establishing and maintaining trunk alignment while seated, establishing eye contact for 3 to 5 seconds during conversational exchanges, and making appropriate transitions from one task to another. AB achieved criterion of 80% correct for 20 trials over three consecutive sessions in these tasks. However, she continued sporadic tantrums in transitions between activities, and required verbal and visual prompts to establish and maintain eye contact.
2. The second goal was for AB to improve receptive language skills. Tasks included having AB identify pictures of common objects, independently point to pictures of verbs (e.g., *want*), and respond to two-step directives during activities. With the use of PECS, AB achieved criterion of 80% correct for 20 trials over three consecutive sessions in pointing to pictures of nouns and verbs and in following two-step directives.
3. The third goal was for AB to improve expressive language skills. Tasks included labeling action verbs, independently initiating a conversational exchange expressed vocally or with PECS, and independently using PECS for the purpose of requesting. Using PECS, AB met criterion of 80% correct for 20 trials over three consecutive sessions for labeling transitive but not intransitive verbs; for independently initiating a conversational exchange; and for requesting action, but not for requesting information or clarification.

Guidelines for Writing Progress Reports in Speech-Language Pathology

PROGRESS REPORT

Date

Client

Address

Telephone

Date of Birth

Age

Frequency/Length of Therapy Sessions (individual and group therapy)

Clinician

Supervisor

PRESENTING PROBLEM

(All section headings should be all capital letters and underlined.)

This is a historical overview of the client's communication problem. In the first paragraph, provide a brief description of the presenting problem, including the nature of the communication impairment and initial severity rating. You may find this information in the initial evaluation report. In the second paragraph, summarize therapy history and progress to the beginning of the current semester.

GOALS OF THERAPY

Present the information in a list format or in narrative form. Include the semester goals, not the short-term objectives, taken from your treatment plan.

TEST DATA

Include updated test results performed during the current semester.

PROCEDURES AND PROGRESS

Address each short-term goal with a paragraph of text. Procedures include materials, activities, and, most importantly, therapeutic techniques, such as the types of prompts and cues used to facilitate success. When reporting progress, do not overload this section with numbers reflecting percentages of accuracy in individual therapy sessions, but rather try to describe what the client is or is not able to do.

PRESENT STATUS

Briefly note the client's strengths and weaknesses. Highlight areas that need to be addressed in future therapy.

RECOMMENDATIONS

Include recommendations such as:

1. cessation or continuation of therapy,
2. number and length of sessions per week,
3. individual or group treatment,
4. future therapy goals,
5. referrals, and
6. suggestions for home practice.

Clinician's Name

Supervisor's Name and Credentials

Title

Clinical Intern

Progress Report: Writing Style Worksheet

1. Use the client's complete name.
2. Write age in years and months for clients under age 18, and years only for those older than 18. Remember to use a colon, not a decimal point, between years and months (e.g., 5 years, 9 months is 5:9, not 5.9).
3. Avoid ambiguous terms and colloquialisms. For example, always use a referent, rather than a pronoun, such as *she* or *that*, for the first notation in a paragraph. Be specific: "The clinician used stickers to get the client to say something," should be rewritten as, "The clinician used stickers to motivate the client to use the auxiliary verbs, *is*, *are*, and *am*."
4. Use language that can be understood by the reader. Define all technical terms and professional language, give examples for clarification, and use the phrase, *characterized by*, after a diagnostic label.
5. Use specific, accurate, brief sentences. Avoid verbosity and jargon.
6. Use complete verb forms; avoid contractions and hyphens.
7. Use active rather than passive verbs. Avoid such qualifiers as *somewhat*, *quite*, and *very*.
8. Write in the third person rather than the first person. Refer to yourself as *the clinician*, not as *I* or *me*.
9. Follow the rules for use of numerals described in Chapter 2. In general, use words to express one through nine and numerals for 10 and above. However, as noted in the numeral expressed as *Chapter 2* above, there are exceptions to the rule.
10. Express behavioral data mathematically, where possible. When reporting progress, include the number of trials to criterion and number of consecutive sessions in addition to the percent correct. Writing *80% correct responses* can mean 4 of 5 correct or 8 million out of 10 million. In general, collect data for at least 20 trials over three consecutive sessions before reporting the percent correct. In cases where performance is variable, use such quantifiers as *some* or *most*. Indicate whether criterion levels were reached for your clinical goals.
11. Use operational definitions and operationally written goals. These are statements of observed behavior that the client exhibits as a result of your clinical intervention strategies. Avoid such mentalistic terms as *learn*, *understand*, and *know*, and use operational terms such as *categorize*, *retell*, or *repeat*.

12. Do not refer to *lesson plans* when you mean *clinical intervention strategies*, or to *teaching* when you are *testing clinical hypotheses*. Our jobs would be much easier if we could, for example, eliminate word retrieval impairments by teaching vocabulary lessons.

Edited Progress Report in Speech-Language Pathology

The progress report below, with identifying information changed, includes comments in brackets that relate to information highlighted in boldface type and indicated by the left arrow. In general, there is a good deal of useful information in the progress report, but it is compromised by imprecise and overly verbose writing, or *flabby prose*. Before searching the Internet for the South Beach Writing Diet, please note some of the specific comments.

Date: August 9, 2018

Client: Hillary Bloomingdale

Address: 1000 Third Avenue,

New York, NY 10065

Telephone: (212) 794-0000

Date of Birth: 7/23/39

Age: 79

Frequency/Length of therapy sessions:

Individual: 1 x ~/wk for 45 minutes

Group: 1 x ~/wk for 60 minutes

Clinician: Barack McCain

Supervisor: **Dr. Robert Goldfarb, PHD**, CCC-SLP ← [writing Dr. and PhD (not *PHD*) is redundant]

PRESENTING PROBLEM

Mrs. Bloomingdale ← [form of address, e.g., *Mrs.* or *Ms.* is established by the institution] is a **79 year old woman** ← [need hyphens for *79-year-old*] who presents with mixed (flaccid, spastic) dysarthria resulting from cerebral hemorrhage in 2008. The client's speech is poorly intelligible and can be **characterized by** breathiness, hypernasality, poor breath support, consistent articulation errors, slow rate, strain-strangled voice quality, and poor variety in pitch and volume ← [good expansion of *characterized by*]. Saliva management is a cause of concern to the patient, as she is constantly wiping her mouth with a handkerchief and apologizing for the presence of extra saliva. The client has reported a hiatal hernia, which manifests **itself** ← [delete—redundant] in **gastoesophagael** ← [two spelling errors in *gastroesophageal*] reflux disease, causing pain and heartburn. The client currently receives physical therapy for **right sided** ← [add hyphen] weakness as a result of the stroke. Cognition is intact, and Mrs. Bloomingdale presents **herself** ← [delete—redundant] as a bright, sophisticated, and **highly opinionated** ← [wrong word—it means *stubborn*; also delete modifier] woman.

Mrs. Bloomingdale has attended both group and individual therapy regularly since May 2011. She appears to be **highly** ← [delete modifier] motivated and **utilizes** ← [*Uses* is preferred here and almost everywhere.] the strategies **taught** ← [*Established* is a better word, as therapy involves testing clinical hypotheses, and does not follow a curriculum.] during therapy in order to be understood by the listener. Despite the requirement that the speaker put forth considerable effort in understanding Mrs. Bloomingdale, **she** ← [referent is unclear] is determined to be understood and uses **many different modalities** ← [Specify whether the modalities are auditory, visual, graphic, etc.] to reach **intelligibility** ← [should be *comprehensibility* as context is involved]. During previous semesters, the client was **taught** ← [*trained*] to tap out each syllable with her finger and increase her vocal intensity to improve **intelligibility** ← [*Intelligibility*, based on an acoustic measure, is used correctly here]. She is currently working on improving her articulation, prosody, and vocal quality.

GOALS OF THERAPY

1. Mrs. Bloomingdale will improve her **prosody skills** ← [use the adjective,

prosodic, to modify the noun, *skills*] by using correct intonation and stress patterns.
2. Mrs. Bloomingdale will use **the** ← [delete] proper breath support during speech. Goals 1 and 2 do not have measurable objectives.
3. Mrs. Bloomingdale will **improve** her articulation of /s/ using the auditory discrimination and phonetic placement approaches. ← [Set a criterion for improvement, based on a percentage derived by dividing number of correct responses by number of trials, and maintained over a specified number of therapy sessions.]
4. Mrs. Bloomingdale will **incorporate her speaking strategies** while conversing with peers. ← [This is too general to be a useful goal.]

TEST DATA

No standardized tests were performed during the current semester.

PROCEDURES AND PROGRESS

Authors' note: Only the first goal is analyzed for writing.

1. Mrs. Bloomingdale will improve her prosodic skills by using correct intonation and stress patterns.

A method called *shadowing* was used to improve prosody and increase the naturalness of the client's speech. The clinician read a **passage** ← [add comma] and the client was instructed to repeat **after the clinician** ← [delete—redundant] and follow her stress and intonation patterns. While shadowing the clinician, Mrs. Bloomingdale's speech sounded less **robotic**. ← [Use a more behavioral descriptor.] In addition to shadowing, the clinician **also** ← [Delete as redundant, because the sentence started with *in addition*.] presented the client with written questions with arrows indicating **proper** ← [Use a behavioral descriptor, e.g., *rising* or *falling*.] intonation and had the client read them aloud. Mrs. Bloomingdale had **difficulty managing pitch changes** ← [Use a behavioral descriptor.] **in her voice** ← [delete as redundant] as **appose** ← [misspelled *opposed*] to pitch. **An exercise was done where** ← [delete] the clinician said a sentence while raising either the volume or **pitch** ← [use *frequency* to correspond with *volume*] **of her voice** ← [delete phrase but insert comma] and Mrs. Bloomingdale was asked to identify which aspect was changed. The client's motivation and cooperation facilitated improvement in her prosodic skills. However, **much work** ← [therapy] is still needed **in order** ← [delete] to **further** ← [delete] increase the naturalness of the client's speech.

III. Audiogram Form Report

In settings where audiologic assessment procedures, findings, and terminology are well understood, it is common to use an abbreviated reporting form instead of the comprehensive diagnostic report format. The client's actual audiogram (in expanded form) may serve as the report itself (Figures 9–1 and 9–2). The audiogram report includes graphic or tabular information of clinical outcomes (e.g., pure tones, speech audiometry, immittance), in addition to a written summary section (Stach, 2010). The audiogram form report is commonly used in the exchange of information with audiologists, otologists, and hearing-aid dispensers, and is often the reporting format used in the patient charts of hospital or medical settings. The brevity of this type of report form creates the advantage of reducing time in both the recording and reading of information in the often fast-paced health setting.

IV. Medical Chart Logs/Reports

A typical reporting format used in hospitals or medical-based clinics or centers is the medical chart log or report. The writing of logs or reports in medical charts is extremely brief and includes only the most pertinent information, characterized by the use of standard abbreviations (see Chapter 2), short phrases, or fragmented sentences. This writing style meets the need of quick documentation and reading of information for professionals in facilities where many patients are seen in short time blocks (Bickley & Hoekelman, 1999; Seidel, Ball, Dains, & Benedict, 2003).

University Audiology Center

Name ______________________ Age ________ Date _________

Audiologist __________________ Audiometer _______________

FREQUENCY IN HZ

250 500 1000 2000 4000 8000

DECIBELS IN dB HL

-10 0 10 20 30 40 50 60 70 80 90 100 110

750 1500 3000 6000

Otoscopy
R: ____________
L: ____________

Tympanometry
R: ____________
L: ____________

Speech Audiometry

	SDT dB HL	SRT dB HL	SRS %	SRS dB
R				
L				
Sound Field				

HISTORY:

RESULTS:

RECOMMENDATIONS:

Figure 9–1. Sample audiogram form report format

Audiology Center

Name ______________________ Age __________ Date __________

Audiologist ______________________ Audiometer ______________________

FREQUENCY IN HZ

250 500 1000 2000 4000 8000

DECIBELS IN dB HL

-10 0 10 20 30 40 50 60 70 80 90 100 110

750 1500 3000 6000

Otoscopy
R: TM redness
L: TM redness

Tympanometry
R: type B
L: type B

Speech Audiometry

	SRT dB HL	SRS %	SRS dB HL
R	30	100	65
L	30	96	65

HISTORY:
failed hearing screening

RESULTS:
Otoscopy: redness of tympanic membranes (TM) bilaterally
Pure Tones: mild to moderate conductive hearing loss bilaterally
Immittance: type B patterns bilaterally

RECOMMENDATIONS:
1. medical referral to assess middle ear status
2. re-test post-medical treatment or follow-up

Figure 9–2. Sample audiogram form report.

Although appropriate to the health or medical facility, a more formal reporting format (see prior sections in this chapter) may be necessary when sending reports to other professionals. In audiology, it is common practice to use the audiogram report form (see above) as the medical chart entry.

Common medical chart abbreviations are used in communication sciences and disorders. For a more complete list of abbreviations in our discipline, see the abbreviation list in Chapter 2.

Sample Medical Chart Report Format

Date

Clinical Findings/Outcomes

Recommendations

Name/Signature

Example of a Medical Chart Report: Speech-Language Pathology

Log Note: 9/10/18

Maintain eye gaze 3–5 sec: 18/20 CR = 90%

Transition to task: 4/5 CR = 80% (one tantrum)

Label verbs in PECS task: 10 consecutive "I want"

Point to Boardmaker nouns: 14/20 CR = 70% (used "pizza" as default choice)

Expanded Version:
The client achieved criterion of 80% correct for 20 trials by maintaining eye contact with the clinician for 3 to 5 sec in 18 of 20 attempts. Of the five transitions from one task to another, one resulted in tantrum behavior.

In the Picture Exchange Communication System (PECS) task, the client was able to label 10 consecutive verb pictures, following the carrier phrase, "I want . . . " She did not achieve criterion of 80% correct for 20 trials in pointing to nouns represented in Boardmaker pictures following the clinician's production of the word, with 14 correct in 20 attempts, and pointed to the "pizza" picture in all error responses.

Example of a Medical Chart Report: Audiology

Evaluation: 9/10/18

F/U CAE 13 yo = TM redness AU; Mild to moderate CHL AU; type B tymps AU; abs ARTs AU

Rec: 1. ENT 2. retest

Expanded Version:
A complete audiologic evaluation follow-up was conducted on this 13-year-old patient.

Otoscopy: redness of the tympanic membranes bilaterally

Pure Tones: Mild to moderate conductive hearing loss bilaterally

Immittance: Type B patterns bilaterally; absent contralateral middle ear reflexes

Recommendations:

1. Medical referral to assess middle ear status.
2. Retest post-medical follow-up or treatment.

Professional Correspondence

Correspondence often takes the form of a request for information from an outside agency or professional, referral for additional service, or compliance with a request for information or service.

Professional Referrals/Sending Reports

Often the proper clinical care of a patient requires further assessment or treatment by other professionals in communication disorders or those in other disciplines (e.g., medical, educational, psychological). Patients may be referred to you as the communication disorders specialist, or you may be making the referral. In either case, an exchange of information regarding the patient will be required.

Following the regulations of the Health Insurance Portability and Accountability Act (HIPAA) of 1996, it is imperative that a signed release of information form be obtained from the client or legal guardian prior to providing any information, oral or written, to other individuals, including professionals who may be involved with the client's case. A signed authorization of release of information is necessary even if a report is to be sent to the professional who may have referred the client to you in the first place. It is important to recognize a patient's right to refuse disclosure of information.

Sample Authorization of Release of Information Form

CENTER FOR COMMUNICATION DISORDERS AUTHORIZATION FORM (HIPAA)

Authorization for Disclosure of Protected Health Information

NAME OF CLIENT: ______________________

1. I authorize **The Center for Communication Disorders** to disclose or receive my protected health information, as specified below, to/from:

   ____

   ____

2. I am authorizing disclosure of the following protected health information:

   ____

   ____

3. This protected health information is being used or disclosed at the request of the individual.
4. This authorization shall be in force and effect until one (1) year after the date below, at which time this authorization to disclose protected health information shall expire.
5. I understand that I have the right to revoke this authorization, in writing, at any time by sending such written notification to **The Center for Communication Disorders, 723 Main Avenue, Jamestown, NY 98765**. I understand that a revocation is not effective to the extent that my authorization was obtained as a condition of obtaining reimbursement for services provided.
6. I understand that information disclosed pursuant to this authorization may be disclosed by the recipient and may no longer be protected by HIPAA or any other federal or state law.
7. My health care practitioner will not condition my treatment on whether I provide an authorization for disclosure except if such authorization is required to receive third party reimbursement for services provided.

____

Signature of Client or Parent of Minor Client

____

Date

____

Print Name

____

Relationship to Client

Correspondence Via Electronic Media

Present-day professional correspondence involves interaction via hard copy ("snail mail"), telephone, or electronic media. Increasingly, delayed or instant text-messaging through telephone or computer media has become a popular electronic communication form in average daily interaction. Similarly, electronic communication of patient records through facsimile (fax) or Internet transmission is commonly used in professional correspondence. Reports may be scanned or sent as text documents in email attachments, or faxed from original hard copies to the recipient. Facsimiles may also be the legal equivalent of an original document, which should be familiar to those of us who have served on jury duty.

Irrespective of transmission form, proper professional correspondence etiquette requires some formal introductory commentary to precede the electronic submission. The "cover letter" in electronic correspondence may follow a formal cover letter style (see section below) or a less formal style of a few lines of text (under the heading, say, of "Fax Transmission Sheet") that would include a salutation, reference to an attached or sent document regarding the specific patient, and a closing.

Certainly, all forms of electronic communication, even the less formal, should follow proper professional writing style, form, and content. This applies to any type of professional communication, even the nonclinical. For students, this would include electronic correspondence with professors or clinical supervisors in the academic setting. Emails from students without proper formal salutation, or with use of the colloquial *hey*, may be perceived as rude, whereas errors in spelling or grammar from prospective students may leave the impression of someone incapable of graduate-level work. A simple rule of thumb would be to follow and apply the principles of professional writing in *any* type of professional interaction (see Chapter 10: Writing for Professional Advancement).

Letters to Professionals

Letters to other professionals may be written for the purposes of information request, referral, or gratitude, and may also serve as a cover letter accompanied by an additional report or copies of clinical outcomes regarding a patient. Depending on the nature of the professional relationship, a formal cover letter usually accompanies a written report of information that is sent to other professionals. The formality of a cover letter may be omitted when corresponding with a professional with whom one is very familiar. It may not be conventional practice in some settings, where briefer reporting practices are preferred. (See sections on report forms above.)

There are two variations of letter formats in the reporting of patient information in professional correspondence: one in which a separate cover precedes the formal report, and the other where the report is written in a letter format.

Cover Letters for Professional Reports

Cover letters accompany attachments of professional reports, whether hard copy or electronic. Cover letters should follow a standard professional business letter format. (See sample below.)

Cover Letter Format

Note that all information—including the date, signature, and paragraphs—is flush with the left margin. Both indented and flush styles are acceptable in a cover letter.

Sender Contact Information

Address

Telephone Number

Email Address

Date

Recipient Contact Information

Recipient Name

Title

Address

Salutation
Begin this section with "Dear (title and name):" making sure to use the correct title (e.g., Dr., Ms., Mr.) and spelling of the first and last names. Use

a proper salutation even when sending an email; do not begin with the informal greeting of "Hi."

Body of the Letter
The first sentence should begin with a statement of the purpose of the correspondence, such as for referral, reporting, or request of information on a specific patient. Identify the patient and the type, location, and date of the service conducted or requested, as applicable. If clinical findings are to be communicated, the next sentences should refer to the report and whether it is attached as a hard or electronic copy. In the letter report format (see example below), the report itself may be embedded in the letter in subsequent paragraphs. The last sentences in the body of the letter may thank the recipient for a request of information, and add or refer to your listed contact information.

Closing
End the letter with a cordial term such as "Sincerely," "Respectfully," or "Yours truly."

Name and Signature
Type your name with degree and certification credentials, and place your handwritten signature just above it. For email transmission, provide an electronic signature.

Example Cover Letter for Speech-Language Pathology Report

Speak the Speech
1501 Hamlet Street
Stratford, CT 12345
1-800-SCENEII

September 24, 2018

Sara Booth, AuD, CCC-A
I'm All Ears
321 Blastoff Street
Cape Kennedy, FL 10987-6543

Dear Dr. Booth:

I am referring AB for a complete audiological evaluation. She failed a pure-tone hearing screening bilaterally for the frequencies 500, 1000, 2000, and 4000 Hz at 20 dB HL. Enclosed please find a copy of her speech and language evaluation.

If you need additional information, please do not hesitate to contact me.

Yours truly,

Anne Hathaway, MS, CCC-SLP
Speech-Language Pathologist

Example Cover Letter for Audiology Report

Center for Communication Disorders
Jamestown, NY 98765

September 10, 2018

Andrew House, MD
723 Main Avenue
Jamestown, NY 98765

Dear Dr. House:

I am referring Susan Shore, age 13 years, for middle ear evaluation. She was referred to the Center for Communication Disorders for a complete audiologic assessment as a result of failing a hearing screening in school. Audiologic and immittance findings are consistent with middle ear pathology.

Enclosed please find a copy of the audiologic report, audiogram, and immittance findings. Pending any medical treatment, a hearing retest is recommended. Please contact me should you require any further information.

Sincerely,

Sara Booth, AuD, CCC-A
Audiologist

Letters as Reports

Reports can also be written in a letter format, combining the cover letter and the clinical report in speech-language pathology or audiology. (See sample letter report format below.)

Sample Letter Report Format

Sender Information

Sender Address

Telephone Number

Email Address

Date

Recipient Information

Recipient Name

Title

Address

Salutation

Dear . . .

Body of the Letter
The body of the letter report should include components of the clinical report.

Diagnostic Outcomes

Clinical Impressions

Recommendations

Closing

Sincerely, and so forth.

Signature

Sender's Name and credentials

Example Letter Report: Audiology

Center for Communication Disorders
Jamestown, NY

September 11, 2018

Dear Dr. House:

I am referring Susan Shore, age 13 years, for middle ear evaluation. She was referred to the Center for Communication Disorders for a complete audiologic assessment as a result of failing a hearing screening in school. Audiologic and immittance findings were obtained on September 10, 2018, and are as follows:

AUDIOLOGIC ASSESSMENT

Otoscopy
Redness of the tympanic membranes was noted bilaterally.

Pure-Tone Audiometry
Mild to moderate conductive hearing loss bilaterally was noted.

Speech Audiometry
Speech recognition thresholds (SRTs) are consistent with pure-tone findings. Speech recognition scores (SRSs) are excellent.

Immittance
Type B patterns bilaterally with absent contralateral acoustic middle ear reflexes, consistent with middle ear pathology.

CLINICAL IMPRESSIONS

Clinical findings of tympanic membrane redness, conductive hearing loss, and type B tympanograms with absent middle ear reflexes are consistent with middle ear pathology.

RECOMMENDATIONS

1. Medical evaluation to assess middle ear status.
2. Retest post-medical treatment or follow-up.

Sincerely,

Sara Booth, AuD, CCC-A
Audiologist

EXERCISES

Exercise 9–1. Chapter Review

1. Informed consent is needed:
   a. only if the consumer is a minor child or a disabled adult
   b. to permit HIPAA regulations to prevail
   c. to assure confidentiality of individually identifiable health information
   d. before the clinician uses edible items in therapy
   e. to permit the clinician or institution to charge fees for services

2. "AB will maintain purposeful eye contact for 3 to 5 seconds during 16/20 consecutive conversational exchanges for three consecutive sessions" is an example of a:
   a. long-term goal
   b. short-term goal
   c. treatment plan
   d. progress report
   e. status report

3. In a progress report, the *presenting problem* includes:
   a. the historical overview of the client's communication problem
   b. the goals of therapy
   c. test data
   d. procedures
   e. recommendations

4. The problem with writing, "The clinician used stickers to get the client to say something," is that it includes:
   a. passive rather than active verbs
   b. use of the first person rather than the third person
   c. verbosity and jargon
   d. language that cannot be understood by the reader
   e. ambiguous terms

5. Which is the briefest form of a professional report?
   a. cover letter
   b. progress report
   c. audiogram form report
   d. medical chart report
   e. treatment plan

Exercise 9–2. Change Language from Passive to Active and From Mentalistic to Behavioral

The following is an example of how to change language from passive to active and from mentalistic to behavioral: *Joseph could not be conditioned when an audiological evaluation was attempted.* Corrected example: *The audiologist attempted to evaluate Joseph, but he repeatedly removed the headphones and rose from his chair.* Change the following examples in a similar way.

1. Earphones were fitted for the client, but it was difficult because she was feeling anxious

 ____

 ____

 ____

2. The client understood my instructions

 ____

 ____

 ____

3. Divided-attention tasks are distracting for the patient with traumatic brain injury.

 ____

 ____

 ____

4. John's mother was told that he felt bullied because of his stuttering.

 ____

 ____

 ____

5. Cochlear implants recommended for a 3-year-old may be refused by deaf parents who want their child to remain in the Deaf community.

____

____

____

Exercise 9–3. Rewriting Trite or Slang Words and Phrases

The following is an example of how to change "dead wood," slang, and trite expressions to image-rich descriptions: *Mr. S. came into the therapy room all messed up. His responses were way out of line.* Corrected example: *Mr. S. came into the therapy room with his wrinkled shirt half tucked into his pants. He said that he was on a bus and that the clinician was the bus driver.* Change the following examples in a similar way.

1. My clinical supervisor is so cool. She is just as nice as she can be.

____

____

____

2. The three-year-old nonverbal child was a handful. I had had it by the end of the session.

____

____

____

3. Some people say that hearing aids don't do it for them. They need lots of follow up.

____

____

____

4. Water calorics used in electronystagmography may make some people dizzy.

____

____

____

5. Mike's new AAC device is the bomb.

____

____

____

Exercise 9–4. Practice Writing Clinical Observations

Complete the description, using the strategies highlighted in the section on writing clinical observations. Demonstrate your powers of observation and your ability to write what you observe. *On this rainy September morning, I am sitting at a child-sized table in the Center for Communicative Disorders, waiting for my first client.*

____

____

____

____

____

____

____

____

____

____

____

____

____

____

____

Exercise 9–5. Write Clinical Goals in Speech-Language Pathology

For a child with an interdental lisp, write the following goals:

A. Set goals for the task, with criterion levels.

B. Set goals for the schedule and type of reinforcement.

C. Set goals for the hierarchy of treatment

D. Set goals for generalization or carryover of treatment.

E. Set goals for efficacy of treatment.

In this section, you will observe diagnostic and therapy sessions in speech-language pathology to practice writing a therapy plan, progress report, medical chart note, and a professional cover letter and letter report. Exercises in audiology will provide cases with diagnostic information for you to practice writing cover letters, letter reports, audiogram form reports, and medical chart reports.

Exercise 9–6. Observe a Diagnostic Session in Speech-Language Pathology and Write a Treatment Plan

Please maintain client anonymity.

Exercise 9–7. Observe a Therapy Session in Speech-Language Pathology and Write a Progress Report

Please maintain client anonymity.

Exercise 9–8. Write a Medical Chart Note Using Information Obtained from the Progress Note Above

Please maintain client anonymity.

Exercise 9–9. Write Professional Letters in Speech-Language Pathology

The physician of the client you observed has asked you to send a report regarding the client's treatment plan. Appropriate consent forms have been obtained. Using the information provided below and in the exercises that follow, practice writing:

a. a cover letter that will accompany your report
b. a letter report

Speech-Language Pathologist
Henry Higgins, CCC-SLP

Facility
University Speech-Language Pathology Center
122 Nassau Drive
Cambridge, NY 03511

Physician
John Hopkins, MD
54 Northville Avenue
Southtown, NY 34762

Exercise 9–9A. Write a Cover Letter Using the Information Above

Please maintain client anonymity.

University Speech-Language Pathology Center

Exercise 9–9B. Write a Letter Report Using the Information Above

Please maintain client anonymity in your response.

University Speech-Language Pathology Center

Exercise 9–10. Write Clinical Goals in Audiology

For an adolescent with an auditory processing disorder, write the following goals:

A. Set goals for the task, with criterion levels.

B. Set goals for the schedule and type of reinforcement.

C. Set goals for the hierarchy of treatment

D. Set goals for generalization or carryover of treatment.

____

____

____

____

____

E. Set goals for efficacy of treatment.

____

____

____

____

____

In this section, you will practice writing professional letters and concise clinical reports in audiology. For each exercise, you will write an audiogram form report, a medical chart note, a cover letter, and a letter report. Refer to the corresponding diagnostic reports in Chapter 8, and the background information provided below.

Exercise 9–11. Audiology Reports and Professional Letters

Mrs. Frank would like a report of her son Tyler Frank's audiologic evaluation conducted at the Center for Communication Disorders sent to the County Early Intervention Program. Mrs. Frank has signed a consent form. Write a cover letter that will accompany the corresponding information in the diagnostic report in Chapter 8, and below:

Audiologist
Sara Booth, Au.D., CCC-A

Facility
Center for Communication Disorders
232 South Street
Weston, IL 12534

Exercise 9–11A. Write an Audiogram Form Report Using the Information Above

Center for Communication Disorders

Name ______________________ Age __________ Date ______________

Audiologist ______________________ Audiometer ______________________

FREQUENCY IN HZ

250 500 1000 2000 4000 8000

DECIBELS IN dB HL

-10
0
10
20
30
40
50
60
70
80
90
100
110

S S S S

750 1500 3000 6000

Otoscopy
R: ______________
L: ______________

Tympanometry
R: ______________
L: ______________

Speech Audiometry

	SDT dB HL	SRT dB HL	SRS %	SRS dB HL
R				
L				
Sound Field				

HISTORY:

____

____

____

____

RESULTS:

RECOMMENDATIONS:

Exercise 9–11B. Write a Medical Chart Report Using the Information Above

Exercise 9–11C. Write a Cover Letter Using the Information Above

Exercise 9–11D. Write a Letter Report Using the Information Above

Exercise 9–12. Audiology Reports and Professional Letters

Your patient Don Smith would like you to send a report of his audiologic evaluation conducted at the University Audiology Center to his internist, Dr. Campbell. Mr. Smith has signed a consent form. Write a cover letter that will accompany the corresponding information in the diagnostic report in Chapter 8, and below:

Audiologist
Holly Lightly, AuD, CCC-A

Facility
University Audiology Center
122 Nassau Drive
Cambridge, NY 03511

Internist
Mark Campbell, MD
27 Institution Avenue
Countyville, NJ 42733

Exercise 9–12A. Write an Audiogram Form Report Using the Information Above

University Audiology Center

Name ______________________ Age ____________ Date ______________

Audiologist ______________________ Audiometer ______________________

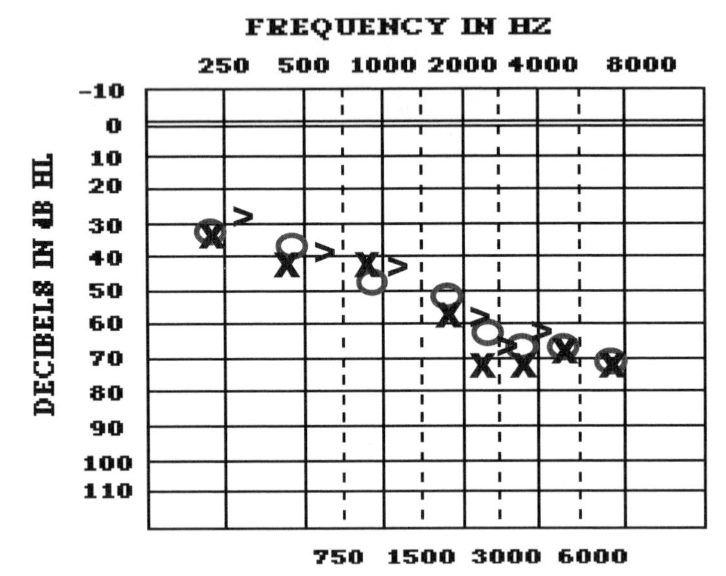

Otoscopy

R: ______________

L: ______________

Tympanometry

R: ______________

L: ______________

Speech Audiometry

	SDT dB HL	SRT dB HL	SRS %	SRS dB HL
R				
L				
Sound Field				

HISTORY:

____

____

____

____

RESULTS:

____

____

____

____

RECOMMENDATIONS:

____

____

____

____

Exercise 9–12B. Write a Medical Chart Report Using the Information Above

Exercise 9–12C. Write a Cover Letter Using the Information Above

Exercise 9–12D. Write a Letter Report Using the Information Above

Exercise 9–13. Audiology Reports and Professional Letters

You are referring your patient Maria Aresta to Dr. Maxwell, an otologist, for medical clearance prior to an amplification fitting. Mrs. Aresta has signed a consent form. Write a cover letter that will accompany the corresponding information in the diagnostic report in Chapter 8, and below:

Audiologist
Donald Saunders, Ph.D., CCC-A

Facility
University Audiology Center
122 Nassau Drive
Cambridge, NY 03511

Otologist
Dr. George Maxwell, MD
1000 Park Road
Springfield, CT 02345

Exercise 9–13A. Write an Audiogram Form Report Using the Information Above

University Audiology Center

Name ____________________ Age __________ Date ____________

Audiologist ____________________ Audiometer ____________________

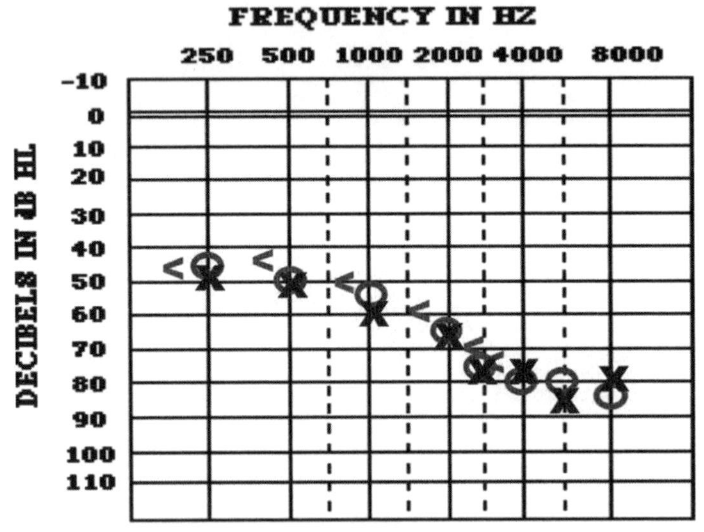

Otoscopy
R: __________
L: __________

Tympanometry
R: __________
L: __________

Speech Audiometry

	SDT dB HL	SRT dB HL	SRS %	SRS dB HL
R				
L				
Sound Field				

HISTORY:

____

____

____

____

RESULTS:

____

____

____

____

RECOMMENDATIONS:

____

____

____

____

Exercise 9–13B. Write a Medical Chart Report Using the Information Above

Exercise 9–13C. Write a Cover Letter Using the Information Above

Exercise 9–13D. Write a Letter Report Using the Information Above

Exercise 9–14. Audiology Reports and Professional Letters

Mrs. Zorros, the mother of patient Lyle Zorros, has asked you to send a copy of the audiologic report to the referring facility; she has signed a consent form. Write a cover letter that will accompany the corresponding information in the diagnostic report in Chapter 8, and below:

Audiologist
Sarah Bell, AuD, CCC-A

Facility
University Audiology Center
122 Nassau Drive
Cambridge, NY 03511

Referring Facility
County Early Intervention Program
200 Northpike Road
Garden Park, NY 22446

Exercise 9–14A. Write an Audiogram Form Report Using the Information Above

University Audiology Center

Name ______________________ Age __________ Date ______________

Audiologist ______________________ Audiometer ______________________

FREQUENCY IN HZ

250 500 1000 2000 4000 8000

DECIBELS IN dB HL

-10 0 10 20 30 40 50 60 70 80 90 100 110

750 1500 3000 6000

Otoscopy

R: ______________

L: ______________

Tympanometry

R: ______________

L: ______________

Speech Audiometry

	SDT dB HL	SRT dB HL	SRS %	SRS dB HL
R				
L				
Sound Field				

HISTORY:

____

____

____

____

RESULTS:

____

____

____

____

RECOMMENDATIONS:

____

____

____

____

Exercise 9–14B. Write a Medical Chart Report Using the Information Above

Exercise 9–14C. Write a Cover Letter Using the Information Above

Exercise 9–14D. Write a Letter Report Using the Information Above

Exercise 9–15. Audiology Reports and Professional letters.

You are referring patient Sam Gould for an otologic evaluation to rule out middle ear pathology in the right ear. Mrs. Gould, Sam's mother, has signed a consent form. Write a cover letter that will accompany the diagnostic report in Chapter 8, using the specific information below:

Audiologist
Michael Reiner, PhD, CCC-A

Facility
University Audiology Center
122 Nassau Drive
Cambridge, NY 03511

Otologist
Zach Trainer, MD
430 Institution Avenue
Farmingville, NY 11427

Exercise 9–15A. Write an Audiogram Form Report Using the Information Above

University Audiology Center

Name ______________________ Age __________ Date ____________

Audiologist ______________________ Audiometer ______________________

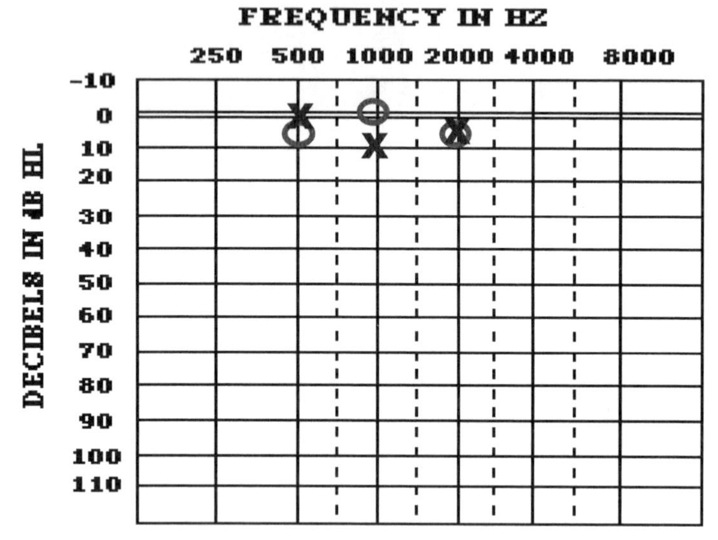

Otoscopy
R: ____________
L: ____________

Tympanometry
R: ____________
L: ____________

Speech Audiometry

	SDT dB HL	SRT dB HL	SRS %	SRS dB HL
R				
L				
Sound Field				

HISTORY:

____

____

____

____

RESULTS:

____

____

____

____

RECOMMENDATIONS:

____

____

____

____

Exercise 9–15B. Write a Medical Chart Report Using the Information Above

Exercise 9–15C. Write a Cover Letter Using the Information Above

Exercise 9–15D. Write a Letter Report Using the Information Above

References

Bickley, L. S., & Hoekelman, R. A. (1999). *Bates' guide to physical examination and history taking* (7th ed.). Philadelphia, PA: Lippincott Williams & Wilkins.

Gladwell, M. (2008). *Outliers: The story of success.* New York, NY: Little, Brown.

Goldfarb, R., & Santo Pietro, M. J. (2012). The use of sets in SLP diagnosis and treatment. In R. Goldfarb (Ed.), *Translational speech-language pathology and audiology* (pp. 313–318). San Diego, CA: Plural.

Health Insurance Portability and Accountability Act (HIPAA) of 1996, Public Law 104–191, 104th Congress.

Office for Protection from Research Risks, Protection of Human Subjects. National Commission for the Protection of Human Subjects of Biomedical and Behavioral Research (1979). *The Belmont Report: Ethical principles and guidelines for the protections of human subjects of research* (GPO Office 887-890). Washington, DC: Government Printing Office.

Seidel, H. M., Ball, J. W., Dains, J. E., & Benedict, G. W. (2003). *Mosby's guide to physical examination* (5th ed.). St. Louis, MO: Mosby.

Stach, B. A. (2010). *Clinical audiology: An introduction* (2nd ed.). San Diego, CA: Delmar.

Stocker, B., & Goldfarb, R. (1995). *The Stocker probe for fluency and language* (3rd ed.). Vero Beach, FL: The Speech Bin.

Yairi, E., & Seery, C. H. (2011). *Stuttering: Foundations and clinical applications.* Upper Saddle River, NJ: Pearson Education.

Writing for Professional Advancement

In this chapter, you will review proper formats for professional resumes, cover letters, portfolios, and electronic correspondence. In addition, an overview of multiple-choice test formats will be provided, with attention to the Graduate Record Examination (GRE®) and the Praxis® examinations in speech-language pathology and audiology.

In the exercises that follow, you will be required to:

1. Develop a personal resume and professional cover letter.
2. Create a portfolio.
3. Write professional letters via email.

Writing for Professional Advancement

There are several written documents essential for advancement as students in academic programs and for securing employment as future professionals in communication sciences and disorders. This chapter will focus on those documents.

I. Resumes

The resume (*resumé*, *résumé*; French meaning *summary*) is intended to be a brief (one- to two-page) written synopsis of an individual's educational background, skills, and experience. In essence, it can be thought of as a large business card. A more detailed, lengthier version known as the *curriculum vitae* (*CV*; Latin meaning *course of life*) is commonly used in academic, legal, and scientific settings (Friedman, 2007). Typically, the student and future professional in communication sciences and disorders will be using the resume format, unless hired by a college, university, or research institution, for which the CV is appropriate.

Although the most common purpose of the resume is for gaining employment, it may also be useful to the student in providing information for the preparation of letters of recommendation, applications for service or leadership positions, awards, or scholarships. The resume is a work in progress throughout one's career; the information should continually be updated to reflect the latest academic or professional developments. As such, the resume also serves as a record of one's academic and professional achievements and experiences. Students should therefore begin to develop their resumes early on during their program of study, adding and modifying the information as it changes during the course of academic and professional life. A good suggestion would be to make modifications as they occur rather than when the resume is needed. This will prevent lapses in memory of specific details and allow easy access to an already updated resume at a moment's notice.

The main purpose of the resume when job searching is to get noticed and land an interview. In writing the resume, particularly for purposes of employment, certainly clarity and style are important, but brevity is of the essence. Unlike the CV, which can go on for pages with detailed information, the resume is meant to capture important details and is confined to no more than two (but preferably one) pages of space. Employers or personnel reviewers frequently must get through dozens of resumes before deciding which candidates to interview, and often do so by a quick overview of the information. Indeed, a study suggests that only 1 minute or less is spent by most hiring reviewers in reading a resume and forming an impression on an applicant's qualifications, with preferences shown for organized, conventional-style resumes (Helwig, 1985). It is therefore in the applicant's best interest to follow a basic guide for resume preparation, as described below (McDaniels, 1990; O'Hair, Friedrich, Wiemann, & Wiemann, 1997; Rosenberg & Hizer, 1990; Seiler & Beall, 1999).

Although there is no standard resume style to which you must adhere, the most commonly used is the *chronologic* format, which uses headings to group items listed, with the most recent first (i.e., in reverse chronologic order). The order and specific titles may differ and should be tailored to the individual, but typical headings of information following the letterhead would include education, certifications/licenses, professional experience, awards/honors, publications, professional presentations, research, professional affiliations/activities, skills, and references. Adding a section on *objectives* is optional, but unnecessary in our very specialized professions as the listed degrees, certifications, and skills will clarify the targeted position. In addition, stating an objective on the resume that is too narrow might limit job opportunities. For example, if a prospective job seeker indicates an objective of hearing-aid fitting and dispensing, an employer of a multiservice site who is seeking someone to conduct hearing evaluations and amplification services may bypass this applicant. Statements of purpose usually belong in the cover letter. (See section below.)

There are numerous professional web-based programs and for-hire assistive services for resume preparation, but most universities offer tips to students (in-person or via the Internet) for free. It is strongly recommended that the student take advantage of these academic services but independently lay out and type the resume on a personal computer, making sure to save it on both hard and soft drives. Because the resume will be repeatedly updated, one must be able to access the information quickly and easily; this will prevent the need to start from square one each time a resume is needed.

Following are *do's* and *don'ts* tips with a basic resume layout to assist with creating a high-quality resume.

Do's

1. Above all, be truthful! A resume, as any written professional document, is bound by ethical reporting.
2. Distinguish headings by using distinctive typeface such as uppercase or bolding; separate items under each heading by using dates, titles, or bullets, making sure to be consistent throughout. Omit headings that don't apply, or add ones that may be more appropriate.
3. List all items under headings in reverse chronologic order; use the present tense for current activities and past tense for previous ones.
4. Use a minimum 11- or 12-point type and standard font (e.g., Times New Roman, Arial). Larger type may be used for headings; smaller fonts may be difficult to read and fancy fonts may transform into indecipherable characters in email transmission.
5. Print the resume on letter size, heavy weight (22–25 lb.) cotton-fiber content, light-colored paper using margins no more than 1 inch left and right and no less than ½ inch top and bottom.
6. If the resume is sent by email as an attachment, confirm that it was received and that it could be opened and was legible for the recipient.

Don'ts

1. Don't include a photograph.
2. Don't include personal information such as social security number, date of birth, military status, marital status, or number of children.
3. Don't puff up the resume with excess verbiage or irrelevant information. A sincere, parsimonious, and focused resume is usually received as well as or better than one that runs on for many more pages.
4. Don't create a resume with "bells and whistles." A too-busy, colorful, or atypical resume style may give the impression of immaturity or lack of seriousness.

Letterhead

The letterhead is typically centered at the top of the document with your name (in bold uppercase letters) and contact information, including address, telephone number (if multiple numbers, designate home number vs. cell), and email address.

Education

List the most current degree first, ending with the baccalaureate degree. You need not list your high school education. Include the name of the institution, city and state where the degree was awarded, the degree and field of study (major and minor areas), and year of completion. If the degree is in progress, indicate the date it will be conferred. List degree honors (e.g., Summa or Magna Cum Laude); inclusion of a grade point average (GPA) is optional but should be omitted if less than a 3.0.

Certifications/Licenses

List the dates and titles of any professional or related certifications or licenses received.

Professional Experience

This is probably the most important section of the resume and the one a reviewer will look at first. In reverse chronologic order, list the dates of employment, job title, employer, city, and state. For students just graduating, it is fine to list practical experiences; just modify the heading to indicate this. Don't include experiences outside the field of communication sciences and disorders, such as part-time jobs undertaken while a student. However, individuals who have had important positions in other fields and have changed careers may use the section on employment history to show evidence of leadership and responsibility that should be highlighted. Importantly, you want to be able to support your experience or skill in specific areas by stating the job responsibilities and tasks executed. This can be conveyed by using action verbs such as *conducted*, *evaluated*, or *performed* rather than passive words such as *assisted*, *observed*, or *participated*. Separate items using a bulleted list format.

Awards/Honors

List the titles and dates of the specific award, scholarship, or designated honor (e.g., dean's list). Separate the headings and respective items when substantive.

Publications

List publications in reverse chronological order, similar to APA-style referencing (see Chapter 5, Referencing Resources), indicating whether journal articles were published in refereed or non-refereed periodicals (designated subheadings may be used if substantive).

Professional Presentations

Follow APA-style referencing (see Chapter 5, Referencing Resources) to list each presentation, the type of session (e.g., paper, poster), and whether the professional meeting is national, state, or regional.

Research

Use this section to indicate the participation in or conduct of research-related activities such as those related to doctoral or masters theses, independent study, or research assistantships.

Professional Affiliations/Activities

Indicate memberships or offices held in professional organizations. Include the dates, position (e.g., member, officer), and title of the organization. Title the heading as *Affiliations* or *Activities* for listing nonprofessional campus or community organizations or volunteer affiliations.

Skills

Highlight special skills such as fluency in a foreign language or American Sign Language.

References

References may be listed as "provided on request" or may include names, titles, and contact information for at least three individuals who have agreed to provide a reference.

Figures 10–1 and 10–2 are sample resumes for a hypothetical student of speech-language pathology or audiology. More examples on resumes can easily be found using an Internet search.

Sample Student Resume Format

YOUR NAME
address, telephone number, email address

EDUCATION
name of institution, location
degree, date awarded or anticipated

CLINICAL EXPERIENCE
name of site, location, position title, dates
describe job responsibilities, tasks executed

AWARDS/HONORS
list title of award/honor, scholarship, and so forth; date

PROFESSIONAL AFFILIATIONS /ACTIVITIES
list professional memberships, committees, dates

SKILLS
list proficiency in a foreign language, computer skill, and so forth

REFERENCES
provide names and contact information or can indicate "available upon request"

Note:

- list each item separately, most current first
- tailor headings to fit individual experiences
- keep to one page

II. Cover Letters for Resumes

Appropriate employment-seeking etiquette requires that a cover letter precede the resume. Whereas the resume is a uniform, universal document to be sent to many individuals, the cover letter must be tailored to fit the contact name, site of employment, job title, and responsibilities of the targeted position. Because the cover letter is usually a first point of contact with a prospective employer, it will provide a first impression of you, and in this case, first impressions do matter.

Keep the cover letter formal by using professional language and using proper rules of writing and spelling, similar to writing a proper letter. It is wise to be concise, limiting the length to one page. A hard-copy cover letter should be printed on good-quality paper, similar to the resume. Although it is acceptable to send cover letters via email, a professional formality must be maintained.

JOHN Q. PUBLIC
1000 Third Avenue
New York, NY 10065
(212) 794-1000
jqp@bloomingdales.com

EDUCATION
Adelphi University, Garden City, NY
M.S. in Speech-Language Pathology, Phi Delta Kappa, 2018
Queens College, CUNY, Flushing, NY
B.A. in Linguistics and Communication Disorders, 2016

INTERNSHIPS
Peninsula Medical Center, Far Rockaway, NY
Speech-Language Pathology Intern, February 2018–May 2018
Conducted bedside swallowing evaluations
Evaluated videofluoroscopic examinations
Provided speech-language therapy to adults with swallowing disorders

Herbert G. Birch School, Flushing, NY
Speech-Language Pathology Intern, September 2017–December 2017
Evaluated preschool children for speech and language
Provided speech-language therapy to preschool children

Hy Weinberg Center for Communication Disorders, Garden City, NY
Speech-Language Pathology Intern, September 2016–May 2017
Provided individual speech-language therapy to preschool children, and group language stimulation to preschool children in TOTalk
Provided individual and group therapy to adults with aphasia

AWARDS/HONORS
AAC Institute Award, ASHA Division 12, 2017

PROFESSIONAL AFFILIATIONS/ACTIVITIES
Student Member, National Student Speech-Language-Hearing Association, 2016–2018
Student Volunteer, New York State Speech, Hearing, and Language Association Convention, April 2018

SKILLS
American Sign Language, Level 4

REFERENCES
Available upon request

Figure 10–1. Resume example for Speech-Language Pathology.

JANE DOE
123 Fourth Lane
Maintown, NY
(012) 345-6789
jdoe@doe.com

EDUCATION
Long Island Doctor of Audiology (Au.D.) Consortium
Adelphi University, Hofstra University, & St. John's University, NY
Doctor of Audiology (Au.D.), to be conferred May 31, 2019
Adelphi University, Garden City, NY
B.A. in Communication Sciences and Disorders, Magna Cum Laude, 2015

INTERNSHIP EXPERIENCE
Long Island Medical Center, New Hyde Park, NY
Audiology Student Intern, January 2018–present
Perform hearing aid evaluations on pediatric and adult populations
Dispense hearing aids

Island Hearing Screening Program, Jericho, NY
Audiology Student Intern, September 2017–December 2017
Performed hearing and outer and middle ear screenings on pediatric clients
Tabulated screening data

Hy Weinberg Center for Communication Disorders, Garden City, NY
Audiology Student Intern, September 2016–May 2017
Conducted hearing evaluations on pediatric, adult, and geriatric clients
Completed (Central) Auditory Processing Evaluations
Evaluated hearing aid function using electroacoustic analysis, real ear

AWARDS/HONORS
Adelphi University Student Leadership Award, 20017

PROFESSIONAL AFFILIATIONS/ACTIVITIES
Student Member, American Academy of Audiology, 2015–2018
Student Volunteer, Annual Conference of the American Academy of Audiology, April 2018

SKILLS
Fluent in Spanish

REFERENCES
Available upon request

Figure 10–2. Resume example for Audiology.

Following is a description of the cover letter format and a sample.

Resume Cover Letter Format

Sender Information
Address
Telephone Number
Email Address

As an alternative, this section can be added at the bottom of the letter or incorporated into the ending paragraph.

Date

Recipient Information
Recipient Name
Title
Address

Salutation
Begin this section with "Dear (title and name):" making sure to use the correct title (e.g., Dr., Ms., Mr.) and spelling of the first and last names. If unsure, it is best to use a general salutation (e.g., "To the Reviewing Committee:"). Use a proper salutation even when sending an email; do not begin with the informal greeting of "Hi."

Beginning Paragraph
The first paragraph should begin by expressing interest in the position, detailing why you are interested, and indicating the name of the person who referred you, if applicable.

Middle Paragraph
The second and subsequent paragraphs should indicate, briefly, your experience and why you would be appropriate for the job. Indicate any other pertinent information such as unique qualifications.

Final Paragraph
End the letter by thanking the recipient for consideration of your application, and indicate when and how you will follow up. It is particularly important that you follow up (after 1 week is appropriate), because letters do get lost in the mail and emails may not open. Add or refer to your listed contact information as well in case the employer wishes to contact you.

Closing
End the letter with a cordial term such as "Sincerely," "Respectfully," or something similar.

Name and Signature
Type your name with degree and certification credentials, and place your handwritten signature just above it. For email transmission, provide an electronic signature.

Sample Resume Cover Letter

Jane Doe
123 Fourth Lane Maintown, NY
(012) 345-6789
jdoe@doe.com

May 1, 2018

Ellen Smith, PhD
Best Hearing Care, Inc.
567 Eighth Drive
Maintown, NY 12345

Dear Dr. Smith:

I am writing to express my interest in the clinical audiology position available at your center. I will be receiving my doctoral degree in audiology (AuD) from the Long Island Doctor of Audiology Program, New York, on May 31, 2018. My advisor, Prof. Yula Serpanos, suggested I contact you regarding this position.

I noted in the job description that you are seeking experience with diagnostic hearing evaluation and amplification fitting in pediatric populations. In my 4 years of academic and clinical training including my current internship at the Long Island Medical Center, I have acquired knowledge and skill in these areas and feel that I am well prepared and qualified for clinical work in this capacity. Please see the attached resume for more complete information on my education and training. A hard copy of both this letter and my resume will be following.

I thank you for your consideration of my application. I will be in touch next week in order to obtain more information. You may contact me if you wish at the phone and email address listing above. I look forward to speaking with you soon.

Sincerely,
Jane Doe
Jane Doe

III. Portfolios

The portfolio, a selection of one's representative academic or professional work and accomplishments, has gained popularity for use in both academia and job searching in many professions, including communication sciences and disorders. The collection of documents comprising the portfolio is housed either electronically or in bound hard copy. In academic programs, students may be required to maintain a *developmental portfolio*, or one that serves the purpose of documenting a student's progress in the mastery of the required knowledge and skill areas. Upon graduation, a *career portfolio* may be maintained for professional use in order to maintain a record of professional development and achievements.

Similar to the resume, the portfolio is a work in progress throughout one's academic or professional career, where materials can be updated as changes occur. A hard-copy portfolio can be compiled in a three-ring binder, and materials can easily be added or removed as needed. The hard-copy career portfolio can be taken to an interview where the reviewer can peruse the documents on site. It is wise to keep a second hard-copy of the items in the portfolio and to save the items electronically. Though electronic portfolios have the advantage of saving space and items into memory, hard copies provide easier viewing of numerous pages and may be preferred by most reviewers; a digital version of the portfolio can then easily be provided if requested.

Following is a suggested list of items to include in a professional portfolio as applicable (McLaughlin et al., 1998; Poore, 2001; Straub, 1997).

- Academic transcript (only for a student applying for a first job)
- Resume
- Copies of degrees, licenses, certificates, attendance at relevant professional workshops
- Samples of clinical evaluations, projects, reports
- Professional publications, presentations
- Copies of honors, awards, or other recognitions
- Performance reviews (e.g., evaluations of clinical supervision, teaching)
- Recommendation letters or reference contact list

Sample Portfolio Checklist of Clinical Work in Audiology

Standard Audiologic Evaluation

☐ Child

☐ Adult

Behavioral Pediatric Testing

☐ BOA

☐ VRA

☐ Play Audiometry

Behavioral Hearing Screening

☐ Child

☐ Adult

Outer/Middle Ear Screening

☐ Child

☐ Adult

Behavioral SOL Testing-Adult

- ☐ PI-PB
- ☐ Tone Decay: Carhart
- ☐ Tone Decay: Olsen/Noffsinger

Functional Testing

- ☐ Stenger test
- ☐ Stenger procedure for hearing estimation

(Central) Auditory Processing Screening

- ☐ Child
- ☐ Adult

(Central) Auditory Processing Evaluation

- ☐ Child
- ☐ Adult

Earmold Impression

- ☐ Child
- ☐ Adult

Hearing Aid Selection/Fitting

- ☐ Electroacoustic analysis
- ☐ Real-ear analysis: Child
- ☐ Real-ear analysis: Adult

ABR-Adult

- ☐ Click-evoked (SOL)
- ☐ Tonal (hearing estimation)

ABR-Child

- ☐ Click-evoked (SOL)
- ☐ Tonal (hearing estimation)
- ☐ Screening

OAE-Adult

- ☐ DPOAE diagnostic
- ☐ DPOAE screening
- ☐ TEOAE diagnostic
- ☐ TEOAE screening

OAE-Child

- ☐ DPOAE diagnostic
- ☐ DPOAE screening
- ☐ TEOAE diagnostic
- ☐ TEOAE screening

Vestibular Assessment

- ☐ ENG
- ☐ Rotational Chair Test
- ☐ Posturography

Calibration

- ☐ Audiometer
- ☐ Sound-field

Sample Portfolio Checklist of Clinical Work in Speech-Language Pathology (Adelphi University Codes)

The portfolio is a developmental scrapbook of evidence of meeting ASHA's standards. Maintain this archive both in hard copy and electronically. In hard-copy versions, page protectors and dividers provide for ease of reviewing. Scan in graded rubrics when using a digital portfolio. See portfolio checksheet for specific contents.

The first page should be the checksheet followed by your most recent transcript and then the Knowledge and Skills Assessment (KASA) form completed as of that date (Tables 10–1, 10–2, 10–3, and 10–4).

The portfolio should include three client studies: one child, one adult, and one culturally-linguistically diverse client. Include a client study from student teaching, if appropriate, as well as one from a diagnostics practicum.

Table 10–1. Sample Documentation For Articulation

	Knowledge				Assessment Skills				Intervention Skills			
	Evidence type	**Rating/ grade**	**Instructor**	**Date**	**Evidence type**	**Rating/ grade**	**Instructor**	**Date**	**Evidence type**	**Rating/ grade**	**Instructor**	**Date**
Articulation 610	Course grade	A	Lederer	F17	Midterm phono process analysis	45/50	Lederer	F17	Final therapy presenta- tion	34/40	Lederer	F17
611	Course grade	A–	Redstone	F17	Video analysis	19/20	Redstone	F17	Client study	42/50	Redstone	F17
Clinical					666 Goldman- Fristoe	N/A	Montano	SS 18	N/A			
Clinical					N/A				Self- reflection: client with dysarthria	Satis- factory	Goldfarb	Sp 18

Name: ____________________

Table 10–2. Knowledge and Skills Documentation

	Knowledge of Disorder (III-C)				Assessment Knowledge/Skills (III-D; IV-F; IV-G)				Intervention Knowledge/Skills (III-D; IV-F, IV-G)			
	Evidence type	**Rating/ grade**	**Instructor**	**Date**	**Evidence type**	**Rating/ grade**	**Instructor**	**Date**	**Evidence type**	**Rating/ grade**	**Instructor**	**Date**
Articulation 610	Course grade											
611	Course grade											
Clinical												
Clinical												
Fluency 620	Course grade											
Clinical												
Clinical												
Voice 630 (611)	Course grade											
Clinical												
Clinical												
Language 603	Course grade											
638	Course grade											
634	Course grade											
Clinical												
Clinical												

continues

Table 10–2. *continued*

	Knowledge of Disorder (III-C)				Assessment Knowledge/Skills (III-D; IV-F; IV-G)				Intervention Knowledge/Skills (III-D; IV-F, IV-G)			
	Evidence type	Rating/ grade	Instructor	Date	Evidence type	Rating/ grade	Instructor	Date	Evidence type	Rating/ grade	Instructor	Date
Hearing 606	Course grade											
Clinical (other than 668)												
Swallowing 646	Course grade											
636	Course grade											
Clinical												
Clinical												
Cognitive Linguistic 624	Course grade											
Clinical					At least one client study (treatment plan, session plan, progress note, self-reflection)	1-2-3			At least one adult client	1-2-3		
Clinical												

	Knowledge of Disorder (III-C)				Assessment Knowledge/Skills (III-D; IV-F; IV-G)				Intervention Knowledge/Skills (III-D; IV-F, IV-G)			
	Evidence type	**Rating/ grade**	**Instructor**	**Date**	**Evidence type**	**Rating/ grade**	**Instructor**	**Date**	**Evidence type**	**Rating/ grade**	**Instructor**	**Date**
Social-behavioral 673	Course grade											
Clinical												
Other												
Modalities (AAC) 672	Course grade											
Clinical												
Clinical												
Screening/ Prevention 666					Speech-Language screening	1-2-3						
668					Hearing screens	668 Grade =						
634												
Other												

Table 10–3. Additional Knowledge Assessments

	Evidence Type	Grade/Rating	Instructor	Date
Basic sciences (III-A): 1 Bio, 1 Phys sci; 1 math; 1 social science	Transcript			
Human Comm Sciences (III-B): prerequisites	Transcript			
600	Course grade			
613	Course grade			
Department policies and procedures (III-H)	Grad manual			
Ethical conduct (III-E) 648	Code of ethics sign-off			
670 (NIH certification)				
Other				
Research and evidence-based practice (III-F) 670	Course grade			
660	EBP project			
Contemporary professional issues (III-G) 648	Position statement activity sign off			
Other				
Certification, specialty recognition, licensure, TSSLD, graduation requirements, praxis, comps (III-H)	Graduation seminar materials			

Table 10–4. Additional Skills Assessments

	Evidence Type	Grade/Rating	Instructor	Date
Oral language (IV-B)	Screening by advisor	Pass or Fail? If fail, results of diagnostic Therapy?		
Written language (IV-B) 648	Critical observation	1-2-3		
Clinical writing (IV-B) 660	Lesson plans; tx plans; progress notes	Mean score from all final supervisor evals		
666	Diagnostic reports	Score from final eval		
Interaction with professionals and families, collaboration, ethics, professional behaviors, counseling (IV-G3)	Supervisor evals	S/NI/U		
648				
660				
661/674 or 662		S/NI/U		
Delivering services to CLD populations (IV-F; IV-G)	At least one client study (treatment plan, session plan, progress note, self-reflection, client reflection)	1-2-3		
Other (e.g., 603 or 638 paper)				

continues

Table 10–4. *continued*

	Evidence Type	Grade/Rating	Instructor	Date
Self-evaluation of practice 648	Essay	S/NI/U		
660	Essay	S/NI/U		
661/674	Essay	S/NI/U		
662	Essay	S/NI/U		
400 hours (IV- C, IV-D: 25 observation & 375 direct; 150 TSSLD)	Dr. Soman sign-off form			
Summative Assessment (V-B)	COMPS	Pass or Fail?		
Exit survey (submit to office)				

U = Unsatisfactory *NI* = Needs improvement *S* = Satisfactory

The client study must include the treatment plan, one session plan (with rationales for goals and procedures), a reflection on that session (how you did and how the client did), the progress note, and a reflection at the end of the semester on that client.

1. *Demonstrating Competency.* Use the KASA form (see Tables 10–1 through Table 10–4) to maintain this record of how well you are mastering material. Simultaneously, the instructor is documenting the same. If you feel you need additional experience in any area, please consult with your advisor.
2. *Remediation Plans.* In the event you do not meet the minimum standard in a particular competency area (e.g., you fail an exam or get a poor score on a rubric in class or therapy), you must meet with the instructor to devise a remediation plan. Your grade will not change for that assessment. However, at the end of the semester, the instructor will determine whether you have successfully demonstrated competency in that area or whether additional demonstration is necessary.
3. *Clinical Practica.* List all practica experiences and the type

    In-house practicum

    Externship or clinical practice in a school

    Diagnostics practicum

    Audiology practicum

For All CSD Students:

- ☐ ASHA Knowledge and Skills Assessment (KASA) / maintained by you
- ☐ Clinical Seminar critical observation and scored rubric
- ☐ Clinical Practica Work Samples
    - ☐ One client study (treatment plan, one session plan with reflection of therapy, progress note, single subject research, or evidence-based practice project)
    - ☐ All supervisor evaluations
    - ☐ Knowledge, skills, dispositions, self-evaluation
- ☐ One graded paper or project dealing with cultural diversity in SLP
- ☐ One graded paper or project dealing with technology
- ☐ Other individual graded papers or projects, such as narrative analysis, therapy plan, augmentative project, clinical case study, parent education materials
- ☐ Comprehensive examination
- ☐ Final self-evaluation
- ☐ Praxis report, if taken prior to graduation

For Candidates Seeking Initial Certification as Teacher of Students with Speech and Language Disabilities

- ☐ School (TSSLD) observation, interview, and rubric
- ☐ Academic Literacy Skills Test (ALST) and the Educating All Students (EAS) test scores
- ☐ Clinical Practice in a School Setting/ Bilingual School Setting
    - ☐ One client study, including IEP, session plan with reflection, progress note
    - ☐ One diagnostic report
    - ☐ Cooperating teacher evaluations
    - ☐ University supervisor evaluations

For All Other Candidates, Including TSSLD Holders or Non-Teacher Track Students

- ☐ Clinical Practicum Externship
    - ☐ One client study, including IFSP, IEP, or treatment plan, and a session plan with reflection

- ☐ One diagnostic report
- ☐ Supervisor evaluations
- ☐ Self-reflection

For All Candidates: Additional Recommended Artifacts

- ☐ Evidence from volunteer work or unique experiences
- ☐ Your resume
- ☐ Letters of recommendation

IV. Professional Correspondence Via Electronic Media

Any professional correspondence should include appropriate content, form, and style, even when communicating via electronic mail. Start with a proper salutation (e.g., "Dear Dr. . . . ") continue with the body or content of the communication, and end with a proper closing (e.g., "Sincerely"), and your name.

Sections of Formal Correspondence

Salutation

Body

Closing

Name

Sample EMail Correspondence

Dear Dr. Jones:

I was concerned about my midterm grade and would like to set up an appointment to review my exam. Would you please let me know when you are available for a meeting?

Thank you,
Maria Silver

Multiple-Choice Tests

Students take multiple-choice tests from elementary through graduate school, often from instructors who have had little or no formal training in preparing them. Professionals may write these questions as part of student assessment in a course, or in clinical practice for assessing reading comprehension or higher cognitive functions. Students in the communication sciences will also need to prepare for two important standardized examinations; the Graduate Record Examination (GRE®), required for admission to most graduate schools, and the Praxis® examination in either audiology or speech-language-pathology, required for certification and licensure.

A multiple-choice item is an objective test question containing alternative response choices. The introductory statement, called the *stem*, presents the situation, poses the problem, and/or asks the question. Each question usually has four or five *options*, or possible responses to a question. The *key* is the option that is the correct answer. The other options are called *distractors* or decoys, which should be plausible but incorrect choices.

The Stem

Examinees often complain that the stem is so lengthy and ambiguous that the test item requires separating the wheat from the chaff more than revealing knowledge and skills. The sentence structure of a stem should be clear and direct. The stem should include all information necessary for the examinee to understand the intent of the item but should not provide clues that will make it easy to detect the key. Rather than having words or phrases repeated in all of the options, they should appear once in the stem. Typical stems use the format of a direct question or an incomplete statement. A stem should avoid the format of filling in a blank, for example, *To evaluate communicative responsibility in stuttering, _____ should be avoided*, because the examinee needs to look back and forth between the stem and the options to try out the choices. Also, a multiple-choice item should not be a disguised true-false question, as in, *Which of the following statements about play therapy is true?*

The Options

The key, or the correct option, must be unequivocally correct, and the distractors indisputably wrong. Distractors or decoys should attract examinees who do not have adequate knowledge and skill, and not those who are confused by such terms as *all of the above except for C*. Although the authors enjoy a pun as much as anyone, examinees can be thrown by a bizarre or humorous decoy. Accordingly, the *levator linguini* should not be listed as a possible muscle of the tongue.

Graduate Record Examination (GRE®)

The GRE General Test is required for admission to most graduate programs in the communications sciences. The exam may be administered in either computer- or paper-based format, and consists of three test sections. Two sections, Verbal Reasoning and Quantitative Reasoning, are multiple choice, with a writing component in the third section, Analytical Writing.

The Verbal Reasoning section (score range 130–170, in 1 point increments) intends to measure the student's ability to analyze written materials and presents questions on reading comprehension, text completion, and sentence equivalence. Quantitative Reasoning (score range 130–170, in 1-point increments) is designed to assess interpretation of quantitative information based on mathematical concepts of arithmetic, algebra, geometry and data analysis. The Analytical Writing section (score range 0–6, in half-point increments) consists of two separate timed (30 minutes each) written tasks that require the student to analyze a presented issue and to analyze an argument.

Adequate preparation for the GRE is strongly advised as many graduate programs include the scores as a critical component in the evaluation of a student's qualifications for admission. Free preparation materials such as a math review booklet and a practice book are available in either printed form or software on the GRE website (https://www.ets.org/gre/revised_general/prepare/). In addition, the site offers fee-based preparation materials (book or electronic software formats) and services such as an online writing practice service for preparation in Analytical Writing. Students may also elect to enroll in formal GRE preparatory courses in traditional or online formats, or seek GRE tutoring services. It is highly recommended that students investigate these options and plan an appropriate timeline for taking the GRE with allowance for a possible re-take of the exam (if a higher score is desired) in order to meet program application deadlines.

Praxis® Examinations in Speech-Language Pathology and Audiology

A pass grade on the Praxis II® subject assessment in speech-language pathology or audiology is necessary for ASHA certification and is also a state licensure requirement, though the pass score for licensure may differ from the ASHA requirement in some states. The hours-long (2½ hours for speech-language pathology; 2 hours for audiology) examination consists of multiple-choice questions (132 for speech-language pathology; 120 for audiology) and is a comprehensive summative assessment of learning outcomes in speech-language pathology or audiology. Therefore, the student should not take the Praxis exam unless properly prepared and at the conclusion of graduate study. Currently, applicants for ASHA's Certificate of Clinical Competence (CCC) in speech-language pathology (Table 10–5) must achieve a score of 162 out of a range of 100 to 200; for audiology (Table 10–6) the passing score is 170 out of a range of 100 to 200 (reported in one-point increments). The examination is administered by Educational Testing Service (ETS), which may change the scoring system. For updated information, go to the ETS website in the specific area below; information on exam preparation and study guide materials is also available on the ETS website.

Table 10–5. Speech-Language Pathology Praxis Examination

Content Categories	Approximate Number of Questions	Approximate Percentage of Examination
Foundations and Professional Practice	44	33%
Screening, Assessment, Evaluation, and Diagnosis	44	33%
Planning, Implementation, and Evaluation of Treatment	44	33%

Table 10–6. Audiology Praxis Examination Content Categories

Content Categories	Approximate Number of Questions	Approximate Percentage of Examination
Foundations	12	10%
Prevention and Identification	12	10%
Assessment	48	40%
Intervention	36	30%
Professional Issues	12	10%

The same exam is used by many states in the United States as one of the criteria for awarding licensure as a speech-language pathologist or audiologist. Whereas it is not the intention of the present authors to give specific test-preparation strategies to readers, it seems appropriate to present something of a guide to how multiple-choice items are written.

The Praxis Examination includes three types of questions, grouped according to cognitive levels, or the mental processes required in the problem-solving situation. (Note: The examples below follow the current exam question format of four answer options for speech-language pathology and five answer options for audiology.)

Level I questions assess knowledge, requiring the cognitive behavior of remembering and understanding previously learned information. There are relatively few Level I questions on the Praxis, because they require memorization rather than application of the knowledge in professional practice.

Examples of Level I questions follow.

SLP Example

The external or superior laryngeal nerve, a branch of Cranial Nerve X, the vagus, innervates which of the following intrinsic muscles of the larynx?

A. posterior cricoarytenoid
B. *cricothyroid*
C. lateral cricoarytenoid
D. transverse arytenoid

Selecting the correct answer of *B* requires only that the examinee recall its innervation, although it might be helpful to recall that all the other intrinsic laryngeal muscles are innervated by the recurrent laryngeal nerve. The question does not require application or interpretation, which might be addressed by a question regarding the effect of impaired innervation to cricothyroid on vocal pitch.

Audiology Example

The ASHA 2005 air conduction pure tone guideline *minimally* requires testing of the following frequencies:

A. 500, 1000, 2000 Hz
B. 250, 500, 1000, 2000, 4000 Hz
C. 250, 500, 1000, 2000, 4000, 8000 Hz

D. *250, 500, 1000, 2000, 3000, 4000, 6000, 8000 Hz*
E. 250, 500, 750, 1000, 1500, 2000, 3000, 4000, 6000, 8000 Hz

In selection of the correct answer *D*, the examinee is required to recall the specific pure tone frequencies that should be tested, but is not asked to indicate procedures related to hearing assessment.

Level II questions assess basic knowledge in context, requiring the cognitive behavior of interpretation, or understanding the *why* and *how* of a situation. The question might present a problem that can be solved by understanding a theory, principle, or technique.

Examples of Level II questions follow.

SLP Example

Aphasia syndromes represent an aphasia type at only one arbitrary point in time, but aphasia is a migratory disorder. Which migration might happen in aphasia?

A. Broca's to Wernicke's to anomic
B. *Jargon to conduction to anomic*
C. Transcortical motor to global to Broca's
D. Anomic to Wernicke's to jargon

Selecting the correct answer of *B* requires that the examinee apply theories and patterns of recovery in aphasia, specifically regarding type and severity of the disorder. Aphasias cannot migrate from fluent to nonfluent or vice versa (A), nor can they migrate from less impaired to more impaired (C, D).

Audiology Example

This auditory pathway is responsible for sound inhibition:

A. *efferent*
B. afferent
C. ipsilateral
D. bilateral
E. bone conduction

Choosing the correct option *A* requires an understanding of and ability to differentiate among different aspects of auditory function (i.e., afferent vs. efferent sound pathways, bone conduction hearing) and sound presentation (ipsilateral, contralateral).

Level III questions assess evaluation and decision making, requiring the cognitive behavior of synthesis of elements into a comprehensive whole. The questions often include hypothetical case information, and simulate the process of designing or modifying treatment based on evidence.

Examples of Level III questions follow.

SLP Example

Which of the following impairments may occur in traumatic brain injury (TBI), but not in aphasia?

A. poor word retrieval
B. poor reading and writing
C. semantic and phonemic paraphasias
D. *disproportionately impaired pragmatic skills*

Selecting the correct answer of *D* requires that the examinee understand clinical characteristics of language impairments in aphasia and TBI, and synthesize the principle that individuals with aphasia communicate better than they speak, whereas the reverse is true for individuals with language and communication impairments secondary to TBI.

Audiology Example

A patient with a mild conductive hearing loss will likely exhibit a speech recognition threshold (SRT) of _____:

A. 0 dB HL
B. 10 dB HL
C. *30 dB HL*
D. 60 dB HL
E. 80 dB HL

In choosing option *C* the examinee must know the decibel levels that define a mild degree of hearing loss (26–40 dB HL), and know that the SRT is closely related to pure-tone thresholds.

EXERCISES

Exercise 10–1. Chapter Review

1. A brief synopsis of an individual's educational background, skills, and experience is called a:
   a. resumé
   b. synthesis
   c. curriculum vitae
   d. course of life
   e. job advertisement

2. Which of the following is a *do* tip in writing a resumé?
   a. Include a photograph.
   b. Include your social security number.
   c. List all items under headings in reverse chronological order.
   d. Highlight your resumé with interesting graphics.
   e. Include your date of birth and marital status.

3. Which of the following is a *don't* tip in writing a resumé?
   a. Use 11- or 12-point type and a standard font.
   b. Use light-colored paper.
   c. Use boldface only for headings.
   d. Add related information, such as hobbies, when you are just starting in a new career.
   e. Use a larger type for headings and a smaller type for details.

4. Which of the following should you leave off your resumé?
   a. Ability to play the cello
   b. Level IV ability in American Sign Language
   c. Poster presentation to ASHA
   d. Poster presentation at a state speech, language, and hearing convention
   e. Poster presentation at your university research day

5. Which of the following should you include on your resumé?
   a. Boy scout or girl scout merit badge
   b. Fraternity or sorority membership
   c. Name of your pastor as a reference
   d. Experience as a sales clerk
   e. NSSLHA membership

6. Resumé cover letter format does not need to include:
   a. sender telephone number
   b. recipient telephone number
   c. expression of your interest
   d. your appropriateness for the job
   e. your handwritten or electronic signature

7. Your developmental portfolio must:
   a. be in electronic form
   b. include a teaching evaluation
   c. include a sample of a clinical evaluation
   d. include a term paper
   e. include information about student loans

8. The treatment plan, one session plan (with rationales for goals and procedures), a reflection on that session (how you did and how the client did), the progress note, and a reflection at the end of the semester are part of a:
   a. client study
   b. diagnostic evaluation
   c. hearing screening
   d. discharge plan
   e. clinical hypothesis

9. The part of a multiple-choice test question that includes all the information necessary for the examinee to understand the intent of the item is called the:
   a. key
   b. stem
   c. options
   d. answer
   e. question

10. The Praxis® exam in speech-language pathology and audiology:
    a. is required with a passing grade for ASHA certification
    b. is required with a passing grade for ASHA certification and state licensure
    c. uses essay questions
    d. uses fill-in questions
    e. is administered by ASHA

Exercise 10–2. Create Your Own Personal Resume

EDUCATION

CLINICAL EXPERIENCE

AWARDS/HONORS

PROFESSIONAL AFFILIATIONS/ACTIVITIES

____

____

____

____

SKILLS

____

____

REFERENCES

____

____

____

Exercise 10–3. Write a Resume Cover Letter

Write a cover letter to your university's clinic director in application for a hypothetical externship position at the clinic site. Use the example resume cover letter (above) as a guide.

Exercise 10–4. Create Your Own Portfolio

Obtain a three-ring binder to create your own hard-copy portfolio. Use labeling, dividers, plastic sheet protectors, and so forth, to craft your own unique professional portfolio. Refer to the checklist above as a guide for information to include. In the section below, create a plan for the items that you will include.

- ______________________________
- ______________________________
- ______________________________
- ______________________________
- ______________________________
- ______________________________
- ______________________________
- ______________________________
- ______________________________
- ______________________________
- ______________________________
- ______________________________

Exercise 10–5. Write an Email Message to a Professor, Requesting Information

Inquire about graduate admission requirements for a masters or doctoral degree in speech-language pathology or audiology. Select a university program (not your own), find the website, search faculty profiles, and remember to start your email message with "Dear Prof. Smith," not "Hey Prof." or "Hi Doc," or "Hello James."

Exercise 10–6. Write an Email Message to a Professor, Asking for a Recommendation

Ask for a letter of recommendation for an externship or clinical fellowship. Go to the online graduate handbook for your program, and learn the procedure for beginning an off-campus placement. If you are completing your degree, go to http://www.asha.org and navigate the site until you find an employment opportunity which you find interesting. Include the following in your request for information: the kind of placement you are looking for; the courses you took with the person who will write your recommendation; dates and grades for these courses; titles of papers or other written work for which you earned a high grade; ages and case types if you are referring to clinical practicum.

References

Friedman, J. P. (Ed.). (2007). *Dictionary of business terms* (4th ed.). Hauppauge, NY: Barron's Business Guides.

Helwig, A. A. (1985, December). Corporate recruiter preferences for three resume styles. *Vocational Guidance Quarterly*, (34), 99–105.

McDaniels, C. (1990). *Developing a professional vita or resume*. Garrett Park, MD: Garrett Park Press.

McLaughlin, M., Vogt, M. E., Anderson, J. A., Dumez, J., Peter, M. G., & Hunter, A. (1998). *Portfolio models: Reflections across the teaching profession*. Norwood, MA: Christopher-Gordon.

O'Hair, D., Friedrich, G. W., Wiemann, J. M., & Wiemann, M. O. (1997). *Competent communication* (2nd ed.). New York, NY: St. Martin's Press.

Poore, C. A. (2001). *Building your career portfolio*. Franklin Lakes, NJ: Career Press.

Rosenberg, A. D., & Hizer, D. (1990). *The resume handbook: How to write outstanding resumes and cover letters for every situation* (3rd ed.). Holbrook, MA: Adams Media.

Seiler, W. J., & Beall, M. L. (1999). *Communication: Making connections* (4th ed.). Boston, MA: Allyn & Bacon.

Straub, C. (1997). *Creating your skills portfolio: Show your accomplishments*. Menlo Park, CA: Crisp.

Index

Note: Page numbers in **bold** reference non-text material.

C

D

E

F

G

H

I

J

K

L

M

N

O

P

R

S

T

U

V

W